THE SPIRITUAL PILGRIM

A Journey from Cynical Realism to "Born Again" Christian Faith

Miles Huntley Hodges

spiritualpilgrim.net

ISBN: 978-1-7376413-0-8 (soft copy)
ISBN: 978-1-7376413-1-5 (hard copy)
ISBN: 978-1-7376413-2-2 (e-copy)

Library of Congress Control Number: 2021915169

spiritualpilgrim.net

CONTENTS

INTRODUCTION

* * *

THE QUEST FOR TRUTH

Life's social rules, and the immense variety in the way those rules are put to social action. I discovered along life's way that there are both unchanging rules of human behavior, especially social behavior, something like the unchanging rules of physics and chemistry, and yet at the same time a vast array of different social patterns, different ways of putting those social rules into action, some of them better than others in the way they bring health (or pain) to human life on this planet.

Most of us only know one of those social patterns, the one we grew up in. The society we are born to – and its operational rules – instinctively become for us some kind of social absolute, producing a disciplined social order that is greatly needed to keep us humans able to work together in some kind of harmony. And often we would be called on to live in full defense of that social order, even at the possible cost of our own lives.

And this social order takes on all kinds of forms: tribal groups, nations, religious sects, social classes, dynasties, all of them in some way necessary for social life to exist at all.

I myself had no idea of the degree of complexity of all this until I was brought out of the very comfortable 1950s Middle-American world of my high school years into a much broader 1960s world of other societies – both abroad and in history – not only through my university and grad-school studies but also my travel, study, research and work abroad during those years. And that "abroad" stretched from America to Europe, to the Middle East, to central Asia, to Central America, to South Africa, by way of both personal travel and residence. And, through deeper study (and eventual teaching), it also led me to all the world's major societies – including those in East Asia, Africa, and South America. And this study also reached back in history – all the way to ancient Egypt, Israel, Persia, Hindu and Buddhist Asia, Greece, Rome, and the world of Islam.

What amazed me was not only the grand variety in it all, but also the distinct patterns of birth, growth, maturity, decline, decay and social death that I discovered in my further research.

And I discovered that I was not the only one to come to understand such historical patterns. Others had taken a similar interest in looking at

1

these patterns of social dynamics, all the way back to ancient Greece's Aristotle, down to modern England's Toynbee. And these social scientists came up with much the same conclusion: that the quality of the moral character of a society ultimately determined its chances for grand success – or grand failure.

And thus it was this moral character of a society that really came to be my focus as I continued my study through my years as a university professor (international studies).

And some of that study was quite encouraging. But some of it was quite discouraging.

Life inside a rational "bubble." What bothered me most was what happened to a society when clever rationalists – I eventually came to term them as "wise ones" or "Sophists" – manipulated a society's moral code in a way designed strictly to advance their own standing within that particular society, and then tragically the people would most gladly but also most blindly follow the lead of these Sophists.

I early on came to understand that human Reason and ultimate Truth are not only not the same thing, but tragically quite often the very opposite of each other. Sadly, Truth is very hard to come by, because of life's enormous complexities. But Reason is so much easier to grasp, especially when clever Sophists make it seem so simple.

Reason posing as Truth does not require much introspection. The people merely have to "sign up" as followers of the dogma the Sophists have constructed, and life thus seems to move ahead with much less confusion.

But where that all takes a society is usually not very pretty. "Crusades" for Truth result, in which Truth becomes an ideological ideal people are willing to live and die for. And many will be called to undertake just such death in order to defend this great Truth. And perhaps there is good cause for just such a stand. But perhaps also there is not. But the people themselves have little basis on which to make such a judgment, because they are usually operating within the "bubble" of Reason presented as a beautiful social picture of blissful victory and grand social success by their Sophist leaders.

World War One gives us a perfect example of such social reasoning, as young Englishmen and Frenchmen were led off to kill (and be killed by) young Germans – as many as possible, the point being? And American President Wilson just could not stand by and watch all the glory being amassed in this great moral struggle of "democrats" versus "autocrats" (a very false political dualism of his own very clever design), and marched young Americans off to do some killing (and be killed) of their own in this pointless war. Then there soon was Hitler, who promised a blinded German people that if they followed him, they would construct a German Empire or Reich that would last a thousand years, which in fact lasted only a dozen years – and resulted merely in the total ruination of Germany. Wow!

And it did not stop there, as, for instance, clever American leaders led the nation to fight for "democracy" in Vietnam, in Iran, in Afghanistan, in Iraq, in Libya, in Syria, all ending up tragically – and quiet predictably so.

But more of this in the pages to follow.

"Truth" as a highly personal matter. Overall, the greatest thing I came to learn in my 80 years of life on this planet is that this "Truth" that I long searched for is a very personal thing. It does not exist as some lofty standard lying above human experience itself.

Truth begins to take shape for us as we begin our engagement in life. It is what we find, often the hard way, about what works, and what doesn't work. But it is also what those around us, especially the ones we relate to easily in a loving way, show us through their own personal experience that they have found to be true, especially if those relationships reach across the many social divides that define our world.

America – originally founded on the quest for Truth. And I also learned, through those many years living, working and traveling abroad, that the country I was born and raised in, and have always called my home – *America* – is a great country, a society that has tried (most often anyway!) to live by what it has long understood to be True.

Four centuries ago this country, this society – at least the Northern portion of it – was laid out by Puritan settlers for exactly that purpose: to show others in the world how Truth can be found by simply taking on life the way God, the very Creator of life, himself showed us in Jesus Christ how we were to live.

It was a very personal matter, shaped not by the commands of kings, princes, dukes, archbishops and bishops. It was found in the commands of God himself, relayed simply through the stories of those who went before us, summed up in the exemplary life of Jesus, God's own Son. This was well laid out in the Christian Bibles that these families brought with them to America. The Bible was thus the source of Truth they lived by.

But that Biblical Truth took its shape among those early Americans in the way that Truth was shaped and put into play right at home, in the way the Christian families that came to settle the New World gave very personal support to their neighbors ("Christian charity"), and in the personal teachings of those assigned by these new Americans themselves to give them much needed counsel in this challenging new land, that is, in the sermons of the Christian pastors who, from their pulpits, weekly gave carefully-considered Biblical counsel to the members of their communities.

Again, it was all very personal.

My own counsel on this matter of Truth. Just last year (2020) I published a three-volume history of America*, in an attempt to bring to the generations coming up behind me a deeper understanding of this great American social and spiritual legacy, one that I have come, step by step, to understand and appreciate deeply over the years. It is a glorious legacy, one that is now theirs to carry forward, or to lose.

But, as my own understanding of this very American legacy itself is as much the result of personal experience as it is the result of long-accumulated research material, I came to the decision to bring that personal perspective behind these writings to the forefront.

Ultimately, what you have here before you is very personal testimony about what I have come to understand as to how societies succeed – and why they sometimes fail. It is about what I have learned through not only my many years of social research and course development but also through those same years of my own quite personal frontline encounters, struggles, occasional successes and occasional failures, in going at life.

I've majorly "been there – done that" over those 80 years of my life. And in this process, I came to this particular understanding, how it is personal involvement, even more than well-thought-out plans and schemes, that is what makes the whole thing called "life" work.

That's because we humans were made that way.

"Been there – done that" involved not only living in various points around the country – including a substantial portion in Washington, D.C. (an eye-opening experience in itself!) – but, as I previously mentioned, also residence and exploration abroad, in all kinds of different contexts.

✱ ✱ ✱

FAMILY, AND "MIDDLE AMERICA"

Family as central to the process. But arriving at this understanding included also being part of a personal legacy that my family or ancestors before me developed as "family tradition." Much of what I did or became happened simply because I was raised in this particular family environment,

---

America, The Covenant Nation – A Christian Perspective. Vol. 1 – *Securing America's Covenant With God: From America's Foundations in the Early 1600s to America's Post-Civil-War Recovery in the Late 1800s.* Vol. 2 – *America's Rise to Greatness Under God's Covenant: From the Late 1880s to the End of the 1950s.* Vol. 3 – *The Dismissing of America's Covenant with God: From the Early 1960s to the Present.* Indianapolis: Westbow Press, 2020.

in this family tradition.

But it's also a legacy that my children, coming after me, have also taken up, and in the process themselves have validated in their own ways, further verifying the wonderful qualities of this family legacy. I have thus learned from their own experiences as well.

Thus I know beyond a shadow of a doubt that *family, even more importantly than government and its officials, is what brings rising generations to the Truth in life.*

I know this very well having also served many years as a street and prison pastor, sadly discovering along another pathway how important the American family system is to its people, and the tragedy that hits our society when the family system is messed with by "progressive" social planners, modern-day Sophists who have no personal, no intimate, knowledge of what actually works in the communities and streets of America. Their Truth is rational, abstract and high-sounding. But it has no bearing on what is actually True about life, since such Truth is not found at their desks but instead through personal involvement in the world they are trying to preside over.

"Middle America" as a witness to such Truth. Thus what my sons and daughters (and my students) have discovered is that the great Truth in our lives is simply to live gloriously as supporting members of a "Middle American" family, finding a serviceable place in a social realm that is not too fancy – requiring only some vision, some understanding of how it works, and a willingness to do the labor necessary to make it work for us personally. There is much joy to be found in living so simply.

Living as "Middle Americans" has indeed worked for countless generations before us. It has been a social approach to life that much of America was founded on, especially in the Yankee North and the wild, wild West. And it is a social approach that, through much testing, has consistently brought Americans – including the many immigrants who flocked here, eager to take up the challenge of living the American way – to grand success. And it ultimately brought America itself forward as the world's leading "superpower." And, it is a social methodology that has also gone on to inspire the lives of many others around the world outside of America itself.

Again, personal involvement rather than social engineering as the path to Truth. But for a number of very bad reasons, "Middle America "is undergoing rejection today, by Americans themselves. This is largely because social planners – self-appointed social authorities off in some bureaucratic office, or before you in the never-ceasing presence of the "media" – have decided that they know better than the rest of Middle America how life needs to go forward, how it needs to be more "progressive."

And we are increasingly seeing the brutal results of these Sophists' grand plans and ideals, however, not for the first time in our history – and very much so in my own lifetime.

Again, very personal involvement at the local level – rather than just grand social ideals coming from some distant social managers – has proven itself to be the best teacher concerning what works and what doesn't work on a very practical basis here in America, and even around the world.

And so, as the professor-consultant-pastor-teacher I have long been, I am inviting the reader of this journal into that personal world, to come to understand how the grand American legacy works – on that very personal basis, one that anyone can – and should – take up.

So let us begin this personal journey.

CHAPTER ONE

GETTING STARTED
July 1941 to August 1971

* * *

MY GROUNDING IN "MIDDLE AMERICA"

Collinsville, the heartland of Middle America! I was born in July of 1941, just before America's entry into World War Two, and raised in Collinsville, a small midwestern town in Illinois, a little to the east of St. Louis. I grew up there with a younger sister, a mom at home, and a father who worked as a chemical engineer in nearby E. St. Louis.

Collinsville was only 10 miles to the east of downtown St. Louis, though actually it was never a suburban retreat for the city of St. Louis. It was a social universe unto itself, fully self-sufficient as a community of around 14,000 people – typical of thousands of such small communities spread across the country.

Family background: Dad's side of the family. My dad, Paul, was the baby of a family of six children, and raised within a professional family, both of his parents being college grads. His father was the class president of his senior class and his mom was its secretary. Reaching back even a generation earlier, his grandfather (my great-grandfather) was actually a co-founder of that same Seventh-Day Adventist college in Lincoln, Nebraska, and well-known for his experimental work with fruit orchards and bee hives. And his mother's father (my other great-grandfather on that side of the family) was mayor of the medium-sized town of Sedalia, Missouri.

But I knew of that side of the family only through the few stories I was able to piece together over time. My Dad's father became a banker, but one who ended up financially and emotionally devastated by the financial gyrations that descended upon rural America after World War One. Even sadder, my dad's mom was physically devastated by the 1918 Spanish flu pandemic, became permanently infirm, and thus a remote personality during my dad's youth. And she died when he was still quite young. He really was raised by his older brothers and sisters, particularly when the family moved to Kansas City, where one of his brothers became a fast-rising lawyer, the oldest sister a corporate secretary, another sister a nurse, and yet another sister a church secretary. And there was another brother, who headed off to New York City, eventually to rise as a technician in the new TV industry located there.

Dad's father had also died before my dad and mom married. And though I came to know my aunts and uncles quite well, Dad seldom talked about his parents. Thus I grew up knowing little about my grandparents on his side.

But I did come to know that my dad grew up in Kansas City as a quite tall youth (6'3"), was considered to be very good looking, and at the same time was quite unsure of what it was that he was supposed to become as a person. Apparently, the family worried about him quite a bit.

Mom and her family. On the other side of the family, my mom, Margaret Blanche Miles, was a pampered only child, who knew little of the realities of the Depression, her parents being able to put her through Baker University during the darkest of those days.

Her parents (my grandma and grandpa!) I knew quite well, and was very, very close to – like being a second set of parents! My grandfather grew up as a farm-boy in a rural community in central Illinois, was well-known locally for his adventurous streak, was the first person in the county to own a car, and as soon as he could, headed off to Chicago to avoid the destiny of farm life. But he had started up a relationship with my grandmother, a local school teacher (also born and raised in central Illinois). Ultimately that relationship led to marriage, with the two of them then heading off to Kansas City, where my grandfather started up a business as a restaurant owner. This business too (like my other grandfather) had its ups and downs during the 1920s, and my grandfather ultimately sold the restaurant and went on the road selling asbestos fire-curtains for movie theaters. He did sufficiently well at this so as to be able, as just mentioned, to put my mom through private college, where she majored in English.

My mom was working as a writer for the *Kansas City Star* when she met my father at Christian Endeavor, a popular way for young adults to meet each other during the 1930s. My father fell head over heels in love with her, becoming totally devoted to her (as he would be for the rest of his life), and wanting to marry immediately. But she held out on that until he finished his engineering studies at the University of Kansas in Topeka.

He met much of the financial burden of university studies through a ROTC scholarship – which led him to be commissioned into the reserves as a 2nd Lieutenant. Thus I came very close to being raised as an army brat. In the end, however, they chose the world of private industry rather than the army. Thus just before America's involvement in World War Two, they came to the St. Louis area for Dad to begin work at Monsanto Chemical Co. – just before I was born.

Dad's job with Monsanto was considered very strategic for the war effort and thus he was never activated to service. Consequently, I had very little sense of the war and its deprivations, even though I spent my first years going through it.

My sister, Mary Virginia or "Gina" (or just "Sis" to me) was born a year after me, and we remained close growing up – though often closer in battle than in peace!

Denver, my other home. In growing up, my sister and I moved back and forth seemingly constantly between St. Louis (that is, Collinsville) and Denver, where my grandparents now lived. My grandfather at that point worked for the Union Pacific Railroad as a dining car steward or manager, at home three days and on the road three days in constant succession.

Gina and I loved Denver. My grandparents owned a beautiful home on 8th Avenue just across from Cheesman Park, a park that became my summertime front yard to play in, also offering wading pools and all kinds of cultural activities – including an annual popular opera, such as Oklahoma, South Pacific, etc.

My grandparents also owned a cabin home – complete with a little pond I could skate on in the winter – just outside of Evergreen, up in the Rocky Mountains just west of Denver. Evergreen at the time was reached by a winding road along mountain cliffs that used to excite me with fright as we made our way along it. And also, at that time, Evergreen was still something of a frontier town. I used to love to ride into town on a horse to pick up the family's mail!

Indeed, Denver itself at the time also still had something of the Old West flavor to it, founded heavily on the world of cattle and railroads. Years later I was to discover, to my great horror, that after I grew up, not only had Denver become totally "yuppified," Evergreen too had become a fashionable Yuppie suburb of Denver – thanks to Interstate 70!

Eisenhower and Nixon. Also, it was in Denver that I took my first steps into a world that would come to have great importance to me: that of national politics.

Actually, I had just taken my first interest in that world back home in Collinsville the year (1952) that my parents bought a new 13-inch TV set, and I found myself that summer following intently the Republican National Convention, covered fully by one of the national stations. I was deeply intrigued by it all.

But it was in Denver that the "personal" part of that world opened up.

It seems that General Dwight Eisenhower, who had just been selected by the Republicans at that same convention to be its presidential candidate, happened to be in Denver later than summer, when we too were there. He and his wife Amy were visiting Amy's mother (who lived only a couple of blocks down 8th Avenue from my grandparents), and was holding a reception, open to the public at the Brown Palace Hotel in downtown Denver. So off to meet this man I went, where indeed, this 11-year old boy got to shake hands and be greeted – not only by Eisenhower but also by his running mate, Richard Nixon.

That meant a lot to me, something I would never forget, something that brought home to me that the idea that national politics was not really that remote, if you were willing to step forward a little to engage it personally!

Dad's role in my getting "Middle-Americanized"! Fitting into the larger world that awaited me as I made my way step by step to adulthood never seemed to be a very complicated matter. The game-plan was clear to all, not at all controversial, and seemed to be simply a matter of doing what was expected of any normal human being.

First of all, there was the family model placed clearly before us. My dad was the "provider" thanks to his job. Today he would be considered very much the "professional." But back then he was just someone who simply did his job, to put a roof over our heads, put food on the table, and pay the bills.

He and a group of buddies (they all attended the town's Presbyterian Church) bought an old used car together to take them daily from their homes in Collinsville to their work at the East St. Louis Monsanto plant. In that car pool was a Monsanto division chief, my father (the engineer in the group), and several other men who performed tasks at various levels of production. That is, they made up what today would be considered members of distinctly different social ranks. But at that time, whatever their different roles at Monsanto were, they were simply co-workers, just as all Americans were simply co-workers in the American world.

Identity politics? That was a key part of what made Middle America so unique, at a time when the rest of the world had its various societies divided distinctly into a whole array of class, sectarian, ethnic, even tribal and national, groupings. The general idea in Middle America was that in America, you were just "American", nothing more, and certainly nothing less.

What about the Black world at that time? In Collinsville, you would have had almost no contact with such a Black world. Aside from a few families living in town, there was almost no Black presence there. True, nearby East St. Louis had a quite large, though (as yet) by no means dominant Black presence in the life of that community. Indeed, it was through regional sports, involving some of East St. Louis's high school sportsmen, that I came to have my first contacts with the Black community. And my general impression, besides the obvious fact that they had skins darker than mine, was that they tended to be excellent athletes. And that was about as far as the matter went for me personally.

True, there was some "diversity" in Collinsville, in that Collinsville had once been somewhat minorly an industrial town, mining soft coal for home-heating and whatever. A number of people had come to Collinsville from Southern Italy a generation or two earlier to work those mines, now at that point closed. In doing so, they naturally formed their own Italian-Catholic community in town. I did not have much contact with that world either, until the kids coming out of that community left the town's Catholic parochial school and went on to Collinsville's public high school, which I also attended, as did everyone my age in town. But that Italian-Catholic community had become so "Americanized" that in high school there was no discernible difference in terms of any "identity" matters.

Well not entirely. I found that these Catholic girls seemed to be especially attractive, and it was among that group typically that I found myself dating! My grandmother was not wild about the matter. But hey, she was off in Denver, so that hardly mattered at the time.

Mom's role. My mom was an "at-home-mom" as was virtually every other mom in town, at least as far as I knew. Sure, she was college-educated. True, she had once worked for an important city newspaper as a writer. Also, by today's understanding, that should have put her in the professional class, rather than be ranked as something as inferior as occupying the position of "other" or "unemployed" on today's tax sheets. Every woman was an "other" back then, and very importantly so in the scheme of community life, both nationally and locally.

She played the key role of nurturing the rising generation, especially during the critical first years of our lives when we developed our first notions of what larger life was supposed to be all about, and how it was that we were supposed to meet the larger world's expectations of our own performance. That training was vital to us, for it provided healthy development for any of us "Middle Americans."

Yes, she would eventually go on and get her master's degree in library science, and yes, she would then take up the job as the high-school librarian. But that was not to occur until my sister Gina and I were off in college pursuing our own education. Up until then, Mom was at home, making sure that our world was safe, manageable, and enjoyable. That was her first priority.

True, she was quite active outside the home, doing what most "Middle American" women did, connecting the family to the surrounding social world – while Dad was off at work and the kids were in school. She was very busy in church matters, which depended heavily on this unpaid, non-professional work force of committed women to make the worshiping community succeed in its call. She was busy helping at the public library, which also depended heavily on such volunteer support. And yes, she was active in the Collinsville Women's Club (an organization involved in every imaginable activity possible in this small world), even becoming its president at one point.

In all, Middle America found itself built heavily on this kind of egalitarian, volunteering public spirit. It needed no state bureaucrat to tell it how to go about life, much less how to make it better. It was quite good as it was. And any needed improvements would have come quickly from the good citizens of Collinsville themselves, who not only voted in the local elections but also participated in curriculum discussions (which tended to be very conservative anyway) at school board meetings and at open forums at city hall. That was the way American "democracy" worked. That was Middle America being just that: Middle America.

And it all paid the bills. We lived quite comfortably – as everyone I knew did in Collinsville – not at exactly the same income level, but not on the basis of much of an income spread either. In any case, I knew of no one "poor" in Collinsville.

My first experience with a much harder or crueler reality. This is not to say that I lived entirely in some kind of social "bubble"! Something that happened even in my preteen years left an indelible mark on me: a Disney nature movie! I would never get out of my mind a scene that I was exposed to, of an African leopard creeping up on an inattentive younger gazelle and bringing it down, in order to feed its own hungry cubs. It was deeply shocking to watch, at the same time being aware (even at such an early age) that it was very necessary for the survival of the leopard's cubs. Yes but what about the survival of the gazelle?

Unlike everything else in my well-regulated existence, I realized that there was no "rational" answer to that question. That was certainly for me a "first." I can't say it made me cynical (though I would come to know cynicism quite intimately in later years). It just undercut the kind of pleasant assurance I had that all things had quite logical, even straightforward, formulas designed to provide a trouble-free life.

This was my introduction to an existential proposition that things just happen, and some unavoidable decisions would have to be made, not on the basis of some clear reason, but on the basis that they simply had to be made in order just to move ahead, sometimes just to survive. And they were choices that had more the feel of guesswork than rational planning for success.

I would later have this understanding amplified as I came to appreciate the fact that this was a challenge found widely in life. For instance, it was typically the situation facing an army about to go into battle. All the battle plans that had been made will suddenly have to be adjusted, even possibly be set completely aside, once the first shot is fired and the action gets underway, for both sides of the contest.

When finally moving past the typical Cowboys-and-Indians stage in my early life, I would take on more seriously an understanding of the drama facing the immigrant Anglos and the native Indian-Americans when they encountered each other in their struggle for the land. One would be a winner. One a loser. And the struggle would be very ugly. The Anglos were determined to build their communities in the New World, and they needed the land to farm and thus feed their population. And the Indians needed those same lands to hunt, in order to continue to support their own economy. And they would defend their hunting territories (as they always had), brutally if necessary.

Yes, life is a matter of watching the leopard and gazelle going at things. The leopard, though the mightier of the two, did not always succeed in bringing down the gazelle. And when that happened, the leopard cubs would grow ever hungrier, and more susceptible to tragedy.

There were no guarantees about such things. But the dynamic could not be escaped. Survival depended on it.

Such ideas and understandings for a mere youth to have to take on! But it would deeply shape my future venture into the world of social dynamics, where things tended to operate along much the same lines.

My religious upbringing. But there seemed to be the matter of church to offer comfort in the face of such things. The Christian life (as I understood it at the time) was a set of answers to all of such mysteries and contradictions. And I wasn't the only one who tended to go at America's national religion, Christianity (actually coupled with "democracy" and "capitalism") from that perspective. We all worshiped an orderly God, whom we were certain had ordained this perfect order.

Thus it was that in my Middle America, everyone went to church. Besides, there was not much else to do of a Sunday morning anyway, as everything – absolutely everything – was shut down so that people's attention could then be focused on church!

Yes, there was great religious diversity in town. True, there was no synagogue in town, although my family doctor, and his daughter that I grew up with from 3rd grade through high school graduation, were Jewish, and attended a synagogue nearby (which our Presbyterian youth group visited once on something of a religious "exchange.") But religiously involved we all were, regardless of the particular form it took. Religion was a key component of Middle American life.

Yes, I dated Catholic girls, and yes, I was active in high school sports (cross-country, track, and football), and yes, I danced regularly at "Teen Town" on weekend evenings. But the real focus of my social life was the town's First Presbyterian Church. I not only grew up within its religious-moral precincts, I found it to be the center of a lot of social activity for me. My closest friends in Collinsville were always the ones that I had grown up with in Sunday School. And on Sunday evenings, we attended regularly the youth group, Westminster Fellowship. And we went to the week-long Westminster Fellowship summer camps together.

Indeed, so active was I in all this that I not only later became a camp counselor for the younger version of summer camp, I became an officer in the organization, becoming the "moderator" (head) of the Collinsville chapter of Westminster Fellowship, but then also the moderator of the entire Alton Presbytery (50+ Presbyterian churches in the region) and finally vice-moderator of the entire Illinois Synod (all the Presbyterian churches in Illinois).

It was hardly a wonder that I headed off to a Presbyterian college in the fall of 1959 with the idea that I would be preparing myself for the Presbyterian ministry.

Yet oddly enough, it was not my parents who tended to shape this idea into reality. They themselves had really offered no opinion on the matter of what career direction I should take as I headed into the future, although college itself was a certainty. It was my grandmother, with whom I was especially close, who really helped channel me in this religious direction.

My first (very indirect) contact with the world outside of America. Where, however, my parents did play a huge role in shaping the future unfolding before me was the way they brought the world of Europe, more precisely Italy, and even more precisely the city of Venice, into the Hodges realm. That started up during my junior year in high school.

My father was finding his advancement up the administrative hierarchy at Monsanto to be not particularly to his taste. He was an engineer, a scientist at heart, not a corporate executive. And the corporate politics involved in career advancement was for him a most unpleasant dynamic. He was a researcher, whose work his own boss was taking credit for in order to promote himself in the corporate game.

My mom stepped in at one point and urged my father to join Toastmasters Club in town, in order to help my father develop the necessary public speaking skills he would need to compete in the corporate game. That would serve him in important ways in the future, though it did not change anything immediately for my father politically at Monsanto.

Eventually, sick of corporate politics, Dad was about to quit Monsanto, when his boss's boss, valuing my father's work greatly, stepped into the picture. Monsanto's chemical company plants, sitting astride the Mississippi on both sides of the river, were using the river to dump unwanted chemicals. Clearly this was going to have to come to a halt, at some considerable cost to the company. But it was going to take someone with a visionary mind to tackle such an immense challenge. And this Monsanto chief saw in my father exactly the person best suited to take on just such a challenge.

And since this took my father completely out of the corporate lineup, but promised to make him very much an independent force within the company, he was quick to say yes to the offer.

But he would need to take on a huge amount of research – and experimentation – to get "stream pollution control" up and running at Monsanto.

Two things happened at about the same time (1957) for my father. First of all, he signed up for some of the first graduate courses offered at St. Louis's Washington University, on this new subject of pollution abatement or control. And secondly, the Italian government was putting pressure on the chemical plants in Maestra, on the Italian mainland opposite the water-surrounded Venice, to do something about the terrible pollution coming from those chemical plants. Somehow, Monsanto got brought into the deal, and soon Monsanto had my father flying off to Italy to review the situation there. It turned out to be a great opportunity for him to actually get very busy undertaking serious efforts to do something quite real about the problem.

It very quickly came to the point where it was clear that my father was going to have to relocate himself to Italy, to Venice. And with that came the opportunity for my family to move itself to Italy, at least for a season (4 to 6 months?). My mother jumped at the chance.

But my sister and I balked at the whole idea. Our world was there in Collinsville. And I had just started up a relationship with a girl I met at summer church camp, and leaving that behind made no sense. Exchanging that relationship for what, Italy? I knew all there was to know about Italy (so I supposed), just from my own involvement in Collinsville's Italian-Catholic community. I could "do Italy" just fine right there in Collinsville.

So, it was agreed. With my mother's departure for Italy, my

grandmother would move in with us in Collinsville and take over family management during our parents' absence.

And wouldn't you know that within two weeks of the transition, I got dumped by my new, all-precious girlfriend! That hurt, although in no ways did it change any thoughts I had about having turned down the opportunity to move to Venice. Coming to an understanding of what exactly I had missed by way of an invaluable experience would have to wait a few years.

Four months later my parents returned, deeply changed by the experience.

We had known virtually nothing of "life abroad" prior to that. And why should we? We as Middle Americans believed – almost as some kind of religious doctrine – that America was the most perfect place in the world, and that the world should therefore model itself on our social-cultural ("Christian/democratic/capitalist") ways.

As I would eventually come to discover, yes indeed, America is a very great place. But so are other places.

But discovering that fact however brought no loss of appreciation of the wonderfulness of my America. I learned that the world is full of great places, great in different ways, but still "great." And the greatness of one place does not diminish the greatness of other places!

But we Middle Americans didn't know that. Or at least I didn't know that. Not yet anyway.

Yes, but now my parents did. And as a follow-up to their amazing life lived right on Venice's Grand Canal, they undertook Italian language study, not becoming great at it, but henceforth always very supportive of the idea of Italian culture itself.

Thus it was that a much larger world was about to open up for me, though at the time I was still quite clueless about any of it!

✳ ✳ ✳

THE CHANGE OF DIRECTION (1959-1960)

Hanover College: Biblical criticism and the loss of my Christian faith.
The decision to become a Presbyterian minister did not outlast my first semester at college. In my very first Bible course, the professor delighted in exposing all of the "myths" of Scripture. This was the theological vogue of the day. Stripping the Bible of all its supposedly merely superstitious miracle stories would certainly produce a stronger, more reasonable foundation for the Christian faith. At least that's how my Bible professor thought (and others like him).

This was hardly a new idea, Thomas Jefferson himself proposed exactly the same idea back in the early 1800s, which, by the way, did not bring Christianity, or anything else, to a higher realm. And it certainly was not going to have any different effect now, 150 years later. Nonetheless, the professor undertook the task with something of a vengeance, leaving us all disillusioned and gasping in his assault on our Sunday School worlds.

Then he flew off to London the next semester during spring break, and committed suicide.

My Christian faith began to crumble under the shock – though, for a while, I held on to the social aspects of the Christian faith in order not to become totally unanchored. This was not all that difficult, for most of my Christian faith had been built on Christianity's social aspects anyway. Indeed, I had no clue at the time about anything like "spirituality." I don't remember ever hearing such a concept mentioned during my growing up years.

Anyway, I had long been encouraged by my high school math and art teachers and now also a college art professor at Hanover to take my interests and apparent strengths in math and art seriously – and consider architecture as a life work. Thus, towards the end of my freshman year I arranged a transfer for the coming fall semester to the architectural engineering program at the University of Illinois in Champaign-Urbana.

The Empire State Building. But that summer (1960) intervened, to change my life and the direction it would take for the next 25 years. In early June I joined my family on the train headed east to New York City (my family had already boarded the train in St. Louis and I joined them as it passed through Indiana). Then upon arriving at this massive metropolis, we spent a few days touring it prior to our departure for Europe for the summer. We of course did the requisite sites, including a trip to the top of the Empire State Building.

What a different perspective on the importance of the individual, whom I was taught to extol (almost worship), that I got, looking down on the ant-sized people on the street below. As I gazed further out upon the city, I had the sensation that the loss of a few thousand people here and there would hardly make a difference in a city this size – much less in the world. This was almost as deflating an episode as the loss of my Sunday School religion at Hanover College.

I would have great difficulty, for a long time after that, believing that individual lives counted that much in the greater scheme of things. A few lives perhaps (hopefully even mine), namely, those of a handful of great leaders and thinkers. But the vast numbers of the rest of us were destined to live our lives much like worker ants live out their lives, quietly and insignificantly.

Europe (summer of 1960). On the other hand, the next three months touring Europe with my family opened up such a world of wonder and beauty that it came as a powerful counterpoise to the loss of my small, smug WASPish (White Anglo-Saxon Protestant) cosmos. Spaces in Europe were small, but more ingeniously designed in their miniature scope (miniature in comparison to the vast, unchanging cultural layout of America, which I knew quite well through the many car trips our family had previously made across the country, here and there) – and quite unique in particular character as the European cultural scenes shifted every hundred or so miles.

We landed in Amsterdam and I became entranced immediately with the canals, bridges, narrow three-story homes and shops, and the people everywhere on bicycles – speaking a tongue totally unknown to me. From there we moved up along the Rhine River through Germany, across Switzerland to Austria, and finally down into Italy to Venice.

You can imagine how I kicked myself for having stupidly passed up the opportunity not just to visit but to have actually lived in this magical place. But by this time, I had already come to the decision that I would never pass up such an opportunity again. In fact, I was determined to return, to spend extended time at least at one of the many marvelous European communities I was discovering along the way.

And it was not just the sites that intrigued me. I never lost an opportunity to engage any of the locals possessing enough English to converse with me about what they understood about their own culture, their dreams, their understandings about life. I did so in the cafes, in museums, along the docks, but most often at the bed-and-breakfasts we stayed at, as Dad drove us from city to city.

Anyway, we spent an entire month covering Italy from North to South. In the process, I fell particularly in love with Florence, which I explored from end to end, and to which I would years later send my son Paul and my daughter Elizabeth to live and study the local language and culture.

Then we returned to Switzerland and crossed into France. And there is where I was able to put to very good use the French I had learned that first year at Hanover, talking deep into the night with a French grandma owning the bed and breakfast, and her very young granddaughter, who was just as excited to hear me explain about the deeper character of "Middle America", a subject I had not previously seen the need to investigate, much less do so deeply in order to explain it – as I now found myself doing when the subject (at this point, often) came up.

In France I was anxious to visit the Reims Cathedral, for I had just written, as an English assignment my second semester at Hanover, a 20-

page paper describing the cathedral's origins, its physical structure, its role in French life. And now being there (and other similar cathedrals wherever I found the opportunity) I was so easily carried to another time, another world.

And Paris was awesome, especially when I discovered the Caveau de la Huchette, a jazz club in the Latin Quarter, where I showed up several nights running to dance with the very stylish French girls!

From France and then Belgium, we crossed to England. London was, of course, magnificent!

Then I left the company of my mother and sister (my father had already flown back to his work at home) and headed across England on my own.

But I had just got myself seated on the train heading west, to discover that my BritRail pass was missing. Thus I now realized that to complete my journey, I would have to use my limited cash reserves to pay the way (I found out later that my sister had hidden the BritRail pass as a sisterly prank, and then forget to put it back before I left on my trip!)

Anyway, one of my stops was at the Stonehenge historical site, where one evening I found myself actually alone out on the plains where the massive Stonehenge structure was located, taken aback at the obvious technical difficulty it had to have been, thousands of years ago, to bring those stones in from afar (there were no mountains nearby) and raise them up to the heights where they still stood even today. What must human life have been like so long ago? Who were these people, existing even well before the Celtic invasions hundreds of years before Christ (and thus, no, not originally Druid worship sites)? Who were they? And would our work today come to have as lasting a quality as this work did? Was modern culture really that strong?

From England and Wales I headed to Ireland, again, finding myself deeply engaged in conversation with the locals about how they understood and undertook life.

Then I headed on to Scotland, where I found myself falling in love with bagpipe music (years later I would buy myself a set of Scottish bagpipes, and go at the challenge of playing one!). One evening in Inverness, I sat for a long time in the presence of two men who had simply come together to play their bagpipes, the three of us transported by their music into a world that had been around for a very long time before even our arrival on the scene!

Anyway, I finally arrived in Edinburgh, with absolutely no more cash in hand, but also missing – thanks also to my sister's prank – the information mentioning the hotel where I was to meet my mother and sister. Meanwhile, I found a bed-and-breakfast where I could put meals on the bill (for future payment), but figured I would have to go to the American consular offices to find a way of connecting with my family. But it was the weekend and those offices would surely have been closed. Then the thought occurred to me (God's own intervention!) of showing up at the entrance to St. Giles Cathedral Sunday morning, and looking for the possibility they would come there for Sunday worship. And wouldn't you know, there they were – already waiting for me on the steps of the cathedral!*

I loved the European experience I had just had, all of it. Such a wonderful delving into a world with deep cultural roots, something rather lacking in my beloved America.

I never regretted anything up to that time as much as I did, having to get on that plane in mid-September to head home. Europe had stolen my heart.

✱ ✱ ✱

<h3 align="center">BACK TO EUROPE (1961-1962)</h3>

Getting ready (1960-1961). The very first thing I did upon entering the University of Illinois that fall was to transfer out of architectural engineering and into the humanities program.   I knew that I had to follow out this new line of inquiry into life – even though it had no practical occupational applications.

That school year (1960-1961) at first was lonely and insipid in comparison to the thrill of life I had experienced in Europe. It was however always made bearable by the knowledge that I would be spending the next year (my junior year) as a student somewhere in Europe – presumably France. Thus during my sophomore year at the University of Illinois I continued my French studies, but also took up German, and delved into the history of Western Civilization, a subject that still commands my deep affections.

Things however did pick up socially in the spring semester quite a bit with my work with the University's Sheequon spring carnival and with some Beta Theta Pi fraternity activities (I had become a member of that fraternity the previous year at Hanover), in particular the various dances they sponsored during the course of the year.

Mob mentality. But yet another event on campus that I got to experience first-hand would add further to my understanding of the realm of social

---

*Ironically, it would be that same entrance to St. Giles Cathedral that would be the setting for a life-changing vision I was to receive many years later, as a call to full-time service in Christian ministy!

dynamics.

Time was creeping up on the first of May, when by some kind of tradition, a "panty raid" by boys on the girls' dorms was expected to take place, as some kind of rite of spring. For reasons not clear to me, the Inter-Fraternity Council decided that this event was not going to happen. And somehow they seemed to succeed in getting an agreement on the matter across campus.

Although I was a "fraternity boy," I had found it necessary to finance, at least partially, college expenses by working in the kitchen of yet another fraternity, for the work took care of the need for my meals, which were then free to me.

Anyway, May Day arrived, then came the evening, and nothing yet had happened.

But it was our own efforts at the Lambda Chi house to clean up the dishes after dinner that got things up and running. Instead of simply dumping the dishwater out back, one of the kitchen crew decided that dumping it on a crewmate was far more interesting. Well, one thing led to another, and very soon I realized that a lot of guys had come out from fraternity row, to join in the developing water fight. With this, things gathered momentum quickly. And then someone called out for a grand assault on the girls' dorms across campus. And by this time, a wild herd of young men had assembled. And yes, they headed for the girls' dorms. And yes, it was by this time a full stampede!

Along the way one young man jumped up on a bulldozer parked along some road work, and began driving it back and forth. Scary! Then the wild pack headed across faculty row, mowing down the hedges that lined the sidewalks leading to the faculty homes.

As we approached the girls' dorms, the group gathered at a fire hydrant, which someone opened up, only to have a campus cop drive up and shut it off, only to have a young man jump out of the crowd, grab the astonished cop's monkey wrench and turn it back on again.

At this point, I decided that I had had enough of the "fun" of participating in such mass action, and headed home.

Along the way I gave deep thought to the actions of those individuals, who, on their own, would never have dared undertake such behavior. But mob psychology had overtaken them, and they moved accordingly.

That in itself would continue to haunt me, when I came to understand through this experience how noble individualism could be converted so easily into mob action, very destructive mob action. This was a new facet of social dynamics I previously had no reason to give any thought to. Now it was a major piece in my understanding of wars, of battles, of strikes, of riots, and how easily they are taken up by otherwise very cautious individuals. You just needed the right chemistry present, and social reason could be easily replaced by uncontrolled social passion. And I would get to see a lot of this kind of behavior in later years, some of that quite soon.

Geneva. School was ending and my plans to spend my junior year at a European university were coming into being. I was to be placed through the Presbyterian Junior Year Abroad Program somewhere in Europe. Because of my ongoing French language study, as well as actual use the previous summer, my expectations were that this placement would naturally be at a university in France. Thus I was quite disappointed when I first learned that I had been placed at the University of Geneva in Switzerland – French-speaking to be sure, but not France.

But I quickly learned upon my arrival at Geneva (August of 1961) that this was in fact most fortuitous for me – for Geneva proved to be perfect for my personal needs.

As it turned out, Geneva was a small, breathtakingly beautiful city located along the edge of the huge Lake Geneva, with the Alps rising up sharply at the very edge of town. Though small in size, Geneva was magnificent, with its multitudes of international diplomats and jetsetters and was incredibly cosmopolitan in its ways. It was a perfect learning place for someone who wanted to be immersed in the broader cultural coloration of the world. It was a town of Russian and Chinese Communists, of Southern African guerrilla leaders, of Arab modernizers, of sophisticated Europeans – and yes even religious leaders out of the Reformed Tradition of the 16th century Genevan, John Calvin, from which my Presbyterian tradition came.

I proceeded immediately to become entranced not only with Geneva, but with a Norwegian miss, Tove, who was in Geneva also attending my summer French class, studying the language prior to becoming a Scandinavian Airlines stewardess. We quickly hit it off. As we adventured together around Geneva and beyond, I encountered a chemistry for living that I had never known before. At the end of the French summer session in late September, Tove returned home to Oslo, supposedly to bring her family the news of a deep change of plans in her life, for she now intended to return to Geneva in early November to become a regular student at the university, with me. I in the meantime hitchhiked from Geneva to Oslo to meet her parents – only to find upon my arrival there that her father had other plans for his daughter! Thus sadly did I, a few days later, find myself hitchhiking back to Geneva, without my true love in company with me. I was alone, in an aloneness I had never known before in my life. The cold, damp grayness of the late October weather I encountered – first in Copenhagen (where we had originally intended to spend time together exploring the city's many attractions) then all the way back to Geneva – seemed most appropriate to my mood.

My German friends. On the other hand, almost from my first day back in Geneva I found myself in the constant company of a German student, Adam, who would become something like a brother to me. Before classes for the fall term had started, he whisked me off to his home in Munich to pick up my spirits – and to teach me how to drink beer! And upon our return to Geneva to start that fall term I joined him in his wider social circle of German friends. Thankfully during the previous school year I had taken up German study, and was competent enough to follow not only their activities but also their conversations, even their more complex ideas (Adam was the only one in the group with a command of the English language, so all group conversation was conducted in German). In fact, by the end of the academic year next summer, I was fully fluent in German.

What a group! They played harder, skied harder, stayed up longer and ventured out more often than any people I had ever encountered before! I immediately was absorbed into their company – and for most of the rest of the year in Geneva I became something of a German! For a midwestern boy from Illinois this proved to be quite soul-stretching!

But that soul-stretching came not just in their ability to teach me how to let go of my highly structured world, how to plunge into realms discovered by means well beyond those of mere cultural curiosity.

Most importantly, the Germans introduced me to a world of post-authoritarianism, an authentic way of warding off the tendency to do group-think – such as I had seen displayed in the mob action on the Illinois campus the previous school-year. They were very cautious about jumping to quick political decisions, but went at social issues carefully, rather than passionately. And I quickly learned why.

They, of course, had survived as children the bombing of their homes by American and British bombers during "Hitler's war." Then after the war they had to come to hard decisions about where they stood on the matter of what their parents had done during the war, not only to the Jews, but also to their Slavic neighbors, in fact in one way or another, to most anyone not identified as German (the Italians largely excepted, thanks to Hitler's Fascist mentor Mussolini).

One thing was certain about my German buddies. They understood the great dangers of political crusading, of surrendering their better senses in following a charismatic individual into some kind of great political campaign.

In short, they showed me that a cautious approach to social issues was, in the long run, the most likely way to produce good social results.

True, they could have great fun, even be on the wild side at times. But when it came to politics, they were a very introspective breed. Indeed, my German friends were true conservatives, in the very best, the very wisest, sense of the word.

And so it was that I learned a great deal from them in terms of social dynamics.

Kim. In the early months of 1962, I became stretched in a new direction, as a relationship with a young American also at the University of Geneva, Kim, began to take off. Kim was all the sophistication I was not. Though she was only 18 and 2½ years younger than me, she was much wiser in the ways that were just beginning to open up to me, she being the daughter of a ranking American NATO officer living in Paris and having herself lived in many different cultural settings growing up.

I never was really quite sure what her fascination was for me – even though our relationship was to continue as we both later returned to the States. In fact it was to last for three years – and be for me my first truly deep relationship with a female. She was another major part of my coming of age.

Southeastern Europe on a motor scooter. But our relationship had only just begun when I decided to take the month of spring break from mid-March to mid-April to point my Vespa motor scooter eastward and head off alone into a part of Europe I had not yet explored. My purpose was much the same as it had been when I was traveling through Europe with my family: to engage as many people as possible in discussions about their culture, their personal understanding about life's ultimate purposes, except that much of this would be undertaken this time with people living in the Soviet sphere of domination, "behind the Iron Curtain" as we described it in those days. It would also include my first venture into the land of Islam (Turkey).

The trip lasted a month and marked another one of those turning points in my life. I had a couple of close encounters with death, once nearly sliding over a precipice in the snowbound Alps as I headed toward Austria; another trying to get out of the diesel fumes I had been swallowing for an hour as I followed a school bus along the twisting Aegean road in Greece, nearly going off the cliff as I avoided an oncoming car when I finally made a desperate attempt to pass the bus.

But it was oddly a different day that the reality of death touched me deeply – symbolically, but very tangibly. It was a tough day. I had set out from Edirne (near the Bulgarian-Turkish border I had just crossed) toward Istanbul – about a 7-hour trip by my Vespa. I was three hours underway when I remembered that I had left my passport with the hotel clerk back in Edirne and had to return to pick it up. It was a sunny but very windy day with the gusts coming off the Black Sea so strong that one of them blew me off the road, and it took a Turkish shepherd and me together to get the Vespa back up on the road.

That afternoon, once again on my way to Istanbul, I passed a dead dog lying along the side of the road – not the first time I had seen one. But something about that dog lying there in the finality of its death struck me deeply. It lasted only a couple of seconds as I passed. Perhaps it was only my profound fatigue that made me react so strongly. But from that moment on I would no longer hold the youthful view that I was going to live forever. The ultimate and irreversible reality of death truly impressed me – in a way that remained lasting, and building, over the next years.

Also an event in Istanbul would leave a deep mark on my understanding about life and its easy patterns. At one point I got a bit lost in wandering through this ancient city, and found myself facing what presumably was the city dump. And I was shocked when I saw the grey matter that the dump was made of actually moving! And when I looked again, what I realized that I was seeing were filth-covered humans, a fair number of them, living in the dump, presumably scrounging for whatever bits of food they could find there.

This was poverty such as I had heard about previously... but had no idea of its reality. Indeed, in America, being "poor" had a very different meaning than what I, at that point, was observing. American poverty did not mean that you were starving. It meant only that you did not possess the wealth or the status that qualified you as "Middle American."

What I was observing there in Istanbul was true poverty, the kind, unfortunately, that exists quite readily here and there around the world, and has always done so. From that point on I was quite aware of the fact that whatever constituted the American idea of a crusade to end poverty in America, it had little to do with the dynamic I saw before me there in Istanbul.

Actually, things weren't always that serious on this trip. I enjoyed immensely meeting university students from Hungary, Yugoslavia and Bulgaria and managed to get to know a number of them quite well in a very short time (either German or French, or even occasionally English, seemed to be useful in this or that situation).

But even then, such encounters could have some larger, very dramatic outcomes. Thus, for instance, a university student I had spent several days with in Budapest escaped from Hungary later that summer and came to me in Geneva unannounced, because I was the only contact she had in the West. I was able to help her gain refugee status through the European office of the United Nations located right there in Geneva. And I was able to send her on to Paris, where her brother, who himself had just escaped Hungarian authorities, was discovered to be living (he had given the slip to a Hungarian delegation he was part of while on a diplomatic mission to Egypt).

It is also possible that the Soviets, whose Hungarian police followed me closely the whole time I was in Budapest (as one of the first Westerners allowed into Hungary after the 1956 riots, and subsequent boycott of Hungary by the Western powers), also made the connection, for when I applied for a travel visa to go through Russia on my way to Helsinki that summer, I was rejected on "security grounds"!!!

Spring and summer (1962). Anyway, I returned to Geneva in April with almost no money in my pocket and almost no gas left in the Vespa's tank – and took up where I left off with my German friends and with Kim. Studies at the university and at the nearby Graduate Institute of International Studies (I was allowed to take graduate courses focused on international diplomacy and history) continued until mid-July.

Then with exams over, I sold the Vespa and took off hitchhiking toward Oslo to see if I could restart my relationship with Tove. Along the way, I took a side trip to Berlin.

Things were very tense at that time in Berlin. The Berlin Wall had gone up the previous August just as I arrived at Geneva (it was strange that fellow students asked me what we were going to do about the wall, as I had absolutely no say in the matter, of course!), and Europe was still having a hard time accepting this development. And now, almost a year later, in hitching a ride into Berlin from West Germany, I found security to be very tight and very intimidating, a reminder of what life under absolute State authority was like.

And American-supported West Berlin was such a contrast to Communist East Berlin, which you could see across the newly constructed wall. West Berlin was "jumping" – bright lights, bars and restaurants everywhere, in fact a great place for me to celebrate my 21st birthday!

But curiosity got the better of me, and I decided to cross into East Berlin to have a closer look. It was scary! I had to turn my passport over to an East German agent at a booth that was once a ticket window for the city's subway, when you could still go from East to West in the city. It was dark down there, symbolic of the general atmosphere in East Berlin. When I came up on the Eastern side, the area was flat, with some distant buildings still in deep disrepair. And nobody was really there, except a couple, off in the distance, who stared at me the whole time. It was creepy. It was depressing. I soon made my way back to the station, gladly got my passport back ...and enjoyed a couple more days in West Berlin.

But at this point I made an important decision. I would not be heading onwards towards Oslo (and Tove) but instead to Paris (and Kim). And so off I went.

Thus my last month in Europe was spent with Kim and her family, first in Paris, then at a villa located on the Mediterranean coast, where Kim and I found ourselves doing all the fashionable things that one does at the French Riviera – morning, noon and night! It was exciting now being part of Europe's fashionable "jet set."

Then in late August I returned home to the States.

✳ ✳ ✳

GRADUATE SCHOOL (1963-1968)

My senior year at Illinois (1962-1963). I tried to adjust to midwestern life during my senior year at the University of Illinois – but it again seemed so bland in comparison to my European existence, that I was restless throughout that year. Kim, who was now at Connecticut College for Women, spent Christmas with me and my family; then in late January I traveled East to interview at Georgetown and Columbia – and to visit Kim in Connecticut; and in March she came out to visit me on campus. Those were the only high points for that long, slow year.

Interestingly, I was invited (and, strangely, accepted) to be one of two student members on the University's Champaign/Urbana Ministerial Council. At this point I was into existentialism rather than Christianity – and had not entered a church to worship during my entire year in Geneva – and was at this point, my senior year, attending the Presbyterian campus church purely on social rather than theological grounds. I didn't hide the fact. But somehow it seemed not to bother anybody.

I really could not figure out what they thought was important – they seemed to be so all-accommodating to everything. The associate pastor at the campus church even told me – on a trip we made to Chicago to work with the Black community in South Chicago over the week break between semesters – that what was ultimately significant about Christianity was its moral teachings. Did I not believe these to be right and good? Yes, of course. That's why we were going to Chicago.

But such logic only impressed me all the more that there was nothing theologically very profound about Christianity, at least Christianity such as the adult world seemed to be practicing. Anyone of a sound mind most likely had a pretty good idea of the difference between good and evil. I was certain that you didn't need to be a Christian to do that (Kim and my

German friends, for instance, did not presume to be "Christian" in any meaningful way)

Thus when I went off to graduate school at Georgetown I bid the church goodbye, without a bit of remorse – or even thought.

Political "Realism" digs in. Meanwhile, Georgetown University itself was an additional source of my continuing social-political journey. And it would have a huge impact on the way I was to move further into the adult world.

Anyway, if I had ever supposed that I was going to graduate school with the hope of replacing my lost Christian faith with the rising and highly Idealistic "Humanist" faith, typical of most Silents, a strong dose of "political realism" at Georgetown – plus life itself in the nation's capital – clearly blocked that option.

I arrived there at the height of the Kennedy era. Among other things that distinguished this social-political era, American youth now entering the adult world – a quite patriotic sub-generation of "Silents" – had answered quite readily Kennedy's call to "ask not what your country can do for you; ask what you can do for your country." These Silents signed up in great numbers as American social-cultural emissaries sent as volunteer members of the American Peace Corps. They were sent in huge numbers to the Third World of Asia, Africa and Latin America, to present to this rising post-imperial world the "true path" to freedom – that is, doing things the "American way." The presupposition was that these countries had a real cultural choice to make in stepping into their futures, as if the culture they had been living under – probably for many, many generations – could be easily put aside so that they could freely take up American (rather than Soviet Russian or "Communist") ways. All that was needed was for Peace Corps volunteers to show these good citizens of the "Third World" the way to do so.

Washington's bureaucratic lifestyle. I myself did not join the movement, as I was in Washington (or "DC" – which was the way we locals usually called the city) to study, not serve. But I did take up a part-time job (20 hours a week) at the Peace Corps Headquarters in DC – from 1964 to 1966. This would be my first experience working inside the Washington bureaucracy.

At the time all this seemed quite okay. The Peace Corps was a nice organization to find yourself working for, although it was not a hotbed of idealism or patriotism, or much of anything else. It was just a bureaucratic job after all.

Thus it was in those days that I first learned about how bureaucracy is supposed to work.   In Washington, "corporate production" is not about cars, or washing machines, or dresses, or lumber. It is about social ideas, ones that are supposed to guide the nation. In other words, grand social ideas are what Washington supposedly produces, in massive quantities.

As far as the ideas themselves, the only ones actually creating those ideas are the political leaders: the president, the members of Congress, the federal justices, etc. Everyone else is there to support – that is, give flesh to the bones of – those ideas. That's what the massive bureaucracy that constitutes the rest of Washington society does.*

It does not require a lot of brain power to be a bureaucrat. You simply take a place somewhere in the system and perform a small or finite function in the process of putting those ideas into action. You sit at a desk, with an in-box on the left and an out-box on the right of your desk, and papers or folders that are to be moved from one box to the other as your job. It actually does not take long to learn exactly what it is that you are supposed to do with those documents. You do not need to be an expert at some particular social or technical field. You only need to know what it is that you are expected to do between those two boxes.

Furthermore, there is a professional game at the heart of bureaucratic life, in which the object is to rise in government or "G" ranking by changing positions from one agency to another, with each move involving 1) an increase in the size or number of staff that operate below you 2) and a larger budget that you and your staff have to work with. So you may start out at the Department of the Navy as a very low level clerk, advance a step or two to a higher position in the Department of Commerce, then later switch yet to an even higher position in the Department of Education, or the Department of Transportation, or the Department of Agriculture, and so on. It's what you do with your life, rise up the bureaucratic ranks. Interesting, if you are "into" that kind of lifestyle!

An additional dose of "Realism." Also instructive for me was a story that was passed around at Peace Corps headquarters at that time about an American youth, one of the first to join the new Peace Corps, who was sent off to India to show villagers the capitalist or entrepreneurial ways of America, through the establishment and management of a new chicken farm at the village.

The American volunteer was not at all unsophisticated, and had

---

*Except for the massive Black population that inhabited DC's extensive slums, made up of individuals who came to Washington possibly hoping to find employment in the city as some kind of laborer, such as the dynamic in Detroit, or Chicago or Philadelphia. But Washington involved almost purely white-collar (office) work rather than Blue-collar (industrial) work. Thus unemployment in those Black neighborhoods was extensive, along with all the social problems that accompanied such unemployment.

learned not only the local Indian dialect – and, even as an English major in college, how to raise chickens during his Peace Corps training! – but also the necessary diplomacy he would need in order to get the village on board with his chicken project. Thus upon his arrival at the village he went very slow with his project, getting the village elders to understand and then be enthusiastic in support of the idea of raising chickens commercially.

It took some time before things were finally ready to go. But by the end of his two-years in India, he had a real chicken business going full speed in the village. Then once back in the States, he headed off to grad school, but never let the village get far from his thoughts.

After a year back at home he decided to return to India to see how his chicken business was doing. He wrote to the village elders to let them know of his intentions, and they replied that the village would be more than happy to see their "hero" again.

And thus it was that he arrived at the village, and a very enthusiastic reception by the villagers. But he noticed that the chicken cages were empty.

When he finally had a chance to ask the elders what happened, their reply was a shock to him, nothing that he had anticipated. "Oh, Sahib," they said, "the village will ever remember you as a great man, who left us the ability to put on such a chicken feast for the neighboring villagers, one that had never been seen before."

And so that was that. His two-year effort to institute capitalism in the village had become the basis for what mattered even much more in Hindu culture, the ability to put on an extravagant show of wealth – and its possible service in offering grand charity to others – something that would make the village stand out forever in the regard of everyone locally.

That lesson dug deeply into my own thinking.

Other cultures did not just go away because brilliant American culture suddenly showed up. I would soon get to see this dynamic repeated by the American military presence in Vietnam. And I was not at all surprised by the results. Rather, I was deeply disappointed at how American leadership seemed so unable to get past its own cultural thinking in order to work seriously with the way other cultures operated – and have done so for a very long time, and for reasons very clear to the locals.

Thus it was that part of my political "Realism" began to take clearer shape in my Washington years.

The DC Alpha male. Something else I learned about quite quickly reminds me of what I learned in watching that Disney nature movie as a child: life can have some very interesting ways, even shocking if you are not expecting them.

I came to DC out of a very Middle-American world, with its own ideas about society, what it is supposed to look like and how it is supposed to work. My world was built on the foundations of family, a father working a job to support that family and a mom at home to shape the inner life of that family. And there were certain social expectations and social boundaries that my sister and I were expected to learn, and develop ourselves along those same lines. There were simply things you were expected to do, and not do.

One of the first things I learned upon my arrival to Washington was about the many sexual affairs my President (Kennedy) had with numerous women, supposedly including the famous Hollywood actress Marilyn Monroe. I can't say that this came as a shock (I already knew enough about the private lives of men of power in history). But discovering that his brother Bobby, whom I supposed was the more "moral" of the brothers, shared in the "deserts" as well, was a bit shocking. Wow! On the other hand, young brother Teddy as the family's "problem child" came as no surprise, for instance, the stories circulating widely in DC about how many times the family had to use its influence to get him back into Harvard!

I realized that something outside of the Middle-American norm applied to those of great social power. As everywhere else in nature, the strongest male got all the privileges with the opposite sex. And DC was full of such men of power, and women who knew how the game worked.

For instance, two years into my presence in DC – when I found myself actually living in the Georgetown neighborhood – next door to me was a group of young ladies that had come to DC to start out their careers. One of those was a recent winner of the Miss Indiana pageant, and had come to DC to get a job on Capitol Hill, more specifically in Senator Birch Bayh's office. And she knew exactly how to work his male staff members to secure that position. Needless to say, she succeeded.

And then also, I had a housemate and fellow student, Joe, who worked part-time in the evenings as a Senate Office Building elevator operator, who used to keep me informed on what went up and down the elevator after visiting hours were over!

And when I was typing up my master's thesis on Congressman Clark Thompson's IBM Selectric typewriter in his office at night, how many times it was that I had to cut work short because the Administrative Assistant would show up with a cutie in tow, and needed the room for "business."

And then Courtney (a guy's name back then!), a law school student at George Washington University and someone I met while working with an afterschool program for kids, and who subsequently would became a very close friend, was a young man with huge ambitions with respect to the opposite sex. He was a true Alpha Male, destined also to rise high in the DC political game (he eventually became Administrative Assistant to newly appointed Illinois Senator Smith, then soon thereafter Nixon's legal-liaison with the Pentagon). And when my sister Gina returned from her life in Europe, Courtney wanted to date her on her visit to DC. I warned her, though she informed me that she knew quite well how to handle such situations. And apparently she did!

And that was just what happened in DC. The DC news media was well aware of these goings on, although the DC rules were that you were expected to look the other way, especially when DC's moral behavior was likely to shock the rest of the nation! Beyond that, you were not supposed to get caught in your adventures, because DC goings-on were never supposed to leave DC!

But that would change with the arrival of the 1970s, and the appearance of the young Boomer moral crusaders taking their places in the DC news business. But by that time I was only a spectator of such doings, living in Alabama, watching in amazement at the new morality arising in the nation's capital, and the incredible moral hypocrisy that went with it among the DC veterans who were playing along with the new political dynamics. Ah politics!

My master's thesis on South Africa. In completing my first year's required coursework at Georgetown (1964), my professor-mentor suggested that I do my master's thesis on the African nationalist movement in South Africa – and I accepted, thinking that I was going to be studying one of those exciting epochs in the expansion of world liberation. But as I looked more deeply into the South African situation, I found out that he had assigned me a quite different task: coming up with an explanation of why a smaller group of Whites could so successfully intimidate and hold in servitude a larger number of Blacks – and probably continue to do so for the foreseeable future.

In this I was forced to take a view of human nature that differed quite strongly from that of the "Liberal" world around me.

First of all, South Africa was a very complex mixture of ethnic groups, so that it was not a mere mirroring of the Black-White dualism that America itself was increasingly sensitive about at the time. South Africa was not just Black or White. If White, it could be Dutch-speaking or English-speaking White. If Black, it could be Xhosa or Zulu in tribal makeup (the two groups did not like each other very much). Or it could be Indian, of either the Hindu or Muslim variety. And it could be "Colored", descendants of the original inhabitants of the Southern Africa region, the "San" people (Bushmen and Hottentots), intermixed with Portuguese, Dutch and other blood, who as a distinct racial community now actually spoke Dutch.

And South Africa was not a country moving out from under the distant European authorities of the English, French, Portuguese or Belgians. It had been, since the 1600s, self-governing in the same way that the American colonies, including the original Dutch colonies of America (the forerunners of New York, New Jersey and Delaware) had also been self-governing since the 1600s.

And as far as Black-White issues went, the Bantu tribes (primarily Xhosas) had themselves invaded the region, coming South along the coast of the Indian Ocean, at about the same time (the mid-1600s) that the Dutch moved into the area from the opposite direction by way of the South Atlantic. These Dutch built a settlement at the Cape, and then moved on into the interior behind the Cape. In fact, the ever-expanding Dutch Whites did not meet the ever-expanding Bantu Blacks until a century later (the mid-1700s) at the Great Fish River, about mid-way over what is today South Africa.

Then in the early 1800s, the British moved in to take the Cape away from the Dutch community (that was calling itself "Afrikaners" in the same way Anglos in the New World were calling themselves "Americans.") Many Dutch Afrikaners in the early-to-mid-1800s decided to escape the new British authorities by heading into the open lands of the interior, open because the newly assembled tribe of the Zulu had done a pretty good job of killing off all of the enemy Bantu tribesmen, largely depopulating the area.

Then later in the 1800s, gold and diamonds were found in abundance in that interior region, within the rather young Afrikaner republics of the Orange Free State and the Transvaal. And it was the enterprising British, not the Afrikaners themselves, who tried to start up their own mining operations in these Afrikaner regions. However these British entrepreneurs were forced to bring in not only European workers but also Blacks from the neighboring tribal territories to work their mines, because the Afrikaners were farmers (Boers) and not interested in such underground work.

Finally Afrikaner resistance exploded over this, and the Boer War (1899-1902) broke out, in which the British distinguished themselves with their barbarity in sending Boer women, children and the elderly into concentration camps, to break the will of the resistant Boers (which included, in the Boer armies, a large number of Dutch-speaking "Coloreds"). The outcry of the rest of Europe over such behavior was so great that finally the British broke off the war effort, ultimately turning the whole area (including their huge Cape Province) back over to the Afrikaners as the "Union of South Africa", but bringing this South Africa into their British Empire on a voluntary basis (part of the peace deal) – in time to join the British in fighting World War One.

Meanwhile the population of the Black tribal lands (some now independent territories or even states) had exploded in size (no tribal wars to keep the population in balance with the land, as had been the ancient pattern) and Blacks began to pour in huge numbers into the White cities, especially in the Transvaal, looking for jobs, especially in the years following both World Wars One and Two.

The Afrikaners attempted to control this flow with a policy of controlled immigration, built on the policy of racial, tribal, etc. classification, the heart of their program of apartheid or "separateness."

But by the beginning of the 1960s, European "imperialism" was in disgrace, and the British, French, Portuguese and Belgians were being pressured to give up their imperial holdings in Africa. And by extension of the same logic, the world – with America taking the lead in the matter – began to pressure the Afrikaners to give up the policy of apartheid, threatening serious consequences if they did not.

But the Afrikaners understood clearly that his meant having to turn over their 300-year-old society to the now-numerically-dominant Bantu tribesmen (most probably the Xhosa).

As I looked into the matter, I came to realize that there was little likelihood of the Afrikaner being convinced of the need to conduct social surrender. As cruel as apartheid could be, the Afrikaners were simply not going to allow the collapse of their world. Thus I concluded my 250-page study with the assessment that it was most unlikely that anything significant was going to change with respect to South Africa's social structure, at least for anything like the foreseeable future. No amount of pressure, domestic or international, was going to cause the Afrikaners to give up their long-standing place in the scheme of things there in South Africa.

My conclusion did not please everyone, some accusing me of siding with the "Fascist" Afrikaners. Actually I wasn't siding with anyone. I was merely describing the political dynamics of this particular society, such as I came to understand them through some serious research into the matter.

Thankfully, my thesis mentor and professor was impressed with my work, and urged me to stay on at Georgetown and take on doctoral studies there. It was a thought, a good thought.

Kim and I go our separate ways. Most of my first two years at Georgetown proved to be incredibly tough for me emotionally. Besides a serious spiritual loss of the ability to believe in anything high or grand, even at times in myself, I found life tedious and uninteresting. At first I could afford an apartment only across the Potomac in a nondescript neighborhood of Arlington. I would, however, be able in my second year to move into DC itself in finding an apartment just off Dupont Circle, a big step up. But still,

I had no social life apart from an occasional visit to or from Kim.

Our visits tended to swing between delightful and painful – for I found her both warm and intimidating. She was very demanding of performance – from both me and herself, which made it impossible to be truly relaxed in her company. Also I always seemed to be having to play catchup with her obvious sophistication.

I was therefore entirely caught off guard when on her third Christmas visit with me back in St. Louis I realized that she was pressing for a deeper commitment from me as to our future together. She would be graduating in June and we talked about going together to London to the London School of Economics, she to study for her MA and me for my PhD. That had seemed fine with me, until London wrote back stating that it would admit both of us to its Master's program – and I of course was just about to receive a Master's degree from Georgetown. Unfortunately, I didn't realize until much later that this was a standard admissions practice for doctoral studies in England, and that my Georgetown work would probably have all transferred toward the PhD after I took some qualifying exams in London.

Anyway, I made the decision that I would not be going to London – which then put Kim in the position of having to decide what to do. She indicated a willingness to decline the London invitation – except that faced with this possibility, I could not, would not, ask her to do that.

I really couldn't say why I was encouraging her to go on without me – except that at that moment I had a vague feeling that my life was much too thin emotionally to carry the responsibility of another person's permanent commitment, a person especially as high-powered as Kim. I felt myself panicking at the prospects – even as much as I deeply cared for her.

This all proved to be a major crisis in our relationship. And after several follow-up phone conversations in January (1965) in which it became obvious that nothing was going to change for me, our 3-year relationship simply came to an end. I certainly didn't want our relationship to end. But under the circumstances I wasn't able to move forward with it either. Kim, in her decisive way, withdrew completely.

Depression and detachment. The spring of 1965 was a low-water point for me. However, I did find my apartment in the Dupont Circle area offering me a reasonable 25-minute walk to and from the University, and found these walks to be the only thing that seemed to give me any peace. Unfortunately, I made the mistake of trying to remedy my loneliness by reading more existentialist literature, which merely made my sense of spiritual malaise all the deeper.

I finally decided simply to stop pressing life for its answers – and called my parents, to ask them to fly me home for an emotional R & R (rest and relaxation). Then while back in Illinois I drove up to Chicago to visit Sis, somewhere along the way got interested in Greek dance and language, bought myself a new navy blazer, a set of repp-striped ties and khaki slacks – and decided to put all further questions about life on hold. I returned to Georgetown determined to party.

Of course I continued my studies, moving on into Georgetown's PhD program in the summer of 1965, as well as into Georgetown itself residentially – finding a townhouse, only a couple of blocks from the university, to share with three other grad students.

But I now moved forward as a detached observer of the human scene. I focused the remainder of my graduate work on social change and revolution, trying to find the main causes or forces that shaped human culture and civilization. But I never allowed any of this to draw me in emotionally. I simply observed, analyzed and described – coldly but accurately enough.

My father encounters the ugly world of political journalism. An event that occurred about this same time in my father's life brought my father into this same "Realist" world. A reporter for the *St. Louis Post Dispatch*, St. Louis's leading newspaper and also owner of one of its main TV stations, asked my father if he would be willing to be interviewed about the pollution-abatement work my dad was doing. My father had been appointed several years earlier by the Illinois governor to serve on his new pollution control board as its technical expert, whose input was considered to be very valuable in finding practical ways that Illinois industries could take up strong anti-pollution measures – without bankrupting themselves in the process. Indeed, my father's work was becoming so well-known that he had been back and forth between St. Louis and Washington, consulting with congressmen about his work, and what could be learned of a practical nature from that work. It was, after all, the mid-1960s, and the issue of pollution control was just becoming a big political item.

So my father agreed to sit down with the reporter and discuss quite frankly the problems, the difficulties, the breakthroughs, etc. in trying to deal with the problem. He spent a full hour with the reporter in doing so. And overall, my father thought the interview went well, that the young man now understood the difficulties my father faced in taking on this challenge.

How shocked he was, however, when the interview was soon presented on TV, briefly (a minute or two in length only) in which the reporter had skillfully gone through the interview, cutting and snipping here and there, actually redoing his own questions posed to my father. And then he presented the whole thing as a discovery of a major "coverup", one in which he, this young crusading reporter, caught the evil Monsanto Chemical

Company attempting to hide from the public.

My father, ever the engineer, lived in a very orderly world, one of logic and reason. He had no idea that people could be as devious as this young journalist in presenting a pure lie as the truth!

Anyway, he was so upset that he tendered his resignation to the Illinois Pollution Control Board. But the governor begged him to stay, and Monsanto reminded him that his work was invaluable, if the country was going to be able to make the transition, and still stay alive economically. So my father backed down, and continued his work on the Board. But his heart was deeply broken.

He told me this story on one of his visits to DC soon after this event. Ever the Realist, I told him that this was just how politics works. It's all about developing the right kinds of public perceptions that advance your career. That's all the journalist was interested in. He probably couldn't care less about the pollution issue, something however that absorbed my father, heart and soul.

The difficulties involved in trying to live above human deception. Unfortunately, there was nothing you could do about this kind of human behavior. It was/is/always will be part of our human world. All you could do personally was not to allow yourself to be thrown off course by such behavior. It's going to happen, especially if you are involved in something of deep public concern at the moment. You just have to keep going, and not get distracted by such evil.

I knew enough from my own study of history that being able to address public opinion, without being caught up in it at the same time, was what great American leaders of the past (such as Washington and Lincoln) had to do in order to succeed in doing truly great things politically and socially.

Sadly, however, my reading of history at that point did not seem to give me any understanding of why these "greats" were able to do this, of how a deep spiritual strength that these particular individuals commanded was based on a very intimate relationship with God, so that they could avoid being drawn into a dependence on public opinion itself. They reserved that sense of dependence on a very trustworthy God.

Unfortunately, it was only later, much later, that I came to discover the importance of this kind of a relationship with God as the source of enormous strength supporting awesome social leadership.

At the time, I was simply not finding this insight in the history books I was reading, or just found myself not able to understand or absorb the deep meaning of this dynamic when I might have run across it in my readings. Which of those it was that shaped my understanding, or lack thereof, of this component of truly great American leadership I'm not certain. Anyway, that key portion of my understanding of life's "realities" was just not there, not yet anyway.

In any case, living in DC, I myself got to see this self-promoting dynamic, one that had hurt my father so deeply, all around me – every day. It's what feeds DC social life. Nothing other than such politics is ever "produced" in DC. And if you intend to work and function in DC, you had better understand the rules of the game!

And so I got to actually counsel the one individual who had himself inspired me almost every step of my own journey! I learned (as I would someday even from my street guys as well as my students) that counsel is mutual in all significant human relationships! It goes both ways!

Party Time. At the same time that I entered the Georgetown PhD program I also entered something of a Georgetown party program (!), centered on some of the foreign students at the University, in particular the sons and daughters of European diplomats posted to Washington. It started out for me when in the late spring of 1965 the daughter of the German 1st Secretary invited me into the "junior dip(lomat)-set." There I also met and started dating Stefania, daughter of an Italian NATO general. I had no car, but double-dated with Faisal, the Saudi ambassador's son, who was dating Stefania's sister, and who owned a Ford Mustang. It was quite a group – with parties both Friday and Saturday nights, every weekend – not infrequently formal in attire (I thus spent my scarce funds to buy a used tuxedo).

And now living in Georgetown itself only expanded my social life even further, as our townhouse became one of the major gathering points – sometimes almost nightly – for the junior dip-set, especially the German contingent.

Interestingly, rather than finding my studies undermined by this hectic social pace, I found myself more relaxed and concentrated when I did study. And my work showed it.

Martha. Stefania returned to Rome with her family for the summer. While she was gone a new relationship opened up for me when Martha, a summer intern in her Texas Congressman's office on Capitol Hill, came into my life.

She and a number of other females moved into a townhouse next door to us in Georgetown (along with the Indiana beauty-queen previously mentioned!). And my friend Courtney, who was over visiting me at that time, made it a point to send an invitation across our back fence for all the girls next door to have dinner with us. And thus I met Martha.

Anyway, Martha and I hit it off immediately, in a whirl of activity that had us together virtually all our free moments. Needless to say, when

Stefania returned from Rome at the end of the summer, she found that the DC world she had left behind for a few months had changed dramatically. I felt sad, for I truly liked Stefania a lot. But as I still understood things, you can't have these feelings about more than one woman at a time. I chose – not entirely gladly. But choose I did.

At the end of the summer, Martha decided not to return to her teaching job in Texas but to stay on permanently in her Congressman's office, and moved to another Georgetown townhouse with some of her friends, only a couple of blocks away. Our relationship continued on its hectic course.

As I was laying low with the junior dip-set because of my switch in relationships, Martha opened a new set of social affiliations with some of the Capitol Hill crowd. But we tired quickly of the incessant jockeying for status that all social events on the Hill entailed. Eventually I returned to the junior dip-set, with Martha in tow. I found this world forgiving and still welcoming, and both of us found it to be much more to our liking.

Engagement. Martha continued to work for her Congressman for one more year. Then the second year, at my urging, she enrolled full-time for some special post-grad work in history at George Washington University – at least for a semester.

But she wanted to get married. And she let it be known that she was not going to wait around forever. In the early spring of 1967, she returned to Texas.

I had not always dated Martha exclusively – though certainly predominantly. I had found other interests along the way, though none of them were ever serious. I just somehow could not get focused on Martha, being about as panicky at the thought of a permanent commitment with her as I had been with Kim.

But for some reason not entirely clear to me, I soon found myself in my phone calls to Texas talking with Martha about the eventual possibility of marriage. Before I knew it, the date was set: the coming October 14th, her parents' anniversary.

She returned to DC for a few months and then went off with one of her former Georgetown roommates to Europe, supposedly for the whole summer – somewhere along the way meeting my parents in Vienna to pick out her crystal glassware.

Breaking off the relationship. But with Martha away I found myself in more relationships. Thus I realized that there was going to be no wedding in October.

I was taken by surprise in mid-July when I received a phone call from Martha, announcing that she had returned early from Europe because she was missing me so much. My reaction was one of panic, for I knew that the moment that I had been dreading had arrived: I was going to have to confront her with my feelings. I did – and she again took off for Texas. I felt sad, glad, dismayed, guilty, and I'm not sure what else during the blur of the following weeks. My family was also dismayed – for they liked Martha very much and were looking forward to the wedding.

Grandmother passes on. If that were not enough emotional confusion, I then learned that my beloved Grandmother was in a hospital in Denver, dying of cancer. I flew out to Denver and found her in a semi-coma – wrestling with death in the most dispiriting way.

It made me all the more convinced that the Christian faith was largely worthless, for it seemed to bring my grandmother, a longstanding pillar of the church, no visible comfort at this critical moment in her life. I was sad, even bitter about this.*

Moving ahead. I was also still feeling enormously guilty about what I had done to Martha. Indeed, I felt as if my feelings or emotions were no longer my friends but my enemies, as I wrestled with them.

Towards the end of that week in Denver something inside of me resolved to forget my emotions and "stand up and be a man." I was going to go through with that wedding – and put all this useless torment behind me. It was much the same way I resolved my existential depression several years earlier: just deciding that I wasn't going to spend any more time worrying about things that have no logical resolution.

At the end of September, I drove out to Indiana to be a groomsman for Courtney, as Martha arrived there to be a bridesmaid for his English bride-to-be, Valerie (who had also been a roommate of Martha's in DC). I knew that Courtney was as paralyzed as I was over the thought of marriage – even more so. And thus watching him go through the process gave me no small amount of encouragement.

Two weeks later, in mid-October, Martha and I got married in Galveston, Texas, as originally planned. It was a small wedding, mostly family, and only a few friends, such as Courtney and Val.

We then returned as husband and wife to DC for me to finish out my last semester of doctoral studies before I took the last batch of my doctoral exams the following spring.

For a while life seemed pretty uneventful – until April of 1968.

_____

*It was only much later that I learned that, fairly soon after my return to DC, she found the strength that her faith was supposed to offer, and faced her end quite peacefully.

Washington Burning. I had been fairly preoccupied with finishing up my doctoral exams and hadn't paid too much attention to the news. But at 5:00 p.m., as I was finishing my last comprehensive written exam, the proctor spoke up and announced that we had to finish and quickly return to our homes: a curfew had just been imposed on Washington, D.C.

What??!! Then it all came back to me. Martin Luther King had been assassinated the day before in Memphis. Trouble had been expected – even in DC.

Apparently, things had gotten bad. I could tell how bad by the large cloud of smoke that hovered over the city ahead of me as I made my way on foot through the deserted streets of Georgetown toward Dupont Circle where Martha and I lived. Martha met me at the door with bags packed: we would be fleeing across the Potomac to Virginia to stay with Courtney and Val until this all blew over.

Dr. King's Last Sunday Sermon. This was all very eerie to me also because just the previous Sunday, we had been at the Episcopal National Cathedral, where we went most Sunday mornings.

This attendance at the Cathedral however had not been so much to worship God as to touch the deeper roots of our waning WASPish heritage. Neither of us was at that point really a believer in God. Martha had been raised Baptist, but like me had abandoned the faith some years before. But we were both hungry to build on something loftier than our little lives.

Anyway, we were quite surprised to find the area around the Cathedral a buzz of activity that particular Sunday. "Dr. King is preaching" we were told when we inquired about all this activity.

So there we were as Dr. King preached, his last Sunday sermon ever.

Now as I reflected back on this sermon, I remembered how he spoke, as it now appeared quite prophetically, about how his work focusing on the advancement of Black civil rights was coming to a close. He did not approve of how the Black Panthers had taken over the movement, and anyway he made it clear that he was presently refocusing his efforts in promoting the lives of the poor, White as well as Black.

He had also commented on how, with the Black movement initiative passing on to others, things might take a nastier turn. Indeed, how quickly and ironically his prophecy had all come to pass.

America in moral-spiritual crisis. While we were in Virginia with Courtney and Val, Courtney decided to answer the call that went out for lawyers to come to the DC courthouse to take up the defense of those arrested for pillaging or burning businesses in the District. I accompanied him back into DC, but actually only to observe up close how all this chaos was being handled.

So I found myself at the Courthouse, sitting out among a massive number of individuals awaiting their cases, listening to the conversations around me to get a sense of the actual dynamic of "burn baby burn", something that by this time had become something of a Black Power mantra. But what surprised me most was that there was something almost of a party atmosphere filling the massive waiting room. Indeed, sitting right next to me were two young men who decided that they had enough time before their case was due to come up, to head out to a place where they were certain they could get themselves some new shoes! And I am quite certain they were not talking about purchasing those shoes.

What struck me most about the whole thing was that this had nothing to do with Dr. King, or civil rights, or anything else political. The activity that got these people in trouble had nothing to do with standing up for Dr. King and the horror of what had happened to him. It seems I was more impacted emotionally by his death than they were. For them, the whole mess seemed simply to amount to economic opportunity afforded by the breakdown of law and order!

I also felt as if I was observing the results of something similar to what happened with the wild mob charging across faculty lawns anxious to conduct a panty raid on the girls' dorms at the University of Illinois. It was just mob mentality in action.

We stayed only a few days with Courtney and Val, moving back to our apartment when things quieted down. But we still lived under a 3:00 p.m. curfew enforced by members of the National Guard, whose military convoy would pass in front of our apartment a couple of times an hour. Could this be our Washington, D.C., capital of the Free World? It really played to my growing sense of cynicism.

What was happening to America at this point? I knew I was watching the passing of the age of American innocence (and childish presumptuousness). Hippie kids had recently been camping out in large numbers just a block away from our apartment, in a rather contrived effort to demonstrate "flower power." "Peaceniks" were beginning to beat a steady path into town to protest the Vietnam war – evidencing spirits themselves that bespoke war rather than peace. And now DC was a city of several burned-out sections (one within a few blocks of where we lived)!

Sadly also there was a new mood in the air, in the largely bi-racial Dupont Circle area where we lived (in fact, only a block away from where I had lived several years earlier). On a couple of previous occasions, we residents of the area had come out to work together to clean up the trash (broken wine bottles mostly) that littered the streets and sidewalks.

There was a very positive neighborhood spirit at the time, one that I liked immensely. But with Dr. King's assassination, that spirit had become very icy, as Blacks now looked on Martha and me with clear contempt as we passed by.

But we had had no role in Dr. King's assassination. It didn't matter. This was how "identity politics" always works. Tragic, but not an uncommon tragedy in America. Even more tragically, it was one that would appear on the scene again and again in the years ahead.

Our plans to move on. Martha and I for months had been making plans to leave the States at the end of that summer – to follow the trail-of-conquest of Alexander the Great across Asia, all the way to India, eventually to settle in Belgium for me to do my research work for my doctoral dissertation. As the summer approached, I was ready – very ready – to get on with my life, and to get away from this madness that seemed to be infecting my people. Thus in August – an apparent American failure in Vietnam (given the seeming success of the Viet Cong's "Tet Offensive"), Johnson's announcement of his future departure from office, the King assassination and consequent burning and plundering of America, another Kennedy assassination, a disappointing Poor People's March on Washington, and a madcap Democratic national convention later, all in that same *annus horribilis* (horrible year) of 1968 – we gladly bid America goodbye.

✳ ✳ ✳

THE EXPATRIATE LIFE (1968-1970)

Asia – following the trail of Alexander the Great. Martha and I bought a used VW "squareback" (station wagon) in Brussels, Belgium, and then headed east, down through Germany, Switzerland, and Italy to Greece, then picked up parts of the trail of conquest of Alexander (300s BC). We crossed Turkey, Iran, Afghanistan, Pakistan – encountering some of the most incredible driving conditions along the way, not to mention people and places.

By the most amazing timing, we hit historical sites well beyond the tourist season, traveling as we were in September, October, November, etc. For instance, at the Roman Colosseum, we saw no one else there at that time; at the ancient Roman city of Pompeii, there seemed to be only a handful of people touring the place; there were not a lot of people on Athens' acropolis; we were the only ones at Mycenae, Olympia, and Sparta (although Sparta was mostly still not excavated at the time); we were the only ones at the ancient Cretan capital of Knossos (on both of our two days visiting there); there was only another two or three people at the ancient city of Corinth; no one else was at Alexander's home of Pella or at the ancient Hittite capital at Boğazkale , and on and on. It was weird and wonderful. But it allowed us not just to tour the sites, but to sit and reflect on the historical perspectives that just being there allowed.

Iran. In Iran's capital of Tehran, we stayed with the family of one of my former Georgetown housemates, a very pro-Western family. They were able to explain to us the complexities of the Westernization of a proudly Muslim (although Shi'ite Muslim rather than Sunni Muslim) society, that also had not forgotten its origins as the ancient empire of Persia (the European West's constant enemy). And although where we were located in Tehran was fully modern, we were warned not to venture into the very traditional southern part of the city, where the hatred of Westerners ran deep.

It was at this point that we realized the delicacy of the cultural situation that America's close ally, the Shah, was dealing with. But (at the moment) he was generally very popular among his people, even out in the very conservative countryside. He had brought visible upgrading to the roads, city centers, schools, etc.

As a consequence, except for certain pockets of the country, we were well received as Westerners, in particular as Americans, especially since there seemed to be no others of that category around! Even here, we seemed to have this venture into the East all to ourselves!

Afghanistan. When we got to the Iran-Afghan border, our car got bogged down in the mud in the five-mile stretch of no-man's land between the two countries. We were finally able to get a group of Afghan soldiers sent to get our car out of its mess. Then we had to spend the night at the Afghan border sleeping in the car.

Early the next morning we were asked to take on an Afghan traveler, who had run out of travel funds, had managed to get to the Afghan border – and needed to get into Herat, where he could then continue on his own. We were told that he was head of the country's Chamber of Commerce. Yeah, right – as if we were stupid enough to believe such a fishy story! But we took him on anyway.

When we got to Herat, we took him to the airport, where he took a flight onward to Kabul. And indeed, we knew by that time (he spoke excellent German) that he was indeed what he claimed to be. Before he departed, he invited us to look him up when we got to Kabul.

The drive the rest of the way across Afghanistan was peaceful and largely uneventful, almost anyway. It was at one part of the road that we passed a group of men along the road, waving their hands wildly at us. We thought that was very friendly, until (at 100 kilometers an hour) we went sailing into a crude iron pipe poised across the road, to stop travelers (few of whom were actually on the road) so that they could collect "passage" money from them. Thankfully the bar merely creased the upper left portion of the car. Had it been a few inches lower, it would have taken off my head. As these guys came running up, I was furious. I pointed out the glass lying about. Obviously, we were not the first ones to have experienced this misadventure. They shrugged their shoulders, and we continued on. We would have to have the car repaired in Kabul.

We were rather shaken by the experience, even though it was not the first time that strange (and dangerous) things had come our way. Nor would it be the last of such episodes either.

But after all, we had willingly, gladly actually, undertaken an adventure that everyone back home thought qualified us as being totally insane. Where we were going was uncharted territory. And indeed, we took on each day with no way of knowing how things would turn out for us that day. But that's just who we were, adventurers.

I mention this particular episode because of how it led to other amazing things. When we reached Kabul on the other side of the country, we took a few days to enjoy its interesting primitiveness. And then, with the car repaired, we found ourselves ready to move on into Pakistan. But in the meantime, we were advised not to do so just yet, but to wait until a violent uprising going on just across the border in Pakistan had a chance to settle down (this area was "Pakistan" only on the map, but actually a very, very independent-minded Pashtun region). We took the advice. A British couple we met in Kabul did not, and soon returned with their car badly damaged and one of them badly bruised and cut up. We knew we were therefore going to be in Kabul for a while.

At this point we decided to take up the invitation to visit our Afghan Chamber of Commerce friend, Muhammad, and sent word to him where we were staying. Finally, a hotel clerk came to our room to tell us that someone waited for us in the lobby. But when I went down all I saw there was someone who was obviously an Englishman, by his very dress and demeanor. But wouldn't you know it was his nephew, Nasir, who indeed was an architect, schooled at the University of London and well-experienced in the field in England itself. We would spend the next days (a week really) with him, and friends.

Indeed, it was nearing the end of November, and Nasir's brother and family invited us to their home to help us celebrate our American Thanksgiving holiday. What a wonderfully gracious family they were. And it turned out also that he was the country's leading surgeon, who had trained in the field in Houston under the direction of the famous heart surgeon, Denton Cooley! Wow!

But the "wow" did not stop there. We even got an invitation to a fashion show put on by the Afghan Queen, and found ourselves in the most amazing company in the process.

Even after we moved on, we would keep close contact with our Afghan friends, for a number of years anyway, when several moves and changes later in our lives broke the lines of communications. Then when I heard that Soviet-backed "reformers" had taken over the country in 1978, producing a civil war that killed thousands, among them numerous Westernized Afghans, a deep chill hit me. I feared that this statistic most likely included our once-close Afghan friends.

Pakistan and India. Finally we headed south through the famous Khyber Pass and descended down into Pakistan, a land full of people and animals crowded into the country's living spaces. The situation was so tight, the roads so crowded that they were almost impassable, that finally we left our car in Pakistan and headed on into India by train, making the mistake of buying cheap 3rd-class tickets for an overnight journey. We could barely breathe, the train was so crammed with people. The next morning we switched to the 2nd-class, but soon discovered that Indians had the habit of invading the 2nd-class cars when the 3rd-class car could take on not another individual. We finally decided to go 1st-class, which turned out to be not very expensive, and an excellent way to meet very interesting individuals.

We finally arrived in New Delhi, and settled in there for over a week, right off of the very Victorian Connaught Circus. There was so much to see and do there. At first we loved the food dearly, until we finally tired of one curried meal after another (even a fruit dish was curried), and found that the American Embassy opened its restaurant on Friday noons for Westerners (not many actually) to come there to buy hamburgers and shakes! Otherwise we had something of a wonderful love affair with India.

India was such a contrast, of elegance in its historical sites and poverty in the streets. And India, like Pakistan, was a very crowded country. I had no idea of how India could possibly continue to expand its population (actually at the time, it had only half the population that it does today!)

But I admired the way the Indians went at life. Poverty did not mean misery. It only meant going at life in a simpler way. I remember sitting at a window at a railroad station's restaurant gazing out at the yard below me, where a woman was seated on the ground, assembling a small fire of cow "chips" to prepare a meal for her small children frolicking around the yard. There was an amazing "completeness" about the scene. She was doing what she knew to do to push on in life, and the kids seemed perfectly happy with the life they were delivered.

It was at that point that it dawned on me that life simply calls on us to find ways to accommodate ourselves to it, as so many of our own American ancestors had done in the wilds of America. It was not our job to push life into a well-ordered box, although that seemed to be our goal in life these days, at least in my well-ordered American world. And in finding ourselves in such a well-padded box, we seemed to spend a great deal of time looking over our shoulders at life, afraid of what might happen to us if we were forced to live outside that box. So we did everything in our power to make our box even more secure.

Yet, there in India was grand elegance, splendid reminders of that at Delhi's Red Fort, where the palaces were breath-taking with their marble work detailed with semi-precious gems and their hand-cut marble screens.

It led me to inquire more deeply into the story of the Mogul dynasty that had built this splendid work (including the Taj Mahal which we would later visit), of the family's rise, its dominance – then its decay and ultimately its fall.

I would never forget this. It would later become the inspiration for my "four generations theory" – of the typical rise and fall of most all societies (at some point in their existence) – eventually presented in my university course work, and in my recent publications on American history.

And, of course, we just had to make our way to Varanasi (old Benares), a "holy city" (both Hindu and Buddhist) located along the banks of the great Ganges River. There we found Hindu temples, even Muslim mosques, and Mogul palaces alongside common homes and shops, as well as the great Buddhist shrine at nearby Sarnath. We watched Indians coming to the water to bathe in the holy waters and to offer floral wreaths in thanksgiving for some event in their lives. We saw Indian dobymen washing the people's clothing, just upstream from where the dead were being burned at the river's edge and their ashes scattered into the holy waters of the Ganges. We saw semi-naked holy men at prayer. We saw sacred cows wandering the streets, not to be touched, even to be pushed away from food stands where they munched away on the produce offered there. We passed religious processions in the streets, etc., etc., etc. It was so unlike anything you were likely to run into in America (even a monkey visiting us through an open window as we took breakfast at our hotel!)

On to Nepal. There was no practical way to get to Kathmandu, Nepal's capital, except by flight. So we had the privilege – and the glory – of flying over the foothills of the Himalayan Mountains. And we arrived in a world that still belonged to an age several centuries ago. It was primitive in a medieval sort of way, and also glorious in that primitiveness.

However, It was not until we got to Nepal that we also encountered the craziness that we had left behind in America. In Kathmandu you would periodically run into some sunken-eyed Westerner who would finally remember that his or her body needed something besides the inexpensive and readily available opium to sustain it. They would occasionally drag themselves to the local Chinese restaurant to get some cheap food before disappearing again into some hellhole to continue their drugged existences. Periodically they would be flown out of Nepal in body bags. Such a dismal end for people who had come so far to "find themselves."

Back to India. We flew back to India and arrived at a still-quite-Victorian Bombay (the future "Mumbai") just in time for Christmas. It was strange to note that Hindus found ample reason to celebrate Christmas, in a very typical Indian way – with bright colors everywhere, music blaring out onto the streets, and the people parading everywhere, happy to be caught up in the event.

All of this obviously had no connection whatsoever with the Christmas I was familiar with. But for me at the time, Christmas anyway was just a beautiful family holiday on the calendar, to be celebrated for whatever purpose and by whatever manner you chose to do so. Beyond that it had no particular meaning. (I was not anti-Christian at the time. Just not part of that religious world).

We spent a good deal of time with an old friend, Deepak, who was at that point a professor at the University of Baroda, India's sort of "Harvard." He was now happily married, with children. We spent time together just relaxing, taking meals along the Indian Ocean, visiting the ancient Buddhist Elephanta Caves, and visiting a Bombay movie set where they were filming one of India's many productions.

Deepak was the picture of happiness, especially in his marriage with Purnima, a marriage arranged by his family of course. I remember when he got "the letter" commanding him to return from St. Louis (he was attending Washington University the same time as my father) to Bombay. As a majorly free spirit at the time, he knew exactly what his father's intentions were, to end that freedom with a proper marriage.

He explained to me that his father at least had offered him not one but three candidates.   He looked over their resumés (!) and announced that he would start with Purnima. And after a single date with her, he told his father that he would not need to check out the other two candidates. Purnima was an excellent choice – beautiful, well-educated, a skilled dancing teacher, and of very good family. Indeed, Deepak could not say enough positive things about the wisdom of the way marriages were "arranged" in India. I suppose he had a point!

Time to head back West. I think that part of the reason for both my expatriate existence – and my decision to include Asia as part of that experience was a sense that I would find some of that "transcendence" that my soul craved so much: a sense of sharing in some of the "wisdom" of countless generations that went before us. I wanted to plant my personal soul in some of that antiquity.

But in any case, it was time to get back to "reality." I had a dissertation to write, and the need to find employment back in Belgium, where we planned to establish ourselves for the immediate future.

The hand of *Fortuna*. In the course of the trip I began slowly to develop that rising sense of some unseen hand surrounding and protecting Martha and me during all this venture into the unknown. Things that had been happening along the way seemed to me to be much more than mere coincidence. And it certainly was more – much more – than just good luck. This "hand" not only had an invaluable presence, it seemed to have some larger purpose behind that presence. Slowly this "hand" began to take for me identity simply as *Fortuna*.

I certainly would never have called this *Fortuna* "God," for this in no way conformed to my Sunday School teaching about the nature of God. But nonetheless, I did have a keen sense of the outside support of some kind of mysterious force. The very decision to head East across Asia with only the crudest of maps available to guide me and no sense of what I would do if breakdowns or banditry or sickness or something should afflict me – this was possible for me only because I had this strong sense of *Fortuna*.

Most importantly, in very life-and-death moments, this hand of *Fortuna* came through for us, when we were in desperate need of assistance. A couple of the most dramatic instances occurred on the trip back from India to Europe.

The Baluchi Desert. One such instance occurred when I lost my way from the road (path) through the Baluchi Desert, for the road was drifted over constantly by shifting sand. At one point, I found myself hopelessly mired down in sand in the middle of the Baluchi Desert. I could not dig myself out.

I feared being stranded out there, for in such a defenseless plight Martha and I were perfect targets for murderous thieves. But as I got out of the car to consider my situation, I looked up, and – wonder of wonders – saw two men working off in the distance. They saw our plight, and came up to help us get ourselves dug out and redirected back on the road (which they had been working on).

How odd it all was, since they had been the only people I had seen all morning along the road (it was just desert after all!). And I had passed very few cars or trucks since heading out that morning. Yet there they were a few hundred yards off to help us! (angels in disguise?)

The wintry heights of Turkish Armenia. Another such instance occurred a short time later as the car climbed the snow-covered road to the top of Turkey's Armenian Mountains.

Constant snow storms had killed 14 people in those mountains the previous week. And arriving at the Iran-Turkey border, we learned that the border authorities were about to close the main road across those mountains, the road that would bring us to Erzurum in Turkey on the other side of the mountain chain. The next morning, I pleaded with the authorities to let us pass on ahead, as we were running out of money. And everyone was aware that once closed, the border would not be reopened for months. They finally relented and let us proceed.

And so there we were, heading up along a heavily snow-covered road with conditions worsening with each mile. Then it happened: we got hopelessly stranded in a huge snow drift which effectively blocked the road ahead, and prevented us from even being able to turn around and head back to where we had started from. We unloaded everything we were packing, in order to lighten the car. But it proved to be to no avail. We were stuck – completely stuck – with snow coming down heavily around us. And there was no prospect of help, as we had seen no one on the road since we left the border. At that point we realized that we were thus destined to become statistics added to the number who had died from this horrible snow storm.

Then miraculously a truck full of Turks appeared out of the snowy haze. Thankfully they were determined to help, rather than take advantage of our hopeless situation. They dug us out of the drift and then swung in front of us so that the truck blasted its way through the drifts before us, plowing a path for us through the mountainous heights. And then when we came down on the other side, to more drivable conditions, they drove off. (More angels in disguise?)

Looking for work in Belgium. Upon our return to Brussels in February (now the year 1969), we faced the immediate problem of finding work – for we had indeed spent all of our money in those six months of wandering.

I had been warned in Washington by the Belgian consul that getting a job in Belgium would be an impossibility, as work visas were virtually unattainable. But I was not one to let such details slow me up. I had received considerable training in Washington in computer programming, and once in Brussels I went from American corporation to American corporation located there in search of employment as a computer programmer. In the meantime, Martha found a job teaching English at a language school – paid under the table of course!

But I was turned down in interview after interview – not because they did not want to hire me, but because they knew there was no way they were going to be able to get me a work visa. The Belgian government wanted to place Belgians in this newly opening field of computer programming. I grew discouraged after about the 10th similar interview outcome.

Fortuna comes to our aid again, and again! Being discouraged by this was something new to me. I would never have thought simply to arrive on the scene in Belgium to begin looking for a job if I had not had this sense of this mysterious *Fortuna* being "with me." But now it seemed to be failing me.

IBM. And then IBM-Belgium contacted me! They had heard I was interviewing, and wanted to know if I would be willing to be interviewed by them! As it turned out, they desperately needed a programmer/analyst who could work directly with their new American customers in Brussels in developing customized computer operations. Their Belgian staff were having difficulties with the subtleties of American business language. They badly needed an American to bridge that gap. Therefore I was exactly what they needed. And not to worry about the visa. They could get one granted on the basis that I possessed skills (native English-speaker) that they could not get from a Belgian national. I was hired on the spot!

Fortuna had come through for me again!

At about this time Martha was hired by an English-speaking Catholic school in Brussels – and we were on easy street! Indeed, *Fortuna* was busy for us both!

I enjoyed the work immensely. And I had the great satisfaction of being able to solve some programming problems that had some of the other IBM technicians stumped. And I was able to work closely with both Toyota and Ampex offices in Belgium.

But any thought of being able to work for IBM and at the same time press forward on my doctoral research was soon dispelled. IBM left me little time and energy for such an enterprise. I simply had nothing left of me by the evening energy-wise, nothing able to undertake the rigors of doctoral research.

But by the fall, *Fortuna* performed yet another miracle for us when Martha got an even better job teaching at the American military school in Brussels. We could live easily (even splendidly) on her salary alone. So I resigned from my job with IBM and turned my attention to my doctoral work. Life was good.   No, it was perfect!

Friends. It was an active time socially.   We received visits frequently from our families, and both Val and Courtney's cousin (also a former roommate of Martha's) came to visit.

And of course, I met a number of young Belgian professionals through my IBM days, and for the year and a half we were Belgian residents, we remained close to them – especially our Walloon (French-speaking) friends, Pierre and Anne, and our Flemish (Dutch-speaking) friend, Victor. Indeed, Victor became like another brother to me.

At Martha's school we became close friends of a number of American teachers, expatriates and adventurers like ourselves and most like my German friends in Geneva – in their tendency to travel forth at every opportunity. We did a lot of traveling with them.

And I met two Americans (from Tulane University in New Orleans) who were, like me, researching their doctoral dissertations at the Royal Library in Brussels: Bob and Newt. We established the almost daily habit of having three-hour lunches over beers at a nearby cafe, designing solutions to the problems of America, and the world!*

All in all, Martha and I found that our Belgian life was every bit as stimulating as the life I once knew in Geneva.

Researching "identity politics." Multiculturalism had become for me a matter of supreme interest. Of course that summer of 1960 traveling through Europe and discovering the wonder of many different cultures – and the discovery, by way of contrast, of how very American I was – constituted the huge startup of this interest. And my 1961-1962 school year in Geneva had only taken that interest deeper. And my research on multicultural South Africa (1964-1965) had pushed me to ask questions now of what politically this could mean to a society. And my trip across Asia had stretched my familiarity with multiculturalism beyond even the realm of Western culture itself.

And so now I was in Brussels, Belgium, taking up the matter as serious doctoral research, trying to understand the political-social implications of Belgium being a society separated deeply by the language line of Dutch-speaking Flemish in the north and French-speaking Walloons in the south.

At one time (the 1800s, when the country was formed) Belgium had been more or less unified by the fact that the country's political elite, even

---

*Newt would have the opportunity to put those thoughts to action. After teaching college in Georgia, he ran for the U.S. House of Representatives, was elected, and quickly rose in the ranks of the Republican Party, eventually becoming House Speaker, and the force behind the "Republican Party Revolution" of 1994!

in the Flemish North, were fluent in French, as French was the language that the upper classes of Europe expected everyone to operate in.

But the nationalist impulse unleashed by World War One, and the German occupation of Belgium during that war, had encouraged a reaction by the Flemish (Dutch is after all merely another German dialect) against the country's francophones (those who speak French). And World War Two and another German occupation had not softened Belgium's cultural animosities either.

The challenges – and dangers – of multiculturalism. In any case, I was very aware of how much language shaped, defined, and directed culture, especially in this age of nationalism. Language is the means by which a society's dreams, its understandings, its plans are conveyed to the people. It is very, very hard to sign onto a society's cultural doings if you do not speak the language of that culture.

Yes, I am well aware that Liberals somehow believe that multiculturalism is a blessing to a society because it promotes "diversity" and diversity supports "freedom." At least it is supposed to do so in theory.

Actually I never saw that to be the case out there in the real world. In all my research into the dynamics of multiculturalism I came to understand quite clearly that multiculturalism was not a natural blessing. Instead, it was a very dangerous challenge – one that had to find some kind of larger solution to it, before it tore a society to pieces. The American Civil War presented a clear example of just those dangers. So did the Russian and Chinese Revolutions. So also did Gandhi's revolution in India, which set Indian Hindus against Indian Muslims and against Indian Sikhs – even destroying Gandhi in the process. The world around me gave constant witness to that truth. And it would continue to do so in the future.

Switzerland. But what about Switzerland? Wasn't it multicultural, with parts of the country speaking French, parts speaking German, parts speaking Italian, and other parts speaking variants of an ancient Latin form called "Romansh"? Wasn't it a multicultural society, seemingly always found in a constant state of peace?

The answer to that, as I well knew personally, was "yes." But I also knew why, and it had nothing to do with the Swiss fashioning themselves into some kind of higher species, able to operate in the upper atmosphere of Liberal enlightenment.

The Swiss were in fact a very down-to-earth or socially practical people, who had created a multi-cultural confederation of 26 very self-sufficient cantons. It was at the local level of the canton where the real business of government (and everything else) took place.

The point at which Switzerland approached the character of a nation was almost solely in its own self-understanding as a people united against the larger world. In fact, it was in the requirement of Swiss military service that there was a larger or "national" political call placed on the Swiss. And this was strictly a defensive call, one to protect the country from the intrigues of the larger powers surrounding their small but mountainous world. In short, Switzerland was basically a defensive alliance of 26 rather autonomous cantons.

The language issue was for the Swiss of significance only at the canton level, where there indeed, one or another of the languages supported the cultural identity defining that particular canton. True, the Swiss tended to be multilingual, in their ability to speak across cantonal lines. But still, they were first and foremost French, German, Italian or Romansch-speaking Swiss (there is no "Swiss" national language).

And the Swiss had no aggressive foreign policy. Indeed, their policy was to stay out of everyone else's business, and keep everyone else out of theirs. Beyond that, they needed no nationalist cause (such as what drove World Wars One and Two) to define them. In fact, they laid very low during both wars, using their considerable mountain defenses to keep the warring parties out of their country.

Indeed, in virtually everything, they have performed as diplomatic "neutrals", joining none of the European alliances – except for the multinational organizations, the League of Nations and its successor the United Nations – whose European regional headquarters in fact have been located in Swiss Geneva. They have even refused to join the multinational European Union.

So yes, the Swiss found a very effective answer to the challenge of multiculturalism. But for the rest of the world to be able, or even be willing, to go down that same "confederational" rather than national road was, and still is, most unlikely. The crusading spirit of linguistic or sectarian nationalism in our world has always been much stronger than the kind of self-restricted and purely defensive instincts that have long directed Swiss behavior.

Bi-cultural Belgium. Yet, something (sort of) along those lines I realized was beginning to redirect Belgian cultural politics, even as I first took up the subject in late 1969. And Charles De Gaulle was a big help in this matter!

De Gaulle hated the English-speaking world, and blocked British entry into the European Common Market. And step by step he also removed French participation from the North Atlantic Treaty Organization (NATO), because it was clearly led by the United States. When he failed to get other European nations to join him in this NATO boycott, he kicked not only all American troops out of France, but also NATO headquarters (which had been placed in France) out of the country as well.

At this point NATO shifted its operational center north, to Belgium, where the administrative center of the new European Union (the Common Market and its evolved successor organizations) was already located. In doing so this gave Belgium something of a very key international status as the "center" of the New Europe, politically, economically and now militarily as well. And American corporations followed that shift in also moving their European headquarters to Belgium, which I well knew, having worked (via IBM) in these new offices.

And this shift proved to lift Belgium above the linguistic squabbles that had previously bedeviled Belgian politics, when political actors had previously played on cultural sensitivities to advance their particular careers. Now Belgian politicians had a higher purpose, competing to be the better party to lead Belgium even further forward in its new role as administrative center of the New Europe.

Lessons learned. Of course, as I was doing my research (and ultimately writing) on the subject in the period 1969-1970, this new dynamic was only in its infant stages. But I saw where things were going to be taking Belgian society... and how its new higher national purpose would help it move past its linguistic or cultural quarrels.

And I would never forget what I learned in digging deeply into just this kind of social dynamic. It would serve me well in later years in understanding the most likely paths that this or that sectarian social or political movement was likely to take a society, and where a higher and more unifying purpose might better take that society.

And I learned especially the key role that leadership played in the process, for vision and resolve to move toward higher things did not just come by nature to a people. It had to be designed and presented before the people by those who could explain, and – most importantly – give clear personal example to the people of what these higher things were all about.

A true leader needed only to "inspire" the people. If he had to become a "dictator" in this matter, it was clear that the groundwork for a higher social purpose was still lacking. The people were still unable (most likely because of continuing sectarian or cultural differences) to let go of their social prejudices, and move with their leader to new things. Stalin faced that problem, Hitler did not. Gandhi, despite a willingness of both Muslims and Hindus to work together to get the British to "quit India," could not find a way to get Muslims and Hindus to work together after that. Indeed, the two Indian groups became bitter enemies. Mao never figured out how to get rural and urban China to work together – and nearly ruined China, twice. And so on.

So yes, I would watch closely how I saw a society's leaders approach the political-economic-cultural and even spiritual challenges facing a country. Would they merely advance their political careers by cultivating support among one social grouping, against another group in their society (and its leaders)? That was classical political sleaziness, not uncommon in societies that call themselves "democracies", where the people are easily mobilized to action because it is their group duty (quasi-patriotism or just crude sectarianism) to go at some other group, as some kind of great crusade! I saw plenty of that unfolding in America in the late 1960s.

Or were they really able to take that society to higher things, without starting a foreign war as a very destructive cheap-shot version of "pursuing higher things?"

President Kennedy and Dr. King clearly understood things along higher moral lines and tried to inspire Americans to support those higher things.

But Johnson did not have the same confidence in the American people, and tried to put his "higher vision" in place (his "Great Society") through social programs devised by social specialists and backed up by government economic policy and ultimately enforced by the law itself. But turning the challenge over to Washington bureaucrats was not the same thing as turning the challenge over to the American people, who were left very passive in this higher reach – with ironically, the Black community also becoming even more deeply reactive to "Middle America."

Johnson, also tried to bring the nation to higher national purpose by taking on the challenge of fighting the spread of Communism in Southeast Asia. But he really knew very little about the dynamics that drove Vietnamese society, and turned that country into an even bigger mess.

Thus tragically, disaster resulted from his efforts, both domestically and overseas.

And I had been in Washington (1963-1968) to see that all unfold!

✳ ✳ ✳

BACK IN THE USA (Mid-1970)

As I approached completion of my research in mid-1970, Martha and I debated whether to settle permanently in Europe or head home. We both loved Europe very much. But we knew that our futures really belonged in America. So in the late summer of 1970 we returned to the States.

We returned to a more subdued – though still distressed – America. The Kent State massacre had taken some of the edge off the antiwar movement and young people were backing down from the great causes, and getting more "into themselves."

Anyway, I had a busy year writing up the results of my research (most of this effort spent in Texas living with Martha's parents in Galveston) and looking for a teaching job. I knew that I was in for a tough challenge in this job hunt. Even when we were in Belgium, *TIME* magazine came out with a cover showing a student in doctoral robes, filling a gas tank (back then the work of a filling station attendant). The meaning was clear. The job market for PhDs was all dried up.

Indeed, colleges and universities were suffering declining enrollments as America began withdrawing from Vietnam (thus cutbacks in the draft, the great incentive to male college enrollment!). And this was occurring at a time when there was also a huge glut of new PhDs (who had found graduate study preferable to service in Vietnam!) coming onto the market looking for fewer and fewer college teaching jobs. I quickly discovered that with dwindling job openings, PhDs were a dime a dozen.

But again, *Fortuna* smiled. In the summer of 1971, as I was sitting in Courtney's office in D.C., seeking a job from my friend – who was now political appointments chief for the newly formed Environmental Protection Agency (EPA) – a call was forwarded to me from Mobile, Alabama. A fairly new and still growing University of South Alabama was interested in possibly hiring me to teach in the international relations field. I gladly agreed to be interviewed, flew to Mobile, found the interview to be a very positive experience, and was hired.

Martha and I quickly located in Mobile a small cracker-box rental home to live in (a short drive away from the university), moved all our belongings there, and then a few weeks later I happily took up my new teaching duties at the university.

This was also what I believed to be the last that I would ever need *Fortuna* to get me through. I felt that I was now in a position to shape my own destiny. All my youthful preparations for becoming the consummate "self" now kicked into gear.

CHAPTER TWO

THE PROFESSIONAL
September 1971 to mid-1978

✱ ✱ ✱

ENCOUNTERING SOUTHERN CULTURE

Entering Martha's world. What I would find in setting up life in Mobile, Alabama, was that I was entering yet another culture, one that basically looked like Middle America on the outside, but operated internally on its own terms, its very special own terms. I was now living in the American South!

Actually I was now entering fully into Martha's world. She was a Texan, yes. But a Texan whose family roots were deeply planted in North Carolina. Thus she was a Southern "blend."

Her father was a banking executive, and also chairman of some industrial boards, which included a hotel chain that owned a number of hotels across the country. This not only included the National Hotel in DC, located a couple of blocks from the White House (where our parents stayed during their visits to DC) but also Mobile's Admiral Semmes Hotel that put us up (for free naturally) upon our arrival to that city, and where we stayed until we were able to locate our rental home.

Texas. While living with her family in Texas during my dissertation-writing days, I came to appreciate the uniqueness of Texas culture. Status in Texas, though definitely a Southern state, seemed not to follow very closely the South's stricter status system, one that established a person's place in society on the basis of his or her birth – much like the social status system of old Europe, which the South had been following closely since the establishment of Virginia in the early 1600s. Instead, Texas was very "entrepreneurial", something of a leave-over of the wild, wild days of the American West. I remember how some of Martha's dad's Texas friends would brag about how many times they had failed at this or that business venture, only to get up and try again. They were proud of the many comebacks, and not at all embarrassed by the failures. That was something that, if you were not a Texas native, you would find difficult to appreciate. But a Texan understood the meaning of it all. They were a tough breed!

Mobile, at the heart of Southern culture. Mobile was more classically Southern in the way it went at things. For instance, I was quick to learn that the high-achievement mentality that drove the university community did not impress Southerners greatly. Yes, they appreciated the role of "professor." But lawyers, bankers, and commercial and industrial executives ranked much, much higher on the strongly-ranked Southern social system. Even pastors outranked professors, certainly if they were Episcopalian priests, and maybe even Presbyterian pastors (Methodist pastors ranked more towards the "middle" of things, and Baptist pastors seemed to be considered merely the voice of the Southern working classes, both White and Black.)

I was surprised also to discover that local politicians ranked very low on the social scale, also considered more the voice of the lower classes than of the Southern aristocracy, the latter which actually ran Southern society from behind the scenes. U.S. senators and Federal judges were okay, some of them coming from that aristocratic class. But city and county officials were typically drawn from the more ambitious (and usually very colorful) individuals of the Southern working class.

For a Northerner, these loud local politicians had been considered the "face" of the South. I am referring here to the 1960s militant segregationists known so well in the North, Southern politicians who used Black-baiting as a means of getting voted into office. However, and quite strangely, that seemed to have been one strategy that they had largely dropped by the time I arrived on the Southern scene in 1971.

What surprised me most was that Governor George Wallace had dropped the Black-baiting once it no longer gave him an electoral advantage (Blacks now voting in huge numbers). Indeed, he had become a very special friend of the Alabama Black community, setting up technical training schools and junior colleges particularly accessible to aspiring Blacks. He was actually very popular with the Black community, in Alabama at least. And none of this was known – or even wanted to be known – in the American North. In the North he continued to serve as something of a racist "icon" that the Northerners loved to attack, in distinguishing themselves from the racist South. Actually it seemed to me at this point that racism in Northern cities (which I personally was quite familiar with) was far more virulent that the racism that the South was famous for.

The rather isolated university community. Also something I came to realize quite quickly was that the university faculty tended to be made up almost completely of Northerners. There were a few exceptions. But that seemed very strange to me, until, again, I came to appreciate how the Southern status system worked. Professorship ranked way higher professionally in the North than in the South.

Also, coming into full membership in this academic community I found out very quickly that it was not a comfortable fit for me, or for Martha. True, for Martha's part, it was her natural Southern instincts to be not particularly impressed by the professorial sense of special place in society because of their status as "intellectuals." But for both of us, the academic mentality was problematic, because we were adventurers at heart – rather than intellectual system-builders.

And that made us very different from the social world that the academic community lived in. Their world was generally fixed, protected, and very isolated from what went on beyond the precincts of the university itself. Indeed, it was a "complete" world unto itself. But we just could not identify ourselves with that "completeness."

Rather, we found at faculty parties that it was hard for us to find a natural way into the conversation, sort of reminding me of the problems we once had with the Capitol Hill crowd – although for different reasons.

And just in general the way the academic community understood life outside of its intellectualized universe I came to consider to be not only static but also rather unrealistic. And I also discovered quickly that academic politics could be brutal, and usually quite senseless in being so brutal. Just egos at work.

Wow, that did not leave us much to stand on within such a community. And in fact, we were quick to find our Mobile social world elsewhere.

My relations with my students. But my own personal relations with my students were quite different. I had a wonderful, very wide world to introduce them to. I wanted to take them with me, at least in story and lesson, into a much larger world that I knew personally. I wanted them to understand the various cultures that were found here and there across the civilized world, and the way those cultures shaped the politics and economics of those societies. I wanted them to be among the "wiser" of Americans, as we looked out upon a world – supposing (horribly wrongly) that we simply could introduce (or impose) our own social logic on these societies, to make them "progressive" like us.

But even there, which "us"? I also realized that there were many Americas. I came out of the North's Middle America, which I knew well, especially when I had to put it side by side the German, Swiss, Belgian, French, British, Muslim and Hindu worlds, which made Middle America's unique features stand out even more clearly for me.

And I liked Middle America, although I liked other cultures as well.

But most of all, I wanted my students to understand the special qualities of being "American", at a time that the Boomer world (and some of its professorial mentors) thought that discrediting America wherever possible was the most "progressive," the most noble thing to do. America-bashing made no sense to me.

And I had lived, worked, and studied in the self-centered culture of Washington, D.C., a mixture of aggressive Capitol Hill politicians (including importantly their very ambitious staff) and the countless numbers of bureaucrats spread around the area. I knew personally how sex, money and public attention fueled the engines of so many of these politicians who had succeeded in getting themselves elected to power in DC, behavior that would be considered scandalous in most any other environment, but by the rules of DC was kept out of sight of the larger world. And I could go on and on about specific instances I knew of, how this game went.

And I was well familiar, having worked with both the Peace Corps (placing volunteers in this or that overseas program) and the World Health Organization (funding doctors in their research here and there within the Western Hemisphere) noting that the talents needed for such work were only the ability to quickly learn what was expected of a person at his or her desk, moving documents from the in-box to the out-box, no matter what agency it was that you were working with. And I also understood clearly the bureaucratic game of moving upward in status, transferring from one department to the next when a higher "G" ranking position opened up there, for instance, serving in the Department of the Navy, before transferring to the Department of Education, before transferring to the Department of Commerce, etc., etc., etc.!

That was a world unto itself, one that was trying desperately to insert itself ever-deeper into the life of the nation! And yes, I wanted to have my students understand the workings of that world as well, mostly for protective purposes!

✳ ✳ ✳

BECOMING THE CONSUMMATE UNIVERSITY PROFESSOR

The political science department. On the other hand, I found working with the fellow members of my department at the teaching job itself to be quite pleasant. The department chairman, David (a Harvard PhD from Missouri) had no particular social pretensions of his own, was very supportive of whatever it was that I wanted to bring to action, and just in general was a great person to work with. His wife, Janet, was also very gracious, a teacher in the special-education world, who had a lot of ideas to share with Martha.

The only "problematic" individual in the department was a young lady (who didn't stay long) who felt that she had to always be actively opposed to the system, especially the way it worked to favor men. For instance, she blew up at me once when I found myself in front of her as we headed toward the building where our classes were, and made the horrible mistake of opening the door for her. What a male chauvinist I was for doing that! She could open her doors herself, thank you! Wow!

Ultimately she moved on, unable to bring about the "reforms" that seemed to engage her so much.

Next door was a very likable guy, Bob, a quite happy "good-old-boy" that I came to like very much. He had married a very interesting German girl that he had met when posted as a NATO officer in Germany. He now headed up the university's Criminal Justice Program, but also spent about as little time as I did on campus (he was very active with the Mobile police force).

There was an American politics professor down the hall, Joe, who had lost his foot at the disaster of Anzio (Italy) during World War Two.

And there was a quite young Black professor who joined the staff the same year I did, who was actually local – and of "elite" status within that Mobile society! I was amazed to learn, from getting to know him, that there was also a Black Southern aristocracy, one that worked behind the scenes just like the White Southern aristocracy – performing the same roles in directing their respective communities. In fact, the two groups, Black and White, often worked closely together – as I was soon to find out personally. He did not stay long at South Alabama, but was quick to take a job offer from a more prestigious university elsewhere after serving only a single year at South Alabama.

And there was the young couple, Tom and Nancy (he taught constitutional law) that Martha and I spent some time with in the first year or two, who were very nice. But the relationship did not succeed in going very deep or very far, before they moved on to a position elsewhere.

And a couple of years along the way, another woman came to the department (American government), Louise, whom I got along with very nicely. However I later had to be very careful to keep things on that note, after she succeeded in overthrowing the new replacement department chairman for his shortcomings (which I never quite saw at all), and making herself the "temporary" replacement chairman in the process (she was still in that "temporary" position when I left for seminary years later). Ah, academic politics!

The Deep South Model United Nations. Something that awaited me in taking up my job at South Alabama was serving as the faculty advisor for a campus activity, one that had been started up, at least in conception, the year before, and was due finally to swing into operation that coming April: The Deep South Model United Nations. In taking up this responsibility as faculty advisor, I found myself working with a very talented young man, Jim (we would remain close over the next dozen years, as he developed as a very inventive lawyer in the world of computerized legal research – both in DC and then in Texas), and an equally special team he had put together to direct the Model UN Program.

And not only did huge numbers of my own students (international relations and comparative world politics) eventually become involved in the project in signing on as delegates of this or that country, but university students came from all around the South (Virginia and Florida in the East to Texas in the West) to participate. I found myself even involved a bit with these delegates (and their advisors, many of whom I would see year after year) from these other universities.

The three-day event was huge, held in the vast conference facilities at the Admiral Semmes Hotel, and very, very successful in what it was trying to accomplish: to get university students to do some serious research into how the country they were representing would go at a number of United Nations issues actually going on at the time (which we specifically pre-selected for them to research well prior to the event).

And I enjoyed every minute of the program, from beginning to end, including the great party that the staff put on after the event! And in the process, I grew very close to those students, remaining in personal contact with many of them for years afterwards.

In fact, the program was so successful that we began plans to have another such event the following year, and then the year after that, and after that, in fact, the event taking place every spring that I was at the university!

The International Studies Program. By my third year at the university I found myself putting together a new academic program: one so extensive in its academic reach that it would serve to meet both major and minor requirements at the same time, in full and even beyond. The International Studies Program comprised five introductory courses (in the political science, history, economics and anthropology departments), plus the requirements of two years' study of a foreign language (though the students almost always took as many additional language courses as they were able to squeeze into the program), plus an academic concentration of their own design, one put before a board of nine professors (from a variety of departments) as a self-designed contract, for the board to review and approve.

In most cases, my job was to help international studies students assemble this self-designed program. This turned out to be a very big job for me, as we soon ended up with roughly 30 to 40 students in this program every year. And it was my job to find internships that allowed each student to get some practical experience in the international field they had chosen (usually business, but sometimes academics, law, and even diplomacy).

Other professors were called on to help mentor these students, although it was usually me they came to in order to assemble and then undertake the program.

For me, it was hugely time consuming. I still had four courses to conduct in each of the academic quarters (except summers which I took off), each course involving essay exams and a huge term paper – things that involved an enormous amount of time to grade (no, I never turned such responsibilities over to graduate assistants). So all this international studies advising alongside my regular teaching duties was exhausting.

Nonetheless, I loved it! To take students who had never thought much about life beyond Alabama, and to fire their imaginations with thoughts about working or studying abroad, was a very great thrill for me.

Indeed, helping students catch a higher vision of life for themselves was something that I had dedicated my life to, and seemed to be as much a benefit to me as to them. Working this way with my students was my way of connecting to that something larger than myself, that transcendent soul, that I hungered for – though I had no words, no clear concept, for it.

The Fulbright Program. This also played itself out for me in my longstanding work with the university's Fulbright Committee, which I eventually came to chair. What a thrill it was when one year our students received five Fulbright scholarships, one to Germany, one to Belgium, and three to France (out of the total of 50 that France makes available annually to the entire United States). I lived for this sort of thing!

Children? I naturally grew quite close to those students that I worked with on these various projects. They became to me something like my own children, children that Martha and I came to realize that we were not going to be able to have of our own.

And here we were, both teachers (Martha was presently working with "special ed" children, also pursuing a master's degree in the same field), our lives directed to the task of bringing young ones forward in life. So indeed, we turned our full attention to those born of others, but who became somewhat "adopted" into our own world, through our work – which completely absorbed us.

* * *

ENTRY INTO MOBILE SOCIETY AND LIFE

"Downtown Mobile." Step by step, from almost our first days in Mobile, Martha and I found ourselves meeting this person, then that person, people living in the world outside of the academic community. I myself built some of the contacts with that world, for instance, through a local architect who was very interested in expanding Mobile's Sister City program from its present single relationship with Malaga, Spain. He had been in contact with the French, and asked me (with my knowledge of French ways) to help develop a sister-city in that country as well. I agreed.

Also a student of mine invited me to join him as crew on his boat during the annual Dauphin Island Race. I enjoyed the experience very much, sailed with him in a couple of more summer regattas, and decided to get deeper into that world by joining the yacht club he sailed out of (the Buccaneer Yacht Club). But I soon found that in not having a sailboat of my own, the membership itself did not do much to bring me deeper into that world. I would let my membership lapse.

It would be Martha who would really get us up and going with the Mobile crowd. Being a Southerner, she knew exactly how to go at things, and she was very social! For her, one contact led to another, and then another, until we found ourselves amidst a wide circle (actually several circles) of Mobile friends.

One of the things I came to note in entry into this new world was the rather quiet graciousness of the "gentry" class of Mobile. Perhaps it was because they did not need to "work at it" to make themselves significant. They were already significant by way of birth. But this was so different from the kind of ambitiousness that seemed to drive the world I came from, but which also drove local politics right there in Mobile as well.

In any case it did not take us long to find ourselves in "Mobile society", in particular in the close social company with the local "judge" (not really active as such) Judge Inge, and his very aristocratic wife Eleanor. It was through them that our Mobile world opened up, not just through an invitation to one of the all-important Mardi Gras balls, but by becoming part of a small circle that met at the Inge home to discuss the matter of what Mobile needed to do to recover from the enormous economic disaster that hit the city when the US government shut down the Brookley Naval Air Station, ending about 6,000 jobs locally in the process. It was in those discussions that I began to learn how it was the "city fathers" – not the local democratically-elected politicians – that actually shaped not only the social but also the political and economic life of the city.

The Mobile "Colloquium." I was so intrigued by all this that I decided to follow up on these discussions by putting together a "Colloquium" on Mobile and its future, conferences held once a week in early 1973 for six weeks at the university, all six evening sessions led by my new friends Judge Inge and the young and newly-elected county commissioner Bay Hayes that I had come to know personally… plus a few others I had invited to take the lead in the matter (I myself stayed behind the scenes). As it turned out, all these sessions were well attended.

We invited officials (including the young mayor Gary Greenough), businessmen (including officers of the town's Chamber of Commerce), prominent lawyers in town, the newspaper editor, local labor union leaders, pastors, community organization leaders, etc., to present their views on the future of Mobile. The talks were frank, insightful, and yes even inspiring. It reminded me how people could work together – business and labor, Black and White (yes some of these local leaders were Black) – if their goal was to find a higher social goal together, rather than – as we so often find ourselves doing in hard times – going at each other viciously, trying to fix the blame for social misfortune on this local group or that local group.

I had seen that reach to higher things develop in Belgium. I was now seeing the same thing develop in Mobile.

So impressed were the leaders of the Mobile Chamber of Commerce with the results of the Colloquium that they decided to continue these discussions themselves.

And indeed, I was very pleased to see come from all of this, Mobile's decision to become one of the first port-cities in the nation to go largely containerized, not only assembling the considerable amount of investment capital to get things going but undertaking serious vocational retraining of their port labor force in order to make the transition. No one lost his job in the process. In fact, this all turned out to be a huge economic blessing to the town.

And I got to be part of this renewal, of what by this time had become "my town"!

Local politics. It was during that coming summer of 1973 that I decided that I also would get myself more seriously involved in the city's political dynamics, working with an actual campaign for local public office. And it all started simply enough with a summer course I taught at the university.

After that first year (1971-1972) of living in our tiny cracker-box rental home, Martha and I were able to purchase a house (story and a half with somewhat alpine features) on a nice-sized lot in a very middle-class subdivision right across from the university. We moved in (early summer of 1972) and then left the following week for Brussels for the summer.

Upon our return, I set to the task of doing some upgrading of the house, repainting the army green exterior in a warmer yellow, and building a large roof over the large concrete patio behind the house.

To complete that work, we decided that we would be spending the coming summer (1973) in Mobile. And to earn some extra money to help pay for the upgrading of the home, I decided to take on some summer teaching at the university (the only time I would do that!).

One of my students that summer was an older student, a criminal justice major, simply meeting the last of his requirements for graduation. But, as it turned out, he really liked my course, and at the end of it, informed me that he planned to run for the position of county sheriff – and would like it very much if I were to become part of his campaign staff. Loving adventure as I did, I was quick to say "yes."

Indeed, I was already thinking about jumping (somewhat) into this world of local campaign politics. Politics was, after all, my professional field (or so I was believing at the time.) Also, I considered myself quite knowledgeable about such matters, especially having lived in the middle of that dynamic at the national level during my five years in DC. And so I started work with some of the staff, helping (minorly) to think through some campaign strategies.

Then something happened that really jolted me, something that would end my travel down the "local-politics" road.

I really was not keeping up that closely with things developing at the grass roots in the sheriff's race, until I heard that I should be on the lookout for an article scheduled to appear on the front page of the Sunday's *Republican Herald* newspaper (someone on the campaign staff got it put there). This was scheduled to appear just a couple of days before the election itself, and it would be a campaign clincher!

When the article finally appeared, and I was able to read what the campaign staff had placed there, I couldn't believe it. They were accusing their opponent, the rather noble and well-liked 20-year sheriff, of major corruption.

But I knew enough about things that I was aware that none of this was true. And certainly the staff I was working with knew that to be the case as well. And yes, eventually the old sheriff would be able to prove that none of this political "gossip" was true. But he would not be able to clear himself publicly of this supposed scandal before the election itself, only two days hence. That was the whole point!

And indeed, my student-friend went on to be elected the county's new sheriff.

I don't believe that he himself dreamed up such a shady strategy, though I never brought up the issue to him (actually I really never talked to him again after that, except to say hello on a number of occasions).

Could a candidate actually not know of such doings within his own staff? Believe me, yes. I knew that moral self-restraint was not a major virtue to be found among those who could get themselves all worked-up in their effort to bring a beloved leader to success. Staffing a political campaign was a world unto itself, which the candidates had to carefully keep an eye on – lest some of that staff enthusiasm should carry the candidate himself off to political disaster!

Anyway, that was the last of my political campaigning locally. Besides, a new world was opening up to me there in Mobile. And I found it less dangerous and much more inviting personally.

Watergate (1973-1974). This does not mean that I veered away from the world of politics. The study of a society's political dynamics remained front and center in what I had dedicated my professional life to. And there was a lot going on at the time in my nation's capital to keep me deeply engaged, not just personally but also in much of the discussion going on in my classes.

What I saw going on in Washington I cannot say turned me cynical. I think I was already there in that matter! Nothing that happened in DC would ever surprise me. But I still found what was going on there at the time hard to digest.

I rather liked the way Nixon had opened up relations with China and Russia, to work some "linkage" with these other major powers in his determination to pull America out of Johnson's mess in Vietnam, and yet leave something of a workable political legacy behind in Saigon, some kind of reward for all the effort (and blood spilled) to get things to go the "democratic way" in that country.

But he was up against a Democrat-controlled Congress determined to undermine everything he was accomplishing. The Democrats were humiliated by the enormous defeat in the 1972 elections of their own presidential candidate, a dreamy intellectual that was loved deeply by the Boomer-generation crusaders and their intellectualist academic, media, and public-office-holding mentors. They hated Nixon, as a matter of the highest principle.

And a political campaign stunt that went horribly wrong, something undertaken by Nixon's own campaign staff, gave them what they saw as the opportunity they needed to bring him down.

What was particularly galling to me was that behind this push to go at Nixon was Ted Kennedy. It was Kennedy that put together the Senate committee to look into the "Watergate" matter, the same Kennedy who, four years earlier, had left a very pretty young woman (not his wife) to die alone in his car when, heading to Chappaquiddick Island, it went off a bridge and turned upside down in the water. Kennedy somehow got out, she did not. And he did not even alert the police or a potential rescue team about the matter, but spent the night with his family trying to figure a way of covering over this new incident (one of many), so typical of his life.

And now here was "Chappaquiddick Ted" leading the Nixon assault, from behind the scenes of course. Was he doing so for the obvious reason of his own lack of admirable moral credentials, which seemed, however, to have had no negative effect on his standing with his Massachusetts supporters – or with his Democratic Party either? Or was he going at this political lynching operating from behind the scenes because he was thinking of running for president in the upcoming national elections and did not want his role in the inquest to appear to be purely politically motivated, which it was indeed, as everything is in DC?

So yes, Nixon was finally caught trying to cover up the affair. A taped conversation with his chief-of-staff Haldeman revealed him discussing how to make this Watergate event go away, evidence that Nixon had indeed broken the law in trying to head off a more extensive criminal investigation into the matter.

Yes, the post-event cover-up was wrong, very wrong. But it hardly stood out from the behavior that went on rather regularly in DC, including among some of those serving now as his accusers. Indeed, how did the Nixon crime stand out so much more strongly than Kennedy's cover-up action after Chappaquiddick, so-much-so that the day would come when Kennedy would be toasted as one of America's finest politicians, and Nixon would be remembered in our public schools as the "evil president"?

Wow, the depths of political hypocrisy this all entailed!

Of course there was nothing I could do from Mobile about DC political behavior, except comment on that same hypocrisy, and then watch in helpless horror the following year as the American legacy in South Vietnam collapsed so violently (there and even more violently next door in Cambodia), due to further Congressional ideological tampering to undermine what little Nixon had been able to accomplish there. Nixon's enemies were determined to "get Nixon", no matter what the social cost might be. And for the Southeast Asians, that cost was horrendous!

Nonetheless, despite what was unfolding in DC and Southeast Asia, life went on pretty normally right there in Mobile!

Restoring an old house in the Oakleigh Garden District. Martha, meanwhile, was eager to put us in the heart of our opening Mobile world, pressing me to look at the possibility of moving from the university area to the center of "Old Mobile." So, one Saturday in early 1974, we drove downtown to visit Martelle and John (an older couple who had become very deep friends by this time), who drove us around the Oakleigh Garden District – where they themselves lived. This area once was a beautiful neighborhood of rather majestic turn-of-the-century homes, many of which had been turned into boarding homes (or worse) and allowed to run down. However, the area had recently been declared a national historic area, and was just beginning to be "gentrified" by young professional couples moving there and beginning the process of a serious makeover of these once-splendid homes.

I became interested, and contacted a real estate agent who showed us a house in the District at the end of a street, Georgia Avenue, next to a park. The house was magnificent, but in terrible shape. However, it had great promise: fireplaces in 6 rooms, 11' ceilings downstairs and 10' ceilings upstairs, a beautiful staircase, and lots of room.

But admittedly, you had to have lots of imagination to see past the filth and decay. Close friends of ours, Richard and Millie, told us that when they first saw the house they thought we had lost our minds!

But that spring, I tore out the walls of one of the four bedrooms upstairs to open up the stairway and to create an airy openness about the second floor. I built a new bathroom upstairs and fixed up one of the bedrooms with a large closet. And by the summer I was going hard at it, working on the kitchen and an adjoining breakfast room, created by glassing in a back porch.

This activity occupied me totally until we decided to move in in August, when we received a very nice offer to purchase our university home and felt we could not pass it up. Indeed, the really great thing about this venture was that we incurred no extra debt in restoring the Oakleigh home. Indeed, we had enough money from savings and from the equity in the sale of our university home that we were able to pay cash to the plumbers, the electricians and the central-heat-and-air people.

Of course, the house was far from complete when we moved in. Indeed, Martha and I would find ourselves living amidst a lot of construction work (and dust!) over the next couple of years while I worked away at the house. But step by step we finished the kitchen, upgraded the dining room, built a library, and completed the makeover of the three bedrooms (and yet another bath that I installed) upstairs. And we furnished these rooms with some great antiques that we were able to buy locally. One of these was even an antique father clock, over 7' tall, dating from the late 1700s, whose case I refinished myself (14 coats of lacquer, hand rubbed between each coat!).

We now had a beautiful setting to entertain our friends, which was a most frequent event.   Parties and other gatherings happened there often. And we were into the "gourmet thing" with a number of our friends, and found that putting together some extravagant meal was a delightful way to spend a Saturday evening. Indeed, looking back, it seems hard to remember when during those days Martha and I had dinner home alone with just the two of us. But that's the way we wanted it.

The Oakleigh Garden District itself. Oakleigh was by this time a vibrant community of young professionals much like ourselves in interest and activity, lawyers, bankers, shipping agents, etc. There was only one other professor in the group, Woody (a true New Englander) – a young history professor with whom I carpooled to the university most every day. Everyone worked closely together in bringing the neighborhood forward, virtually all of us serving as members of the very active Oakleigh Garden Society. And it was through participation in this organization – and the way that we shared insights as to effective restoration strategies and which plumbers, electricians, etc. were the best to go with – that we came to know our neighbors quite well, and quite far and wide in the Oakleigh district.

And there were a number of activities that added to that sense of neighborliness. Besides the Garden Society, every October there was the annual street dance put on by the first block of Georgia Avenue (the street we lived on, just off the town's main street), an event attended by masses of people, complete with band, refreshments, and just a lot of dancing and socializing.

And there was the Oakleigh Marching Society, just a "fun thing" when we would put on second-hand Mardi Gras costumes, and on the morning of Mardi Gras, gather in front of someone's home (ours in fact in 1979) and join the day-long Mardi Gras parade, for our part, marching from our district down to the center of town (our group usually led by a New Orleans marching band), where we would end up at the Malaga Inn's courtyard, and where we would continue to party (with yet another band), until most of us had to go off to more formal Mardi Gras balls elsewhere (later that afternoon and evening).

And there was the annual Halloween event, in which we would set up one of the houses still under deep reconstruction as the Haunted House, fix it up with "haunted" rooms, dress ourselves up in all sorts of weird Halloween costumes (once I put myself on drywall stilts, becoming about 8' in height) and then scare the living daylights out of the neighborhood kids, particularly the Black kids of the neighborhood, who would typically circle around to go through the visit a second and then a third time, they loved it so much. And we all had great fun doing this for them.

Sailing becomes a serious matter for me. It was when a friend Rodger invited me to join him in crewing with John Van Aken, that my world of sailing really took off. The owner and captain of the 30' sailboat I came to crew was a generation older, Dutch-born shipping inspector for Lloyds Bank of London, and also South African consul for the port of Mobile. He raced his boat constantly through the very long Mobile regatta season. So I found myself serving regularly as crew (it seems most weekends during much of the year), slowly making my way forward as winch operator, then foredeck crew (jib and spinnaker), then finally navigator (plotting racing strategies from the maps and electronic gear). And we generally were very successful in these competitions! For seven years I would sail under his captaincy.

Business partnership with Tony. As an interesting side result, I was to become very close (certainly closest of all of my friends) with his son Tony, who joined us as fellow crewman after graduating from college and then taking a job in town as an international banker. In fact, Tony and his wife Tish were to buy a house just across the street and down three houses from our own home on Georgia Avenue, where he too learned the art of renovating an old Mobile home.

And very importantly, Tony and I were to go in together to create the Mobile Restoration Company, and begin the purchase and redevelopment of other Mobile homes, earning some historic restoration awards from the city for our work. But more about that later.

Eventually, Martha and I were to go on and buy our own sailboat (another 30' beauty), of which I would do considerable upgrading, and which we would cruise rather than race, and which would become a major setting for the entertainment of friends. Also, more about that later.

Summers at home and abroad. Of course, I was not sailing every weekend of the summer, because Martha and I, both being teachers, had our summers off, giving us a great opportunity to do what we loved best: explore. And most normally, we found the object of our summer explorations to be Europe.

Our first summer back in Europe was in 1972, when we returned to Belgium, supposedly for me to do some follow-up work on my doctoral research. I had actually finished my doctoral research and writing the previous year (1971) in the spring, was able to offer my doctoral defense that fall, and finally just that June had officially been awarded the PhD (one of three receiving their Georgetown PhDs in political science that year), sent to me in the mail! Anyway, our summer in Belgium proved to be more social (with our friends Victor, Pierre and Anne) traveling and relaxing at the Belgian shore, and of no great consequence academically. We returned briefly to Belgium also the next summer (1973). But the summer after that (1974) was spent in Mobile, fixing up our new Oakleigh home.

Then the summer after that (1975) we found ourselves again back in Europe, this time living in Paris for the summer. The work I had been doing with the Mobile Sister Cities Program had led to a contract offered by the counterpart French organization (Cités Unies), in which they wanted me to put together a study describing and comparing the development of both the American and French approach to town twinning. This not only had me busy doing a lot of interviewing (including someone in the US State Department, because Sister Cities was actually a part of official American diplomacy), but also doing a lot of traveling around France.

While we were there we were visited by Brenda and Paul, who lived up the street from us on Georgia Avenue, whom we did not know very well yet, but who, when they heard that we were headed for Paris, took up the challenge to come visit us. This was their first trip abroad, so we gave them the special. After showing them Paris, we headed down to Innsbruck (Austria) on an overnight train and then spent the next day climbing the mountain behind our motel. From there we crossed the Alps to Venice, and spent a couple of days seeing the sights in that lovely town. Then we returned to Paris and spent some more time together – in incredible heat (Paris was not used to this heat and air conditioning was rare) before we put them on the plane to go home.

After they left, things just seemed very dull. "Bored in Paris" was not something we had ever expected. Anyway, we suffered the heat for a couple of more weeks, then headed up to Antwerp, to meet my father, who was there on business. The next day we took the train to Luxembourg and headed home.

For no particular reason we stayed at home the next summer of 1976. It did, however, give me the opportunity to undertake and finish the very complicated library project in our home.

But that summer we did get a Sister-Cities exchange visit from France, and became hosts at our home of the youngish (and quite stylish, and yes, a member of the French Communist Party, would you believe!) mayor of Arles and his wife, who were leading the large group.

America having a hard time celebrating its bi-centennial. It was July 4th at the time of their visit, and supposed to be a time of great celebration, for the day marked 200 years since the signing of the Declaration of Independence. But despite the fireworks and grand effort to make the most of the event, it was a sad time in America.

As a political swipe at the Republican President Nixon, a Democratic-Party-controlled Congress had foolishly declared to the world that it was ending America's "imperialist" role in Southeast Asia, and was cutting off all further support, even just financial support, of our allies in the Saigon government, an invitation for the North Vietnamese to do their worst! Consequently, after Nixon had been chased from office in August of 1974, his replacement Ford had to preside over the humiliating escape of the last of the American personnel from Vietnam in April of the following year.

Furthermore, what we Americans left behind in that country as our legacy was the horror that the Communists then unleashed on the many Vietnamese who had supported the American presence in their country those many years. They would pay heavily for that relationship, either killed on the spot or dragged off to prison camps where they were treated to a very brutal "re-education" of their social thinking (brainwashing), the process so harsh that many died there as well,

And this horror was accompanied by an even greater one next door in Cambodia where the collapse of the American-supported political status quo in the region led to the Communist (Khmer Rouge) "Killing Fields" that brutally depopulated Cambodian urban society.

And most Americans suspected that behind it all, our cowardly retreat had brought all that on.

And that's where things stood as we supposedly celebrated two centuries of American greatness. But things weren't feeling so great at this point.

Nonetheless, we in Mobile made the most of the visit of these new French friends, timed with what was supposed to be a wonderful 4th of July celebration.

And indeed, Martha and I enjoyed their company enormously. And we would be invited the Arles Mayor and his wife – and accept the offer – to stay with them in their summer home in the Jura Mountains the next summer when we returned to Europe.

Back to Europe. So, yes, the next summer (1977) we were back in Europe. Very conveniently for us, my parents were now living in Antwerp (my father was continuing the work that had brought him there previously), and we made their beautiful and spacious home there something of a base camp to work from. Again, Brenda and Paul joined us in Europe, meeting us in Portugal, where we enjoyed enormously the country's wonderful seafood dishes! We then headed through Spain to Morocco, and spent a number of days in the quite medieval (but also very Muslim) city of Fez. Then we headed back to Antwerp, where we all got together with Tony and Tish, who joined us there.

Tony and Tish were at that point finishing up their summer visit to Europe and it was time for Paul to get back to work. But Brenda was able to join Martha and me for an ongoing visit to England, a country which Martha and I loved deeply and which we had visited numerous times when we ourselves were residents in Belgium. We then returned to Antwerp, hung out there a bit longer, and finally headed home. No, this time we were not "bored in Paris"!

One more trip would follow the next year (1978), when again we were joined by Brenda and Paul, who had recently moved to Atlanta, Georgia, but stayed in close contact with us. My parents (still living in Antwerp) lent us their car, and we headed off to the French wine regions of Burgundy (Eastern France) and Bordeaux (Southwestern France), trying to become wine "connoisseurs" through our many visits to the wine cellars of Burgundy and the great wine estates of Bordeaux. It was a very enjoyable summer.

It would also be our last trip together to Europe, although we did not know this at the time. But events were about to unfold that would change the very patterns of our lives, deeply.

CHAPTER THREE

CRISIS
Mid-1978 to January 1983

✳ ✳ ✳

CONCERNS ABOUT AMERICA'S "DIRECTION"

I enjoyed working with college students very much, in class and even off campus when the occasion arose, such as our Model United Nations – and our visits to model UNs put on at other colleges in the region. But in general, I was otherwise finding that my teaching had fallen into something of a dull routine.

And I was not particularly liking the larger world of politics (American diplomacy in particular) that I was supposed to be teaching, or as I saw things, advising future voting citizens about the basics of political reality, both at home and abroad.

Dismal foreign policy. It was now the Carter Era (since 1977) and I was not very enthusiastic about the political "Idealism" that drove Carter.

I had early on contributed to his campaign, hoping that he represented "change" in Washington, which he did – except not in the direction I was hoping he would take things. When he began to claim that he was going to institute a more "moral" foreign policy I grew a bit concerned. I thought this all sounded a bit like Woodrow Wilson's naive (and dangerous, as it turned out) political Idealism earlier that century.

Carter made it a major point in his campaign that he would bring to an end our tendency to support dictators as allies. And he made it clear that one of those dictatorial allies who was going to have to lighten up politically or lose American support was the Shah of Iran. My reaction to this Carter pronouncement was that such public speculation about the Shah was very foolish, in fact, most dangerous in every way possible. He obviously had no understanding at all about the delicacy of Iranian politics.

Likewise, he talked about ending American imperialism by removing the American presence from South Korea… and greatly reducing our role in NATO. Where were these ideas coming from?

Then one of his first acts as president was to turn ownership of

76

the Panama Canal over to the Panamanian military dictator Torrijos. Strategically speaking for America, which depended heavily on its ability to move things (including naval forces if need be) from its Atlantic to its Pacific coasts, this surrender of the canal seemed totally unwise. And why to a "dictator"? So where did he actually stand on his supposedly "moral" foreign policy?

The fall of the Shah of Iran. Ultimately as president, he backed down on his really stupid Korean idea, and backed out of his thoughts of redesigning NATO. And he even began to proclaim the Shah as one of America's closest allies.

But for the latter it was too late to undo the confusion and then the political disruption that accompanied Carter's early back and forth on the Shah. As 1978 dragged along, things got worse and worse for the Shah as Iranian youth took control of the streets, first demanding reform, then demanding the complete dismissal of the Shah.

That same fall, I was teaching the course, Politics of the Middle East, and had a number of Iranian engineering students taking the course. They were particularly excited about the bright new future that seemed to be unfolding for Iran, as things got increasingly chaotic in Iran. I told them to be cautious because, although most of those youth leading the revolt were Westernized individuals like themselves, they needed to realize that their movement was very unorganized and not strongly led, especially in comparison with the other group involved in the dynamic, the Muslim clergy and their own young supporters. This latter group was well organized, and it was my guess that if the Shah fell from power, it would be this group that would take control of the "new" Iran.

They thought I did not understand their country very well. I had to be wrong.

In early 1979 the Shah fled Iran, and it looked as if indeed I might have been wrong about my assessment of things in Iran. But little by little, Iranian politics headed in the direction I was afraid it might go.

And tragically, a year later, one of those Iranian students came to me to tell me the sad news that his parents had written to him, telling him to stay in America and forget about coming home, because of the shift in Iranian politics towards the Muslim agenda ("Death to America"!).

I was not happy about being "right" in this matter. In fact at the time I was finding it very hard to be happy about much of anything.

ATTEMPTING VENTURES INTO NEW FIELDS

Housing restoration as a sideline. But a new project in Mobile offered some possibilities for challenge. As already mentioned, Tony advanced the idea of forming a partnership between the two of us and going into a sideline business of buying, restoring and selling homes in some of the other historic districts in town that were starting to show some early signs of revival. He was a banker by profession and I was a carpenter-architect by instinct – a good combination for such an enterprise. Thus the Mobile Restoration Company was born.

We started out with just the four of us (husbands and wives) doing the work – but soon found that we had to subcontract more and more of the work, especially as we started taking on additional homes. Our work was high quality work, the kind we were proud of. Our very first efforts brought historic preservation awards!

The work was also moderately profitable – and so our involvement grew. Eventually we also moved into suburban development with others, until by the end of the 1970s, we were heavily into the housing construction scene on all kinds of fronts.

Taking on the redevelopment of the house next door (1978-1979). The house next door to ours (a local park was on our other side) was owned by a classic slumlord who rented out rooms at the house by the week(!) and who did little upkeep on the house, but who did put out rat poison to deal with that problem, also poisoning one of our two cats who sadly ate one of the dead rats. The tenants were a rowdy lot. Some, we knew, even were prostitutes, doing business right there next door! And it had come to the point that this was the only house in the neighborhood that had not been bought by a young family and upgraded in the Oakleigh "gentrification" process.

Thus what a surprise it was when we returned from our 1978 summer jaunt in Europe to learn that this house next door had been purchased, not by a young family but by a young slumlord who had plans to turn it into a number of cheap apartments. In our discussions with the new owner, we learned that he planned to put $10,000 to $15,000 in it to "fix it up", enough to create some separate apartments in the house.

Actually, the house needed about $50,000 or more for a decent renovation. Nonetheless, the investment plans of the new slumlord would involve just enough money to put its cost beyond the reach of someone someday wanting to buy it to turn it into a family home. Thus it looked as if the house were to remain a slum forever.

This was a shocking development for us – who were sort of cornered between this house and the park. This definitely would not help our property value any. So we got together with Tony and Tish and worked out a deal with the new owner to buy it off his hands for his purchase price and $5,000 extra. This was way more than the house was worth. But there seemed to be no alternative.

By agreement with Tony, the responsibility for the house ultimately fell to me, because it was a bigger problem for me than for him. Fair enough. Nonetheless, we started the restoration of the house with high hopes that this would work out nicely for all of us in the end. Indeed, the four of us, Tony, Tish, Martha and me, put our hearts into the task, and did substantial redesign to the house, both outside and in. And by the next spring we had a house of some beauty next to us.

Our first problems in the housing renewal business. At the same time that we were busying ourselves with the work on the house next door, we were discovering big problems developing with one of our projects downtown. We had finished the restoration of a two-story beauty in the Church Street East District and had it up for sale.

But unlike our first two houses, we could not find a buyer for the house, because the city, which had asked us to join them in restoring this particular district, was not moving to restore its houses. Their houses just sat there as festering sores, inviting problems for themselves, and for us. Until the city started moving on its part of the restoration effort, our house was destined to sit there vacant. Who would want to buy a beautiful house in the middle of an urban slum?

But not only was it vacant, it was being pillaged. We were pretty certain that the family living in a rundown house across the street from our project house was helping itself to the kitchen cabinets, stoves, dishwashers, water heaters, even major heating/air conditioning units from the house. Indeed, we replaced some of these twice as we looked for a purchaser.

We finally decided to rent the house as an effort to halt the pillage. But even here, we had to make some serious compromises. We found two divorced women with a large number of children who were willing to rent – at a rate that hardly covered the interest costs of the money we had borrowed to fix the place up – never mind the high attrition that renting would bring to the overall value of the house. We knew we would have to repaint and do extensive repairs again when they moved out in order to sell the house. Somehow the restoration business was fast losing its luster.

Worse, the women moved out after a relatively brief period there – because the area was so troublesome for them and their families. And when they did, they left behind a needed paint job, some serious repairs required for the floors and some re-wallpapering.

But thankfully, the people across the street had also moved out, and it looked as if there might be some renewed action in the neighborhood by the city authorities. So we left the house vacant – where it remained as such for the next year or so. What a disaster, as we paid out each month for interest costs – without any prospect of a sale until the city got moving on its part of the agreement!

Problems finding a sale on the house next door. Meanwhile, the house next door was finished and ready for sale. But we came up with only one serious offer, for $10,000 less than the money we ourselves had invested in its purchase and development (not to mention all our personal labor)! As the months went by, we grew anxious – for we were shelling out $780 a month in interest costs for yet another empty house.

By the time summer rolled around, Tony announced that he was backing out of the deal. As we had previously agreed, Martha and I would be the ones ultimately left to contend with any financial problems brought on by the project next door.

Finally, just before the summer began (and we needed to leave for a new summer project), we found a renter who was willing to pay $550 a month. This helped enormously – leaving us with only a $230 monthly shortfall. In the meantime, we hoped that the house would sell.

Urban planning as a new line of study (1979). Nonetheless and still overall, my work in housing restoration, plus my earlier involvement in Mobile's own well-organized effort to reconstruct its economy after the closing of the Brookley Naval Air Station, were activities that arose naturally out of an instinct of mine to want to see local communities take a stronger hand in their own development (I was not a big "let Washington do it" kind of guy!).

And thus I applied for and received a grant to study the history of urbanization (with a personal research project on town planning) during a summer session (1979) at the State University of New York (SUNY) campus at Stony Brook on Long Island.

There we rented a very nice little cottage from a professor who was away for the summer. And we enjoyed the experience very much – for Stony Brook was a small "New England" fishing village on the northern shore of Long Island. Martha was able to take sailing lessons while I studied. We also cooked gourmet-style, experimented with various fine California wines, and did some entertaining of other people on the same study program.

The 1979 energy crisis. One of the strange (actually ominous) features of the summer was the gasoline shortage, ostensibly created by the collapse of the Shah's government in Iran and the skyrocketing oil costs which resulted as OPEC manipulated shortages in the oil market (and American refiners manipulated the retailing in the United States). We had to watch our traveling – for gasoline was not always to be had.

Also, and what we did not know at the time, this oil shortage – and the inflation that it produced – would come to have a much bigger impact on us than simply the shortage (and thus dramatic price increase) of gasoline for our car. It would have a major, even devastating impact on our lives, because of a very bad financial strategy that was about to be put in place in Washington in response to this situation.

Anyway, in returning to Mobile that fall, I threw myself into a new graduate-level course I had developed: the politics of urban planning (presented historically). I enjoyed the course very much, as did the students.

And I was hoping greatly that somehow this would open up some new specialized field for me to devote myself to. But in the end, I never really figured out a way to make it work for me. That was too bad.

Late 1979: financial bondage sets in deeply. In the meantime, the too-bad was becoming horribly-bad!

Because of the new energy shortages, energy prices had unsurprisingly risen greatly over the summer, in fact quadrupling for the second time that decade. But the price inflation did not stop there. These massively higher energy costs were now also forcing prices of finished products and other consumer goods to also have to be raised, in order for producers to be able, after paying for the new energy expenses, to still be able to pay their workers (who also, in the face of this inflation, were wanting accompanying salary and wage increases) and find a bit of profit for their investors.

Thus massive inflation hit the country in all areas of the economy, as prices for most everything (food, clothing, furnishings) joined energy prices in a dramatic increase across the board.

Then just to make the suffering for everyone worse, at the end of 1979 the interest rates on bank loans (including our own) suddenly skyrocketed as well.

This is because Paul Volcker, the President of the Federal Reserve Board, had stepped into things by claiming that he was intending to destroy the power of inflation single-handedly, with an excruciatingly tight monetarist strategy. In other words, he was going to increase the Federal discount (interest) rate charged to banks that borrowed from the government, even increase that rate massively if necessary!

And of course, by increasing interest costs to American banks, those higher interest rates would be passed on to the bank's own customers, Tony and me included.

I had no idea of what the logic behind this move of Volcker's happened to be. Volcker's vastly higher interest rate strategy would make a producer's operating costs – costs already driven sky high because of dramatically increased energy and commodity prices – even worse. Borrowed money was an operating cost for a business just like energy and basic materials. Upping interest rates would force a business to have to raise even further the pricing of its own goods, if it intended to make any kind of a profit at all. In short, higher interest rates were guaranteed to increase inflation, not bring it down!

What was the man thinking? Was his idea of "fighting inflation" one of destroying the entire US economy?

People (like ourselves) whose businesses depended on bank loans suddenly found themselves trapped with business inventories (cars, homes, goods) that would not move. Customers for these goods disappeared overnight. No one was willing to buy a new car or a home when interest rates were now running at 16 to 18% or more (Volcker even pushed things up to where the prime rate was at 22% at one point).

There was nothing a person could do that got caught holding business inventory when these rates suddenly jumped skyward, except pay the increasingly higher interest rates that banks were charging – while waiting desperately for the merchandise to move, for something to happen that would get them out of this trap.

And that is exactly where Martha and I now found ourselves at this point. Here we were holding all of this property, property that we could neither sell – nor could afford to continue to finance. The earnings we had made from our restoration work thus far were quickly eaten up by the high annual interest rates (20%+) that we were forced to pay quarterly on the property we were still holding. Soon our salaries were going to make interest payments, payments that were almost as much as our combined salaries.

What were we going to do? Very quickly our savings were depleted. Then we refinanced the house (at a much higher interest rate) in order to secure cash to pay the quarterly interest obligations. How sad this was: the house was almost completely paid off. Suddenly we went from making $188-a-month payments on a $4000 balance left on the house to nearly $400 a month for a $30,000 balance.

The cash we secured through this refinancing bought us some time with the other interest payments of course. But we knew this would rescue us only for a while.

We kept hoping that the Federal Reserve would bring interest rates back down. But it didn't. Slowly we were being bled to death financially.

Bewilderment. This all came at a very bad time for me – for I was already beginning to get very restless about my life. I was feeling "trapped" – the one thing I feared most from life. I was "trapped" in my teaching job – in the sense that I could not think of any new things to take on professionally that would stir my blood the way I was used to having it stirred. The urban planning idea had seemingly led nowhere. And as I surveyed the professional alternatives – they all seemed to promise merely more of the same thing. It was simply more of being "bored in Paris."

Then just to make things worse, toward the end of the spring next year (1980) our tenants next door announced that they had bought a house up the street and would be moving out. But then our realtor friend Nancy (whom we worked with in a number of earlier sales) brought by a man who was interested in a lease/purchase arrangement. I was a bit leery of the idea – but also desperate to get some kind of action on the house. So we closed the deal. The family moved in. But somehow all his talk about family money, etc. by which he hoped to buy the house sounded suspiciously unreal. It was.

The summer of 1980, back in DC. Anyway, at that point we were off to DC for a 10-week Arabic language program at John Hopkins' Washington campus just off Dupont Circle. But those Arabic classes nearly killed me. I got only about 4 to 5 hours of sleep a night. I found myself cramming, cramming, cramming.

On the weekends we headed over to nearby Annapolis – sometimes with my former student and friend, Jim, who was working in DC at the time. Towards the end of the summer, we even went over in the evenings, just to get away from the pressure. In fact, it was really therapeutic to walk along the waterfront and look at the boats, to buy soft-shell crab sandwiches from the fish market at the wharf, or to drink cocktails on a veranda of a restaurant overlooking the water.

One time I spotted a beautiful sailboat sailing out in the Chesapeake Bay: dark blue hull and light blue genoa sail: Oh how I would love to have such a boat! Thus the seed of what would turn out to be a very big deal was planted in my mind.

That summer I turned 39. I got my first few gray hairs – probably from all the pressure I was under studying Arabic – and from all the money worries that awaited me back in Mobile.

I was also probably losing my mind! I decided to interview with the CIA – as an "operative" (not just as a researcher). I spent a lot of time interviewing and preparing interview papers (when I should have been studying Arabic). I was such a bored, restless and "underutilized" individual. But did I really need to go this far? Anyway, thankfully that fall they broke off the interview process, for apparently the reason that I did not fit their psychological profile for an "operative."

The *Marionette*. I have already mentioned that Martha and I at some point bought ourselves a sailboat, to cruise (not race) and entertain on. It was that same summer that we spotted that beautiful blue-hulled sailboat that we afterwards talked about the matter quite a bit. And thus it was, towards the end of the summer we decided to go ahead and buy a sailboat of our own!

Financially this was a very poor idea. But emotionally, it was the one thing that held off emotional disaster, at least for a couple of years.

So we were able to locate a 30-foot sailboat (Catalina) for sale near Annapolis, about 4 years old and in fairly good shape. We arranged a second mortgage on our house and paid $27,000 cash for the boat. We had it shipped by truck to Mobile where it arrived about the same time we did on our trip back from DC.

Then I spent my days before fall classes resumed working on the boat. I refitted it extensively inside and out and had the hull painted a dark navy blue (just like that one I saw in the Chesapeake Bay). I painted the lettering on the stern: *Marionette*.

The house break-ins and robberies. But tragically also, the fall of 1980 also began the series of break-ins into our beloved house. Seven times (!!!) the house or garage (where all my tools were kept) were burglarized – despite all sorts of measures to alarm the house and garage against intruders.

The first couple of times it felt as if we had been raped. Our house no longer represented the safe haven we had always thought of it being. It was no longer sacred or pure. In the subsequent robberies – in which little was taken because we simply did not bother to replace the stereo, TV, tools, etc. (the treasures from our various trips abroad that were stolen were of course irreplaceable) – we simply felt benumbed. Indeed, there seemed to be little point to the future robberies, except that the robber or robbers obviously felt "at home" breaking into our house.

We lived next to a park – and thus were very vulnerable to any mildly enterprising thief, who could watch us come and go, and then make his move on our house, and then slip away through the park without raising any kind of alarm. The fact that a major drug distribution center was just on the other side of this park, and the fact that the park had been taken over by citizens from that particular part of town, obviously played a key part in our plight. None of them would be likely to report to police a robbery in progress.

Just like the financial mess – we felt totally helpless, vulnerable in this matter. There was nothing we could do to remedy the situation. At one point, we tried to move to another house in the neighborhood. But after a very lengthy negotiating process, just as we thought we were closing the deal, someone (who had been tipped off in detail about our offer) at the last minute came through with an offer just a bit higher than ours. We were stunned.

It was just as well, because we probably would have ended up with two houses – at a time when we certainly needed no more property. But it was another major blow for us. After that, we didn't have the heart to try another move away from our besieged home.

My grandfather dies. Also, in the midst of the boat work and the break-ins, Grandpa died very suddenly of pneumonia, which he caught in the hospital where he was being treated for relatively minor injuries sustained during a mysterious auto accident he had in the parking basement under his apartment building. I flew out to Denver for the funeral.

I didn't really have any great theories or feelings about death. I was sad, but not tragically so. The whole thing was, more than anything else, simply another addition to the increasingly numb feelings I was having about life.

Political-risk consulting. Then for a while, in those same years, it looked as if I might be opening up a new avenue for myself professionally. Hope flickered to life as I began to cultivate business contacts, and found myself serving as a political-risk consultant to various banks – first in Mobile, then all the way over to Houston.

I had quite good and well-proven predictive powers about what was likely to unfold in a given political-economic climate, and found that my work was well appreciated. I helped a number of banks make some informed lending/investing decisions overseas. For instance, I predicted the end to the oil price increase – even the resumption of new rounds of competition in oil pricing, thanks to a most-probable scramble to undersell its oil-exporting competitors that a money-short Russia was most likely to have to resort to, which I realized would then set off a new round of price reductions by oil producers trying to keep themselves in this very competitive market. My predictions proved (fairly soon) to be right on target, and thus helped a Texas bank that hired my services to avoid a major multi-million-dollar investment blunder in the Mexican oil industry.

Eventually I was called upon to present seminars on the subject, first developed as courses with my own students at the university. And soon I found myself publishing articles on this subject as well.

But the bloom on this rose began to fade almost as quickly as it flowered – because the early 1980s was also the time of the international debt crisis. As one banker put it to me: "we've stopped making loans overseas for the time being, because of the danger of default from our Third World customers. If, however, you could show us how to get out of the loans we're already in, we'd be very eager for your services." Of course this was a business operations matter – an entirely different affair from assessing political risk.

So, once again I found this new professional path leading nowhere. My sense of frustration thus merely deepened.

Depression and disaster (1981). As I look back on it, I see indeed that the summer of 1981 was some kind of major turning point in my life. Martha and I had laid plans to sail the Marionette with our Oakleigh friends, Cecil and Susan, cross the Gulf of Mexico diagonally to the Okeechobee Canal that cuts across south-central Florida from the Gulf to the Atlantic, and arrive at Fort Lauderdale. We would then sail onward from there to the Bahamas with Tony and Tish, and vacation there with them for a while before sailing home at the end of the summer.

We expected and had planned for the usual mishaps along the way. But we hadn't planned on running aground at a very high tide at an unmarked bend in a South Florida waterway, costing us our rudder, an expensive dredging process to get us off our grounding, and a week in drydock for repairs. We soon ran out of most of our money. And when it was all over, there was nothing for us to do but sail back to Mobile and forget the rest of the summer.

That fall I grew uneasy and restless, unable to sleep at nights. I worried about how we were going to make our next interest payments on our property holdings. I searched my heart for a sense of where my life could possibly be headed – which seemed largely nowhere, just like our trip to the Bahamas. It seemed that at every turn we had been thwarted by the same Fortuna that once had been our invaluable ally. I was despondent.

CATASTROPHE (1982-1983)

Withdrawal. I had no idea how ripe I was for a major catastrophe. But in the spring of 1982 my life began to shift, slowly but surely. It all started quite simply. I found myself less and less at home, hanging around more and more with my students or spending time with my buddies at the Mobile Steamship Association. I didn't head home immediately after meetings, but just hung out. When I did get home, I would head up to my office in our home to work on drawings of a sailboat that I was designing and planning to build, one intended to be able to sail us around the world.

I was simply slowly withdrawing emotionally from the world of what seemed like massive – and crippling – responsibilities, ones that called on me to perform services and undertake responsibilities that were humanly impossible to meet.

I continued to meet my responsibilities at the university. Those were fairly well defined – though they felt increasingly lifeless or stagnant, not having opened any new vistas for me in several years.

However on the home front I was feeling worse than stagnant. Here was where I felt myself under the obligation to "man up," to find solutions to the burdens laid on us, but obligations that I simply could find no way to carry through on. Thus I began to feel my particular responsibilities as life-crushing.

Actually, Martha never complained or even commented much about what was happening to me – not wanting to add to the emotional burden I had now been carrying for quite a while. Actually, I really had tried not to bring her into our financial problems, and instead tried to handle things myself – though certainly she was always well aware of our deteriorating situation. This was both our understanding of what it meant for me to be that "man."

As the spring of 1982 turned into the summer, I could feel myself disengaging emotionally from the home front, from everywhere actually.

Pulling away (August-December 1982). In early August I told Martha that I wanted to be off by myself. I had a life to sort out – on my own.

I proposed to move into an apartment of my own. But Martha said that she would rather be the one to move out – to live with friends – for she did not want to live alone in a house that was so vulnerable to intruders. So we separated. I stayed in the house, and she moved down by the bay with our friends Susan and Cecil.

Then in early December of 1982 by some kind of miracle (!!) someone came around to see if we would like to sell them our house. We jumped at the chance. We sold the house, and were able to liquidate all our other obligations with the proceeds! Now houseless, I moved into a townhouse apartment. Meanwhile Martha continued to stay with Susan and Cecil, while I tried to sort out the still quite uncertain feelings I had about my life.

At Christmas, now out from under our debt burden for the first time in three years, we decided to take a trip together to Mexico City for a week. It was good to be traveling again. But somehow this was not enough to bring me back into our old relationship. I still felt emotionally very removed from

Martha. Actually, I still felt emotionally removed from most everything.

In fact, the sense of freedom afforded by both the loss of the cherished house and the lifting of my other financial obligations served only to make me all the more determined to be totally "free." I decided to unburden myself of all remaining involvements I had beyond my immediate "self."

Cutting ties. Thus one morning in early January of 1983 (January the 3rd, to be precise) I woke up determined to ask Martha for a divorce. I then proceeded that same day to the Dean's office to announce that I would be quitting teaching at the end of this school year in June. Wisely the Dean, who was somewhat aware of the strain I had been under, advised that instead of quitting I simply take a year's leave-of-absence from my teaching responsibilities. I agreed to do this instead.

Actually at that point, I did not really expect to ever return to the university. A leave-of-absence was just a way of "playing it safe."

Of course I had no such "year's leave-of-absence" option with Martha. Anyway, given the mood I was in, I wasn't terribly focused on the thought of ever returning to anything again. That was the last thing that was on my mind.

From the moment of this declaration things proceeded swiftly. Within three weeks of my decision to cut free of all attachments, Martha and I were divorced (thanks to the work of our lawyer friend Cecil, it all happened very quickly and amazingly amicably!) A few days later she returned "home" to Texas.

And that first weekend back in Galveston she met the Coast Guard commander, Mike, who himself had recently arrived in Texas from his posting in Mobile. In Mobile he had become friends with Susan and Cecil, and it was Susan who was inspired to call Mike, asking him to introduce Martha around to his new friends. She wanted to help get Martha settled in to her new world (actually not so new to Martha!) in Texas. And wouldn't you know, the two of them, Martha and Mike themselves, immediately hit it off.

In any case, by the end of January 1983, I knew that I was now set entirely on a new course in life, with nothing of the old to hold me back.

CHAPTER FOUR

THE WAY BACK
February 1983 to December 1990

* * *

FOLLY

I don't think I had any sense of great purpose behind these developments – except to get away from having to live with a sense of great purpose! Indeed, at that time my only thought was to devote myself more fully to the mindless life of party, party, party.

A slow social comeback. As I stepped into this new world, I ended up making a new set of friends, because most of my former friends found good cause to draw away from me. My behavior was erratic. Then too, I was no longer a professor, but only a clerk working in an import-export firm and I no longer lived in the historic Garden District, but in a condo apartment. Friendship with me was less profitable than it used to be.

But I was not critical. I understood the logic, and would have reacted the same way. In fact I really did – holding myself in some contempt. But actually, I enjoyed not having to measure up anymore! It offered a great sense of freedom. I no longer felt it necessary to play to other people's expectations for me.

I guess I was hoping that I would find something significant for myself "out there" in that wild and crazy world. Certainly this was what I got as a major message from our popular culture. But I knew better – just as I had understood in Nepal watching the very sorry looking heroin addicts. Indeed, I rather quickly discovered that this wild and crazy existence was as troubled and as sad as the polite but heavily burdened world I had left behind. If anything, this new world was inhabited by even more desperate people, looking for something that continued to elude them. Most of them in fact were looking for the professional world I had just left behind!

That first year after the divorce I lived a rather reckless life. Though I broke no laws, I found myself largely uninterested in society's well-being, or anyone else's for that matter. I read no newspapers, watched no evening news. There could have been a major war going on – and it would have meant nothing to me.

* * *

THE FIRST RAYS OF LIGHT

Deeper friendships. But not all of my former friends deserted me. A handful of people stayed the course with me. For reasons I could not at first understand, they did not seem horrified (well, maybe) by my wild behavior. They were not put off by me; just concerned about me.

Both Cecil and Susan, caught in the middle of the growing split between Martha and me, nonetheless remained very sensitive to both our feelings as we struggled to understand what was happening to us. And it was Cecil who as a lawyer offered his services gratis in drawing up the uncontested divorce.

There were also our friends, Terri and Erv, who, as an act of monumental charity, bought the largest of our housing debts from us (the house next door) as a "tax write-off", and who moved Martha's half of our furnishings into their house when we broke up housekeeping. Martha spent a good deal of time with them as well. But Erv would frequently go out to breakfast with me – and just listen. He was (is) a very kindly person – a religious Jew, a lawyer who took on a lot of charity cases for free (pro bono), who would later become for me some kind of representation in my mind of what Jesus – as the Jew he was indeed – must surely have been like.

And there was Stephanie and her husband Skeeter. We used to be jogging partners in the good old days. They had watched from quite close up my growing stress and sleeplessness over the financial crisis and my emotional withdrawal from life. Then when the break occurred between Martha and me, they reached out to both of us. I myself was soon invited to attend prayer meetings with them (they were charismatic Catholics) – though it probably was all a bit too early for me to connect with.

It was Stephanie who used to drop off cards and biblical quotes to try to cheer me up – and who one morning (that fall of 1982, when Martha and I were simply separated) dropped by with an urgent message:

"Miles, promise me you won't laugh when I tell you this."
". . . Yeh, okay, Stephanie."
"Are you sure you won't laugh?"
"Yes, Stephanie."
"I was praying last evening about your situation, and I got the strongest vision of you becoming a minister!"

A stunned silence, followed by a huge grin that was as good an effort as I could make not to laugh! I was touched by her earnestness – though not greatly impressed at the time by her prophetic powers! [Hmmm! ...would you believe it!]

Then there was Martelle, (her husband John in the meantime had died, and had one of the largest-attended funeral services I was ever to witness). Martelle was a great listener. And it was she who first brought me back to the church (sort of anyw– through an invitation to attend a special seminar hosted at her Government Street Presbyterian Church on "crisis", led by a well-known Christian theologian, Walter Brueggemann. I found much of what he had to say on the matter make deep sense, something I had not been experiencing at that point in a long time.

Also, all of this "unconditional concern" which these friends showed me during this time of personal crisis was not something I was used to. In my world everything had its worth, its "price." But their deep concern, which became priceless to me, came without a price.

What I also at this point began to see ever more clearly about these people was that they did not go at life the way most everyone else I knew did. They had a deep sense of "beingness," of who they were and what their lives were about, something that did not depend on how they played the "game" of life.

Of course, I had noticed elements of that character in them some time ago... but had not at that time any interest in giving the matter much thought. But now I was intrigued – very intrigued – about what it was that made them so different from the world around me.   They came to represent to me a vision of personhood that I hungered for.

Thus contact with these spiritual giants – plus those very mysterious "interventions" in my life from the strange world of God – began to draw me forward. I was increasingly curious to know more about this strange new world that was just beginning to reveal itself to me.

God, are you real? Behind my new townhouse apartment was a huge undeveloped portion of Mobile, almost like some kind of combination of grassland, swamp and woodland. I used to spend a lot of time on the patio just quietly staring off into that uninhabited space, collecting my thoughts and just relaxing my troubled soul. Then one evening (I'm not exactly sure of the timing of the event,* but am very clear about the particulars of the event itself) I felt drawn to throw out into that peaceful setting a very strong challenge: "God, if you are real, I need to know, and I need to know right away!"

And almost immediately things began to happen ...in much the same

---

*Certainly some time that spring of 1983.

way that *Fortuna* once acted on my behalf. It's hard to explain, but I began to notice things, often just little things, that I previously would probably have taken no note of, except perhaps to have credited them to small doses of good luck. Things just started to show up, and not just coincidentally. So yes, *Fortuna* was back.

But I now began to understand (gradually) what I should have known all along, that *Fortuna* always was God, the one that was intimately connected, intimately supportive, intimately protective of my doings, doings by someone (me!) however who by no means deserved such "otherworldly" support.

But I now took this opening world very seriously. And though I really understood very little about it, I was interested – very interested – to learn more, to discover what all this ultimately meant.

✳ ✳ ✳

EARLY STEPS TOWARD THE RECOVERY OF A SENSE OF "SOUL"

The journey actually begins in London (summer of 1983).   With my regular duties at the university over, I still had one more commitment to academic life. I was contracted to direct a semester-length university seminar in London on political risk analysis.

But once I found myself in London, I found that my mind was drawn as much to the richness of the English Christian religious tradition as it was to the matter of the country's politics and economics.

And – oddly enough – I seemed to find myself every Sunday morning at the nearby St. Pancras Church – not certain what was "there" for me. Something was. I kept coming back.

It seemed weird to me that there were always more, many more, people on a Sunday morning simply touring the church – there to admire its structure and windows – than there were people there actually to worship (sometimes only one or two others than myself). I felt sad, though I could not yet understand why anything like that should trouble me. But I sensed that this church ought to be treated as being something more than a mere museum.

From simple clerk to computer programmer. I returned at the end of that summer of 1983 to Mobile, not to the university – but at this point to take up a job in a friend's import-export company, where I worked simply as a freight forwarder. No one except my friend, whose import-export business it was, knew anything about me. And I intended to keep matters that way.

But as I basically did nothing but fill out import-export documents all day, I could not help but notice that the process could be speeded up (with fewer potential mistakes) if the process were computerized. So eventually I brought the matter up to my friend, and more importantly, his dad, the actual owner of the business. They thought the matter over and agreed that purchasing a computer (newer, smaller computers were just coming out) was a wise idea.

And would I be willing to do the programming involved (they knew of my own experience as a former IBM programmer/analyst)? "Off-the-shelf" or commercial programs were not yet available, so all of this programming was going to have to be a process of step-by-step creativity!

Well of course. It sounded like a wonderful challenge, and I definitely needed challenges at that time, ones that I was fairly certain I could handle!

And soon I had not only programmed the process of import/export documentation, but also their container shipping and freight forwarding business, and then their own accounting system. I loved it, and started making a decent wage in the process!

And when I did indeed return to the university after that year's leave of absence, I continued to do program consulting and writing for them, for the better part of the next year.

My first personal computer. Then at the same time that this computerization began to develop at work, in December of that year (1983) I bought my own computer as well, for $2500. This was a lot of money at the time, but money I figured was well spent. The computer was about the size of a suitcase (in fact came in some form like that, to make it portable), had a 9" black screen with bright green typescript and worked on the basis of programming and data storage found of two 5¼" "floppy" (plastic) disks. And I also bought myself a dot-matrix printer.

And indeed, this investment would prove invaluable to me, on multitudes of occasions.

A hesitant return to the Christian life. At the same time that I took up my new life in the export-import business (that fall of 1983), I also began attending Martelle's church on Sunday mornings, with her usually at my side – sitting way in the back, teary-eyed, feeling that every sermon was directed to me!

However, I must confess that I did not immediately pull away from my wild and crazy life, nor fully embrace a new religious or spiritual life. Rather I played back and forth between them for the next couple of years – though admittedly the religious or spiritual life gained constant ground against the other life.

By the way, I must state that Martha started down this road a bit earlier and more determinedly than I did. As she had a lot of time by herself down by the bay when we first separated, I came to find out that much of that was spent reading the Bible and praying. I don't know much about how that turned out once she went back to Texas* – except that years later she went through the very lengthy and complicated process of having our marriage officially "annulled", so that she could join the Catholic Church.

As 1983 turned into 1984, I now found myself in church every Sunday, normally the Government Street Presbyterian Church, but also rather frequently an Episcopal church where Betsey, a friend I was dating, attended. Both churches spoke strongly to my spiritual hunger – though my interest in the Presbyterian church was greater because it was the denomination I had grown up in. The Presbyterian church thus offered me a deeper sense of "rootedness," something I craved deeply. It felt like I was "coming home"!

Then when, a year later, (the fall of 1984) I did indeed return to the university, I found myself at that point rather disinterested in academic politics, and more interested in the thought processes of my students and friends – and rather absorbed in some of the fast-unfolding thoughts of my own about life. And in late 1984 I officially joined the Presbyterian church (after a 20+ year absence) – though I cannot say that this marked a dramatic shift in my slowly evolving spiritual life.

Cursillo. That was to come in late March of 1985 when I (very reluctantly) attended an Episcopal renewal seminar (Cursillo) which Betsey marched me off to. This three-day minicourse (thus *cursillo*)[†] on Jesus Christ may not have offered me a great breakthrough in my understanding of Christianity – for I was well familiar with all of its doctrinal aspects, even having taught elements of it as part of my offering of cultural studies at the university.

But it certainly opened my eyes wider to the importance of "relationship" as opposed to "personal self-sufficiency" as the heart of human life. This was my first encounter with the language of having a relationship with Jesus Christ – rather than just being familiar with his basic

---

*Although, in the spring of the next year (1984) I did hear from Susan that Martha was going to be marrying Mike in June.

†The word is Spanish because the movement was started up in Spain in the 1940s ...in an effort by the Spanish Catholic Church to stir spiritual renewal among its members, still benumbed by the violent Spanish Civil War of the late 1930s, plus World War Two. Non-Catholics would be so impressed by Cursillo, that other programs, the largely Episcopalian version of Cursillo, plus Tres Dias and Walk to Emmaus, would be created along very similar lines.

goodness and setting him up as a fine moral example for all right-minded people to follow (which is what I remembered about Jesus from my early Presbyterian teachings).

I didn't do anything dramatic that weekend about having such a "relationship." Yet the idea intrigued me – and began to gnaw at me.

Father Streeter. However, also during that Cursillo seminar, I became friends with an Episcopal priest, Father Streeter, who in an amazing way first mediated that sense of relationship with Jesus Christ for me. He was someone whom I would have carefully avoided in my previous Yuppie life: he was very overweight, rather sloppy in his grooming, a "recovering alcoholic" and a still very heavy smoker. In fact it was he that sought me out – to serve as my first Spiritual Director ever!

His simple forthrightness intrigued me – as well as what I came to learn of his work among the drug addicts and runaway youth living under the boardwalks of nearby Pensacola Beach where he had a beach ministry. And I came to appreciate him also through the eyes of others, who I quickly learned had the very highest respect for everything he was as a man, as a truly great man – with the humblest of hearts.

That friendship continued after that weekend. We got together often, when I would drive over to Pensacola to meet with him over an evening meal (he introduced me to Calamari, of which I am now something of an addict when I see it on a menu!) But unfortunately, this relationship lasted only a few months, when he suddenly died of massive heart failure.

Both his life and his death had a profound effect on me – for I was deeply aware of how, during even our brief time together, he had succeeded in giving me something of a distinct picture of who or what Jesus Christ might surely have been like. That was a spiritual gift of incalculable worth.

✳ ✳ ✳

HUNGER FOR MORE

Events in the late spring and early summer of 1985 now moved so fast for me that I am not sure of the sequence of events. During the spring I was teaching a contract course on the politics of international economics and finance with a group of executives at the Continental Teledyne Corporation. And I was very busy at the university laying the groundwork for a major seminar which was intended next year to bring together a large number of key political figures (including former President Jimmy Carter and former Secretary of State Henry Kissinger) on the subject of peace in Central America.

Prison ministry. But my heart was turning more and more toward spiritual matters. I wanted to be as involved there as I was in the world of politics and economics. Finally the suggestion was made that I accompany a fellow Presbyterian on his monthly visits to the Mobile County Jail where he volunteered to go cell to cell quietly showing portions of a movie on the Gospel of Luke. In early June I finally had my opportunity.

I was so moved by this experience that it became another one of those life-changing moments. As I looked through those bars at the fellows on the other side, the only thought that seemed to grip me was how very similar we probably were – except that they had fallen afoul of the law and I had not. I had abandoned a quite fine marriage, broken the heart of a very wonderful woman, which seemed a greater crime than what most of them had probably committed (the fact that I had heard that Martha was quite happy with her new life still did not exempt me from a deep sense of guilt for having brought on our divorce). Yet I was on the free side of those bars and they were not. I felt a deep sense of connectedness to these men – men whom under other circumstances I would never have had anything to do with. In the following days I could not get thoughts about that jail visit out of my mind.

It was now summer (1985), school was out, and I had committed myself for the summer only to the study of Spanish in an intensive summer course at the university, in preparation for a trip I was planning to make to Central America, to promote my peace-in-Central-America seminar. Basically, my afternoons were free (learning Spanish took little of my time, as I found that my knowledge of French made the learning of another Latin-based language relatively easy).

My thoughts during that free time returned to this issue of jail and those who were locked up there. I grew impatient with the idea that I would have to wait a whole month before I could return again to Mobile County Jail.

Emmett and the charismatics. Another friend who was part of that same monthly jail ministry knew of a new jail ministry that had just opened up in downtown Mobile. It was headed up by a fellow named Emmett, a plumber who had been working for the past ten years as a volunteer evangelist at the G.K. Fountain Prison 50 miles to the north of Mobile. A Mennonite organization had opened up this new ministry in downtown Mobile and had asked Emmett (who, however, was not a Mennonite) to head up their ministry on a full-time basis. So he had left his plumbing business to take up fulltime jail ministry.

One afternoon in mid-June I wandered down to the offices of this ministry – and began a friendship that was to be a major influence in my life.

Emmett was unlike anyone I had ever known before in my quite-Yuppie existence. He was simple, direct, and amazingly effective in his work. There was nothing "churchy" about him. He had little resemblance to any of the professional clergy that I was getting to know through my new church affiliations – except, of course, Father Streeter, whose personality had been much like Emmett's.

The people that gathered around to work with Emmett were equally common folk with uncommon ways. Life at the ministry offices was itself a bizarre phenomenon – at least to me, for I had never before encountered "charismatics" (though Cursillo had presented some of the same features). I had never encountered Christians who were ready at the drop of the hat to pray with someone for some need that they had.

The office of We Care jail ministry was a buzz of activity, for it was not only the office of a jail ministry but also a drop-in center for those with various personal problems. Praise music filled the rooms, prayers seemed to be going on somewhere almost all the time, noontimes produced a gathering of people from here and there for Bible study – and there were the "tongues," those strange sounds that came from the charismatics which to them gave evidence of their coming under control of the Holy Spirit!

This was all new to me. To me Christianity had pretty much been limited to stately Sunday morning worship and weekly good behavior that set one off as "Christian." True, Cursillo had opened up the vision of the Christian life as having a "relationship" with Jesus Christ (I was still working through the meaning of that concept at that time). But this being "empowered" by the Holy Spirit as the mark of the Christian life I had never before even heard of.

Needless to say, Emmett and his friends tried on the spot to engineer on my behalf my "receiving the Holy Spirit", in the form of tongues. It was a grand failure: "tongues" just would not come to me. In fact, in months of trying, nothing like that ever authentically developed for me. But they finally accepted the fact – and we all learned new things about the work of the Holy Spirit through my "failure" at tongues!

I kept coming back to the ministry every afternoon – in part to go with Emmett and some of his friends to Mobile County Jail, or the Youth Detention Center, or G.K. Fountain Prison, or wherever, and in part just to be present at the "happenings" in the We Care offices. I was intrigued by their energy, enthusiasm, and dedication. I wanted very much to have their spirit – even if I never could get into "tongues."

Life Church. Inevitably I asked the question: "where does all of this "style," this energy, come from?" Emmett's answer was simply: "come and see." And so I found myself one Sunday evening driving out to the edge of town to this strange church which the men of the church themselves had built – and which looked on the outside like a prefab warehouse, and on the inside like a huge meeting hall with many hundreds of chairs arranged in rows and people buzzing about, chatting excitedly. It was all so animated – more like a county fair than what I understood church to be.

Then BOOM! The 10-piece orchestra struck up with such volume and beat that I felt I was at a rock concert. It all made me feel uncomfortable – not because I had never "rocked" at a rock concert, but just that I had never associated such happenings with Christianity. For about 30 to 40 minutes the music continued, complete with an approximately 50-member choir and a dance group of about a dozen twirling women in colorful dresses and a smaller number of men in Eastern looking shirts and trousers.

The music did not stay at this loud rock level but step by step moved into a somewhat quieter and more reflective mood, more hypnotizing with the repetition of choruses and certain verses. Then it moved to a very quiet mood – almost hushed and inwardly introspective so that it had more the aspect of prayer than music. Then came the tongues, wave-lengthed to a single note that reminded me of the Om found in Hindu meditation. It was mesmerizing. The pastor then went into prayer, prayer that I know lasted many times longer than the pastoral prayers I was familiar with from Presbyterian worship. But it was a prayer that absolutely drew my heart into it all – the kind of prayer that you might wish would go on forever.

Then it all ceased, and the pastor began to preach – though it seemed more an extended Bible study than the kind of 18 to 20-minute homily which constituted a typical Presbyterian sermon. The sermon went on at some length, though I really was not aware of how long he had actually been speaking until he finished with an "altar call" and I noticed from my watch that he had been preaching for well over an hour! I was amazed, because I had never gotten impatient with the length of all of this. In fact, aside from the fright I first received from the music, I had found myself so "drawn" into this worship that time simply dissolved. I even dissolved – in that while there must have been well over a thousand people there for Sunday evening worship, I felt not overwhelmed by the number but well integrated into the whole. I even felt "close" to God.

Needless to say, I came back the next Sunday evening – and every Sunday evening thereafter while I still lived in Mobile. I was sort of a "Presbyterian" by day and a "charismatic" by night – though I never really got the tongues part that the charismatics felt was so important to the Christian life.

I really grew to appreciate my new charismatic friends. They not only were so "empowered" by their worship, but also truly "moved" by the Spirit to undertake amazing things. While I found that many Christians were willing to take "correct" Christian positions on this and that issue, even buying space in newspapers to present their petitions or sending money to organizations that promoted their positions on these issues, I also found that it tended to be the charismatics who would actually be found out in these hurting places personally doing the work of direct Christian charity and counsel. I deeply admired their personal dedication.

DISCOVERY OF THE "TRANSCENDENT" LIFE

I did not have well-defined words for what was happening to me, but I had a vague sense that I was being drawn into something bigger than myself, by something bigger than myself.

Even as far back as those days during my separation from Martha, I found myself contemplating the sense of *Fortuna* that I always had a sense was "with me" – for better or worse. I'm not sure when I began to understand this hand as the hand of God and when I began actually to find myself in "conversation" with this God. But I certainly had notions of something like this even before the divorce in early 1983.

But the God which or who began to evolve to my understanding over time was not the God of my Sunday School days. This God had no clear persona, no identity such as I had once assigned – and then rejected – as God. This God did not live above the clouds or anywhere "out there" somewhere. Nonetheless, I knew that I was not just talking to myself in these "conversations" I was having with this Higher Power. I knew deeply that I was involving myself in some kind of dialogue with some kind of "Other One" we commonly call "God."

Furthermore, strange coincidences began to occur in my life that I realized could not have been mere accidents. In particular I found myself meeting people at exactly the time when I needed to meet such people – and whatever "message" or insight they had for me at the time. This kind of information-flow I began to take note of – and sense that this is how "God" was answering me back.

Thus not only did I take note of a special presence I gradually began to call "God," but I also became much more aware of other people as part of the "higher" game plan of life. I became very aware that I was far from alone in this universe, but greatly, beautifully joined with the world around me. I began to appreciate the idea of "soul" – my soul – as a wonderful subset of a much more extensive Soul, Cosmic Soul, composed of God, and neighbor.

Certainly all this understanding did not come on at once – nor consistently. For me, my "conversion" from an agnostic to one who believed in the profound reality of God was a very gradual, sometimes erratic, process of movement in this direction. But it certainly went forward, step by step as each of these new events took place in my life.

* * *

A TIME OF DECISION

Frustration. In many ways my life showed a lot of progress since the low point of the divorce. I had found, in my return to the university, that I really was enjoying my work again. I had bought a very nice house in a pleasant downtown neighborhood and felt very comfortably resettled. A new circle of friends was widening rapidly. I was making more than enough money to enjoy the many activities that Mobile offered the community. And, of course, I was feeling once again in deep harmony with the cosmos!

But one area of my life remained highly problematic for reasons never quite clear to me: women! I had been dating Betsey now for a long time – but just couldn't get settled down into a one-on-one relationship with her. She was beautiful, intelligent, energetic, and enjoyed a wide range of interests quite like my own. But something held me back from a full commitment to her – and consequently I found myself over and over again starting up secondary relationships. I don't know what I wanted from a relationship – but these new relationships proved no more successful in providing a solution. As a consequence, I found myself increasing the juggling act by adding to the number of balls I was trying to keep up in the air.* This was no way to resolve the issue.

By the summer of 1985, when I added yet another relationship to the program, I was trying to balance about five different relationships. I was out every night of the week, studying Spanish in the mornings, at the We Care Ministry in the afternoons – and growing exhausted in the process.

The "call" in the night. Then one typical sleepless night in July I was jolted awake by a vision or a dream – I'm not sure which. I saw myself holding a set of bagpipes – and as I looked closer, I saw that I was dressed in a black cleric's gown, European rather than American in style. And as I stepped back from the scene, I realized that I was standing on the steps

---

*It got so bad that both Kit and Debby were working together as newly hired salesgirls at Gayfers Department Store's recently-expanded operations, and discovered over lunch together that the boyfriends they were dating happened to be the same person, namely me. Boy was I in trouble!

before the doors of St. Giles Cathedral in Edinburgh, Scotland.

No words accompanied this vision – but I knew exactly what it meant. It took me absolutely no time to say "yes" to the vision. I then fell back into a deep sleep, the first I had enjoyed in a very long time.

In the morning I awoke, understanding fully what I had agreed to during the night. I was going to give my life fulltime to the service of God, an evangelist or teacher who would help people like myself come out of their isolation and find their way back into harmony with life, with the cosmos, with God.

Stepping back from my relationships. It was not long after this decision that a second decision came to me – again as something of a vision or "word" from God: cut out all dating for a month and give the whole woman "thing" a break. Anyway, the time was drawing near for me to go off to Central America and interview political figures who were to be invited to my Central American peace seminar which was scheduled for the following spring. I needed the break. And it was okay with my women friends – for they mostly had already given up on the idea that their relationship with me was going anywhere anyway.

Indeed, I found that as I stepped back, a true sense of friendship seemed to replace the unattainable expectations for a "relationship." I was surprised and pleased at this discovery. I also realized that what I had wanted all along was soul-to-soul intimacy with them, not mutual and exclusive "ownership."

The Central-American trip confirms the "call." In mid-August of 1985 I was off to Central America for a month, to visit five Central-American countries and to talk with various leading figures of those countries.

The first country I came to was war-torn El Salvador. My very first meeting was an informal one, with a young priest, José, who was assigned by the archbishop's office to serve as an interpreter during my stay in El Salvador. We immediately hit it off – and found that we had a wide range of issues to discuss, including our respective faith stories.

In the days ahead I interviewed party leaders, businessmen, newspaper editors, academics, clerics, etc. But I found that what I enjoyed most was my time with José. I met his mother and sisters (he was the last surviving male member of the family; one of his sisters was even a young widow) and heard the story of family tragedy brought on by the civil war. But I was also moved by the strength of their character, their continuing joy in the midst of such violence, their ability to carry on rather normally in the midst of such mayhem.

At one point I accompanied José in bringing the gospel message and communion to a small parish he had charge of in the mountains (a very dangerous place, by the way, as government troops and leftist guerrillas regularly swept back and forth through these remote areas, killing anyone looking suspicious to them). Here too I heard the same stories – and saw the vitality in the people's eyes and hearts despite the constant tragedy that accompanied life in their country.

In them I saw the countless generations of little people who have carried on life – despite the mighty plans of the "great leaders" to save these same little people. Indeed frequently, as I listened to these leaders, I kept wondering how close some of them really were to these people in whose name they carried on their great crusades (some individuals, however, I sensed really were very close to the common people). I got the distinct idea that their countrymen would be a lot better off if people like them would give up trying to "save" the others – and instead would let them work out their destinies themselves. Their "little people" seemed to possess enormous durability and fortitude of their own. What they needed was inspiration and a bit of guidance. They did not need to be dictated to!

Into my fourth week of interviewing (I was in Honduras at the time) I found that my mind kept coming back to José and his family in El Salvador. So I cut the program short and returned to El Salvador – just to check out my feelings (or instincts) further about these things. That final week in El Salvador confirmed all that I was beginning to understand. God really was with these people – and was somehow going to see them through this present crisis – almost despite the efforts of well-meaning individuals to save them.

Faith over politics. You can imagine what light this cast on my "peace seminar" concept. As I returned to the States, I found that my heart was no longer in this enterprise. I would have more gladly put on a program to bring some of these "little people" north to tell us Yanquis what they knew about the power of life, the enormous potency of their faith, their ability to find ingenious ways to survive, despite our well-intended efforts to save them all.

Ironically (or was it so ironic?) I returned to Mobile to the news that the university president's office was frightened at the prospect of so many major personalities descending on the campus at once. They were deeply concerned about the huge costs involved in assuring security for such a conference. So they made me scale the project way back. Thus, for example, even though former President Jimmy Carter was willing to participate for only a negligible fee, I had to uninvite him. However we had made the ($25,000!) commitment with Henry Kissinger and so we would honor that – turning the event into a Kissinger extravaganza (their idea, not mine!), and that alone.

Ordinarily I would have been crushed. But given what I had come to see and understand in Central America, I actually greeted the news with relief. It meant that I was going to have to uninvite a number of North American and Central American dignitaries – but I really didn't mind. Somewhere in El Salvador I had lost my desire for such a conference anyway. It all worked out for the best.

My last year at the university. I had made up my mind soon after my nighttime call that I was going to definitively cut my 14-year tie with the university upon my return with the fall term. This coming year would definitely be my last at the university.

But what a wonderful year that last year was. Perhaps it was because I knew I was going to be moving on to new things. But I was more relaxed, more alive than I can remember having been in a long time. I enjoyed my classes immensely. I felt so "connected" to everything – even as I was preparing to cut my ties.

The year went by quickly. Christmas came quickly and I headed off to the West Coast to join my parents and sister for Christmas, then to return to Mobile, via El Salvador, where I spent a week with José and his family and friends. Christmas also marked the beginning of the heavy Mardi Gras society balls – which I participated in, juggling things between Debbie, Kit, Mary, Marcia and, as always, Betsey. Nothing much had changed on that front!

✳ ✳ ✳

LAY MINISTRY

Yuppie Evangelicals! But neither had my commitment to Christian ministry changed any. Of course my afternoon visits to Emmett and the We Care office had to come to an end with the resumption of the fall school term. But I had made up my mind to go once a week in the evenings on my own to the Mobile County Jail to continue my work there. But I went only one evening by myself before I decided that going alone at this was not going to work. So I started inviting my friends.

At first there were just a few of us, then a few more, then quite a group! We would gather at the We Care office on Tuesday nights at about 7:00 for prayers. I would give a short biblical thought for the evening, we would pray together at some length, and then at about 7:30 we would be off: some to the County Jail, some to the City Jail (men's and women's sections); some to the Women's and Children's Shelter; and when a number of youth joined the team, we added visits to the Youth Detention Center; and then when we had an overflow (over fifty volunteers showing up) I would take a handful of volunteers out onto the streets around the port to converse with whomever. Indeed, we soon got to be well known by the ladies of the night!

We would go simply to be "available" – to be a presence, to pray, and to offer thoughts from the Bible. On the streets, we would chat with people who approached us, pass on paperback New Testaments if they were interested, and pray with any who desired it. We were never "preachy," just there to let them know that they were not forgotten, not by God, not by Jesus, not by Christians who cared.

We were quite a group: Presbyterians and Charismatics, Methodists, Episcopalians, and a few others – though the Presbyterians and Charismatics were the most numerous.

Some were a bit scandalized that we would regroup later in the evening (not including the youth!) in a back room at a yuppie "fern bar," to snack and drink (lightly) and simply to let the excitement pour forth. We all returned from our respective evangelical visits excited – and eagerly sought the opportunity to talk about it.

We were mostly WASPish Yuppies – some were even rather prominent business leaders – who were discovering the joy of going forth into our world in the name of the Lord. I took particular delight in seeing my very proper Presbyterian friends get "turned on" by all of this. They learned to open up to others about their own faith, to help others similarly open up – and to pray, pray, pray (we eventually added a Thursday evening prayer circle to our list of activities). Needless to say, we became a very close group.

The Kairos Prison Ministry. As if all this were not enough, in the early fall I agreed to be on staff or "team" for a Kairos weekend at the G.K. Fountain Prison in Atmore (about 50 miles to the north of Mobile). This was a Cursillo seminar tailored for the prison environment. Serving on the team meant weekly Wednesday night training sessions in Atmore at an Episcopal church for about 8 weeks prior to the weekend. About half of the 40-man team were Episcopal priests, deacons and laymen, with the other half being mostly Catholic deacons and laymen (no priests on this team). But the team included also a Methodist minister and me, the lone Presbyterian.

As G.K. Fountain was an all-male prison, the team that would go into prison was made up of the men. The 20-or-so women who had been working with us would serve as backups to the men, cooking, praying, and worshiping with us when we returned from a morning, afternoon or evening session. Food was abundant – especially in the form of cookies, which I remembered from Cursillo (I ate so many cookies at Cursillo – yet burned off so many calories in just the emotional intensity of it all that all those calories were used up). In fact, in most important respects it was a Cursillo seminar we were putting on.

Team meetings were designed primarily to build up a very close team spirit, which it certainly succeeded in doing. After eight Wednesday nights and one Saturday all-day retreat together, we were a very close group.

It was at Cursillo that I first saw adult men hugging each other in greeting. This was a shock to this Presbyterian – at first. I later discovered that this was the standard greeting among all "renewal" Christians, including charismatics. And I came to enjoy it – for it symbolized the closeness of the Christian fellowship that we were willing to extend to each other. Christianity for this group was not a Sunday morning formality – but a part of the intimacy with which they/we, as Christians, greeted the world. I liked that sentiment very much – especially after having been so "removed" in my feelings about most other people – and even about life itself.

A very sad note in all this closeness occurred at the communion service that all the team traditionally shared on the last Wednesday evening training session. Someone (some of the team knew who, but I never did) among the Catholics mentioned the fact to a Catholic priest – who then showed up to ensure that the Catholics would have a separate Communion service. Most of the Catholic members of the team were burned. Some even came to the "Episcopal" communion service in protest. That bit of "churchiness" or "priestcraft" (as I later came to term it!) left a deep impression on me. It really was an insult to Christ as far as I was concerned.

The "weekend" (actually Thursday evening to Sunday evening) itself went wonderfully well. There were 15 tables of about 5 or 6 inmates, a table leader and a spiritual director each. I was a "spiritual director" and in fact was called on often to take time out to pray with one or another of the inmates.

I also gave one of the "talks" – drawing on Paul's Letter to the Romans, especially Chapter Eight, which was eventually to serve me as the center-post of my own personal theology. It was an excellent matchup for me to be delivering that particular talk. The talks were always personal and often emotional. My talk in fact brought two of my teammates themselves to tears (it was the story of the collapse of my yuppie world and the "second chance" that God gave this sinner).

One of the highlights of the weekend for me in fact was when one of the guys at my table, who was well known as one of the prison bullies (and who was there at first just to keep tabs on his boys) quietly asked me to pray outside with him – and proceeded to break down into a flood of tears, tears which did not stop for the rest of the weekend. The other inmates were stunned – and moved. [He and I kept in touch for over five years, even through a couple of prison moves on his part – until a combination of my move to Garfield and his move to yet another institution broke the link. I tried some years later to restore the link, but my Christmas letter was returned with "addressee unknown"].

The Sunday evening closing was profoundly moving. Betsey showed up and they were all glad to meet my "girl." We all had become close – inmates as well as team by then.

But I was again reminded of the downside of religion, when only a couple of months later a baby of the teammate I had roomed with was killed in a car accident his wife had, and we all came to the funeral. It was a Catholic funeral – and all the non-Catholics were quietly told that we were not to go forward to receive communion during that part of the funeral service. It felt so strange to be shut out of the highest point of the service – because we were not members of the "true" church. This did nothing to improve my very dim view of denominational differences within the church. I was very "Presbyterian." But I was also "Episcopalian," "charismatic," and even "Catholic" if they'd have me. I didn't care. I was "Christian" to the core.

If there was any label to describe me, it would have been "Evangelical", a category that belongs to no particular Christian denomination.

In the spring I signed up for another Kairos weekend and went through the same process again in May (1986). Even the second time through it was a moving experience. Kairos came to mean a lot to me personally.

✳ ✳ ✳

SEMINARY: YES OR NO?

When the call came during that midsummer night in 1985, I really had not given much thought as to what form that call might specifically take. I certainly did not see myself becoming a minister (a parish pastor). I really don't know what I thought I might be doing – even as I gave notice to the Dean that September that this would be my last year at the university.

As that last school year (1985-1986) developed, I suppose I thought that somehow I might, like Emmett, develop some kind of a street ministry right there in Mobile. The growth of my evening evangelical group certainly seemed to point to the possibility of developing some kind of full-time ministry of that nature.

Admission to Princeton Seminary. My pastor at the Presbyterian church where I worshiped urged me at least to apply to some seminaries. That fall (1985) he encouraged me to look into two seminaries in particular. I did apply to one of them and got accepted quickly – even before all my paperwork was in.

But there was something in the name "Princeton" that attracted me. I felt sheepish about having "freed" myself so fully from the presumptions of yuppie life – only now to be thinking about applying to what distinctly looked like a yuppie citadel. Nonetheless I applied. Then I heard nothing – weeks past the time I knew I was supposed to hear from them. Finally in March (1986) I got the news, about a month late: I had been accepted. I was excited!

I went in to tell my pastor the good news. We chatted for a while. Then as I was about to leave, he told me something very strange. He told me that he was actually surprised that Princeton Seminary had accepted me. He had had many conversations with the admissions office – in concern about my commitment to the church. I was speechless.

Needless to say, I thought about those words a lot after that meeting. I realized that this issue could have been raised only by him – for there was nothing in my application that would have caused any such concern about my commitment to the "church" [the Presbyterian "church"?]. I knew that he had become increasingly disapproving of my close association with charismatics. I know he did not care for Emmett. Yet – he had earlier given me such encouragement to apply to the other two seminaries (which he had close connections with). But in considering the matter further, I decided to just let it drop. Anyway, this only served to confirm the Princeton decision for me. God obviously had opened the door for me at Princeton, in overcoming some serious human opposition!

But even then, I hadn't really made up my mind that I was actually going to go to seminary. I very much wanted to stay in Mobile.

God sells my house out from underneath me! Spring and the approach to the end of the school year was upon me and I still had not made up my mind. One Sunday afternoon, as I was visiting with Betsey's family, the subject came up. The concern was expressed about getting my house on the market if I was going to be leaving Mobile, particularly if I was indeed going to be going up to Princeton in June. I had talked about the possibility of starting up at Princeton with some summer Hebrew language study. Anyway, Betsey's father reminded me that the housing market was very slow, and it would not be wise trying to market an empty house if I left in June before it was sold. Hmmm, it was a thought.

That very same evening, as I was entering the kitchen door to my home, the phone was ringing. It was my real estate agent friend, Nancy, that I had worked with a lot in the past, and who in fact had lined up this very house for me. She too wanted to know what I was going to do. Was I going to be putting the house on the market again? She asked me to get back quickly to her with a price if those were my intentions. (Obviously she wanted the listing!) I agreed, and called her back the next evening with a price based on my original cost plus the cost of some improvements I had made on the house. She said "Fine. I'd like to show the house tomorrow." Wow! That was quick!

The next day she arrived with a friend and went through the house. But we had not yet signed any listing agreement. Later that day she called again to say that she had a purchaser for the house, one willing to pay $1000 more than my asking price, and no realtor costs involved! For she herself was the purchaser! She had just sold her house to someone who wanted immediate occupancy, and she needed to find a place of her own – fast. She always liked the house I had bought, knew that I was thinking of moving, and had added the $1000 as a gift to help me through seminary! The only catch was that she needed the house in two weeks: the end of March. This was wonderful, I guess.

But this left me with the problem of where I was to live for 2½ months until I would leave for Princeton. Two nights later, as I explained my plight to my Thursday evening prayer circle, one of my friends, Bill, spoke up.

Miles! Now I know why I had such a strange thought only two weeks ago. I felt this strong urge to invite you to move in with me into this huge, rather empty house I'm living in. But then I thought what a strange idea, since you had your own place already. Now I know why I had that thought. You do indeed have somewhere to stay until you leave for Princeton – and whenever you return on vacation – and a place to store all your furniture while you are away at seminary!!!

Holy Cow! If I had any doubts about whether God wanted me to stay in Mobile to do street ministry, or to head off to seminary, there could be no doubts now. God himself sold my house out from under me, and took care of all the secondary details as well! I was definitely leaving Mobile.

CHAPTER FIVE

THE PRINCETON DAYS
June 1986 to December 1990

✳ ✳ ✳

SETTLING IN

Honestly though, I wasn't at all sure I agreed with God on this! The wonderful going-away parties only made my departure all the sadder – even somewhat bitter for me. Thus the 2½ days I was on the road from Mobile to Princeton were filled with a bit of frustration, maybe even a bit of anger, with God for having pulled me out of Mobile.

The "Voice." As I arrived in Princeton on a Sunday afternoon, checked myself into the Summer School office, got my room assignment, and was unloading my luggage – a very exhausted and unhappy puppy I was – the "Voice" spoke to my spirit: "Get back into your car, I want to show you something."

"Are you kidding? I'm tired. I just want to get out and walk around a bit – look over the Princeton campus." But get back into my car I did – and headed south along US Route 1 until I came to nearby Trenton – and soon found myself in the heart of the Trenton blight. But oddly enough, as I drove along the unfamiliar streets, a deep sense of peace came over me, peace that I had not known since I began contemplating my departure from Mobile.

I then turned back to Princeton, got that much needed walk, and put the Trenton incident out of my mind.

The next day summer Hebrew started off with a bang – and, as a marathon effort, got more and more painful as the days advanced. Within a week all the students were complaining about getting only 4 or 5 hours of sleep a night because of the workload.

The call to Trenton. That's when I decided to head over to the placement office to see if there was not some kind of local "hands-on ministry" I could get involved in so that I did not dry my spirit to a crisp while I was studying Hebrew. I was shown a portfolio of such internships, and discovered one

109

offered by the First Presbyterian Church of Trenton, which listed a whole line of inner-city activities it hosted, and $5200 annual stipend to boot! I asked the Director of the office if what I saw was correct. He himself was surprised to see that particular internship still listed – as it was one of the most popular around and always one of the first to be picked. Then he remembered that the young man that was supposed to have the internship had decided shortly after spring semester ended that he would not be returning in the fall. Thus the listing was still there, as I saw things, just waiting for me.

I called the pastor, John Nelson, and he agreed to interview me on campus, as he was coming up that way the next day. And, of course, I got the job.

But it was not until the next Sunday, as I followed John's directions into Trenton that I realized: I was right back in the same area where the Voice had guided me to on that first day in New Jersey. In fact I had driven just behind the church at one point in my earlier wanderings. Eerie! But not unprecedented as things seemed to go between God and me!

By the way: I continued my summer Hebrew despite being in Trenton every afternoon working with various urban ministries and Sunday mornings assisting in worship – and found that it greatly improved my effectiveness with the Hebrew. I ended up with A's for both summer sessions – much to the amazement of my fellow students who couldn't figure out why someone would take on ministerial duties in the face of such academic pressure. But the Lord has a way of respecting our tithes, time as well as money!

Scoti. Interestingly, the person that taught me the most during my Princeton years was not even at the seminary – but was affiliated with the Center for Theological Inquiry (CTI), right across the street from the seminary.

I met "Scoti" (pronounced "Scotty") in Trenton, the very first Sunday in June that I came to the church as the new intern, and sat in the many-generations-old Chambers pew where he and his family always sat. I seemed to have somehow parlayed that error into an invitation for lunch with Scoti and his wife Mary and their one-year-old daughter Hannah. I joined them for an elaborate Sunday meal back at their home in Princeton – that Sunday, and then every Sunday thereafter for the next couple of years!

Scoti was the picture of scholarship, with a full beard, a studied look, and a careful intensity in his words. He had been a pastor for 18 years – yet was also ever the scholar, having spent many years in Europe (Germany, France, Switzerland) studying languages and earning a Th.D. degree in Reformation studies from the University of Lausanne. His doctorate on the history of worship in the Reformed Church was eventually published as a major text used in a number of seminaries in this country and in Europe. Now he was in Princeton, having given up the pastorate, to pursue research on the history of the Christian sermon - from the ancient "Fathers" down to the present (eventually published in 7 volumes by Eerdmans, under his actual name, Hughes Oliphant Old!).

My Sunday visits with him - plus my many additional visits with him during the week - were my real tutorial in the traditions of the Presbyterian (that is "Reformed") church. We both shared a similar interest in language, history and culture - and my insights into the general social history of Western civilization and his knowledge of the history of the church blended to make for some great discussions. I can't even begin to describe what he taught me about the long history of the church.

But there was something more than just the intellect that joined us. We shared a deep sense of joined "fortunes." We both were "uprooted" people looking to God to discover what the next turn in our lives would be. How many hours we spent together reflecting on the meaning of the respective journeys that brought us to this point in time. Scoti's position in Princeton was temporary - as the study-grant he lived under was only for a couple of years. And I was just as uncertain as to what the future held for me. We were both certain that the last thing I should ever do was parish ministry! But that left me few practical alternatives. [But how interesting that in time his temporary status at the CTI was converted into a permanent research/writing life in nearby Trenton, supported by the very wise investment decisions of his MBA wife that allowed them to be totally financially self-supporting - and that I ended up finally in parish ministry. God has His own unexpected ways of opening the doors to our future!]

Off to El Salvador again. That first summer in Princeton ended and I headed back to Mobile for a month's vacation - to a wonderful reception from my many, many friends in Mobile. I got back into the swing of things as if I had never left. I had some smoothing over of troubles to perform between the Presbyterians and the Charismatics on the ongoing Yuppie ministry. Also, Emmett had moved to much larger quarters - whichneeded lots of work to make it "comfortable." And as I was going to be returning to El Salvador for a week, I found myself busy gathering a fair-sized team of ministers to accompany me there (including my pastor in Trenton, John). Busy, busy, busy.

But oddly, things just refused to work out. One by one participants in the trip to El Salvador had to cancel out for one reason or another. Also I had lined up building materials from a lumber company and the men necessary to start assembling separate counseling rooms for Emmett, and had just enough time to get the project underway before leaving for El Salvador – when I found out that the lumber company had held up the shipment because of a $.05 increase in the board foot rate that they had quoted me for some of the lumber. They wanted my approval before shipping – and could not locate me, so rescheduled shipment for early next week – which just happened to be too late. For something less than an $8 differential, we had to call the whole thing off. I was fit to be tied.

Then when two more pastors canceled out on the trip, leaving just John and me scheduled for the trip to El Salvador, I felt as if the heavens themselves were lined up against me. That evening a number of my charismatic friends gathered around me to pray that the Lord might show me what was going on.

Again: the "Voice." The next morning, as I was having breakfast at a local Waffle House, on my way down to the shore for a couple of days with Betsey before leaving for El Salvador, the "Voice" spoke: "no more projects." It was a most clear/distinct thought. I knew that this was in answer to the prayer the evening before. There was nothing for me to do but simply yield before it all. I did. And I felt a great peace come over me.

Then the morning that I was to leave for El Salvador I was awakened by the "Voice" again. "Call John and make sure he brings along a guitar pick." That was a strange thought. I tried to ignore it and go back to sleep. But the Voice was insistent about that call. Then I thought how strange anyway: John would have had to have left for Newark airport by now. But the Voice persisted. So, sheepishly I called – not sure what I was going to say that would make sense to John's wife. But instead I got a sleepy John to answer. "Ohmygosh! I'll never make the plane. See you later. I'll get a message to you in New Orleans [where I was scheduled to meet him] about whatever flight arrangements I can make at this point."

But as far as I was concerned, it was all in God's hands now. I was tired of worrying about this and that. If I went on to El Salvador by myself, that was perfectly fine.

God as travel director. I got to the New Orleans airport and was handed a telegram – the bottom of which the check-in clerk carefully tore off, saying that it was against FAA regulations to transmit! I was curious. But what I did get from the telegram was that John was catching a flight arriving 3 hours after the departure of my TACA flight to El Salvador. He would get to El Salvador somehow and meet me at the hotel in San Salvador as soon as he could.

But curiously, the TACA flight was very late getting started. Indeed, as it turned out, it was exactly three hours late! When John's plane pulled in, immediately across the same concourse, everyone but me was on the TACA plane. I met John, we dashed the 20 yards to the TACA gate, and looked out to see his bags being loaded on the plane. They shut the door behind us – and off we went.

I asked John what was on the lower half of the telegram. He roared! He had written that I should pray that the TACA flight should be delayed three hours so that he could still make the connection! Funny thing – John said that something (the "Voice"?) had told him that he would make the TACA flight with me anyway.

With those thoughts we both settled back knowing that God had put the two of us together on that plane to El Salvador and would have His hand on us for the rest of the time together. We were both now working according to His plans, not ours!

Indeed, it was a marvelous, event-filled week, unplanned but full of wonderful things. We visited an orphanage, a medical center for the poor, a refugee camp (actually a very nicely developing village) being constructed by Texas lads from a huge church in Dallas, and the seminary where José was the director (even took communion with them, much to their shock!) We spent a lot of time with José's family and friends relaxing at the beach, or back in the hills, where in visiting his country home (whose street-side walls were pock-marked with bullet holes) we found to be occupied by government troops, much to our surprise when we burst in upon them!

John's wife Teresa met us in New Orleans (as did Betsey) – relieved to see her husband safely back from El Salvador.* We spent a short time together there, Betsey and I returned to Mobile – and, once again, it was time to say goodbye to Betsey as I headed north to New Jersey, to start the regular fall term. I went more willingly this time.

REVISITING AN OLD ISSUE: THE AUTHORITY OF SCRIPTURE

One of the great issues that awaited me in seminary was this matter of Scripture and its authority in my life. It had been this issue which had been responsible more than any other thing for my decision 25 years earlier to drop my plans for the Presbyterian ministry – and even for my abandonment of the Christian faith itself.

In my survey course of the Old Testament, part of our first semester requirement, the issue awaited me – and every other seminarian. For some

---

*Teresa was so very Italian. She warned me ahead of time that if I did not come back with John alive and well, I was not to come back at all! She was kidding, or maybe not!

the issue was no big deal – for their stand in Christianity had little to do with whether Scripture was true or not. But for others, the "evangelicals," (like myself) this was a weighty issue. But I did not come unprepared this time to face this issue.

The Truth that lies beyond mere "fact." Though my thoughts were not by any means well formulated on the matter, I had already developed a strange sense that "truth" was more than what meets the Western or modern eye. Perhaps it was in the strange encounters I had with God (the "Voice"), or in how things tended to work out on their own when we gave over in trust to higher things, or in how prayer could have such a powerful effect upon life's circumstances, or even in how Scripture brought simply to a situation like a prison visit could open up lives – but I knew that "truth" was more than just "facts."

The attempt of the Western mind to reduce all truth to "fact" easily robbed truth of its very essence, life of its very vitality. While our dry analytical thinking could indeed "tame" many of the elements of life, this thinking usually ended up with something that ultimately seemed highly counterfeit. It was like trying to describe in analytical terms the beauty of a great symphony, the breathtaking qualities of a sunset over the Gulf as a storm rolls in, or the thrill of finding deep intimacy in a human relationship. Any effort to bring such elements of life to "fact" would always end up making them meaningless.

And this same meaninglessness is what I thought I saw as the chief feature of the lives of many of us in the West. I certainly had been there. Somehow all that great mental control I had over life had not ever made for a very satisfying existence. And of course in the end it all failed me.

Truth, real truth, could be found only through poetry, artistry – most of that merely impressionistic in its handling of the basic truths we live by and for. But the ancients knew that. The East still does too. Truth is conveyed through story – even myth – if necessary. In such a form Truth does not lose its essence in the retelling.

Rethinking the Genesis story. Thus to me the story of creation in Genesis was/is not a treatise in physics and chemistry. The story is a hymn, a song or psalm of praise to God for the goodness of His creation. It is not to be handled as "fact."   The six days of creation have little, if anything, to do with "days" as we literalists understand them.   Their specific sequence may not even be "factually" important. Indeed, chapter two of Genesis, in repeating the story of creation, rearranges the sequence a bit.

Instead, the Truth found in those opening chapters of Scripture is there to highlight the contrast in the goodness of God and the sinfulness or failure of prideful man. God's intentions in creation were pure and holy. Earthman (the literal meaning of "Adam") had been given a privileged position in the scheme of God's creation – but failed to respect this honor by breaking trust with this holy Creator, who had asked only that Adam should celebrate the glory of it all in fellowship with Him (as one might enjoy a great meal with a friend). Instead, Adam misappropriated his privilege in his effort to obtain for himself independent status within creation, even moral-ethical knowledge which should make him his own judge over life – and thus make him "free" from God's dominion. The consequence of Adam's willfulness was that his life from then on was burdened by a grimness that comes from being so "self-aware" about the shortness of life and the hardships that accompany mortal existence. Adam found himself cut off from Paradise. The biblical "storyline" from that point on was how God then chose to try to bring Earthman back ("redeem" him) from this self-inflicted folly.

I knew many of the details of that story myself – personally.

What a powerful Truth is told in those few opening chapters of Scripture! Such profoundness about the "human condition," related simply through a handful of poetic words. It is an ancient myth that I would come back to often in my thoughts, in my sermons, in my teachings.

The place of Biblical text-criticism within My Christian faith. Certainly text-criticism seems to me to be interesting – in that it discloses some wonderful understandings of how such ancient Truths came to be transmitted through the generations – even across tribes, nations and cultures – as the "story" was told and retold by the ages. But to make more of text-criticism than that is to miss the whole point of the Truth that is contained in the medium of ancient biblical literature.

Thus I was not bothered by the revelations of doublets (where elements of the story seemed to have been simply repeated twice), borrowings from the literature of surrounding pagan peoples (the creation myth and the story of the great flood), the obvious hands of different editors (reflecting the fact that the story we have today was carried forward by more than one tribal group or school of ancient priestly scholars).

To me the Truth of God did not rise or fall on the existence of any of these intriguing features. I was aware that all of this ancient Truth came to us through numerous generations and many different political circles. I no longer expected some kind of single-minded document, as if the whole thing had floated down from the sky one sunny afternoon – to land in the laps of Jewish rabbinical scholars a century or two after their return from captivity in Babylon.

I was bothered, however, by the failure of some of our professors to show any significant amount of interest in the message itself – in the Truth that lay powerfully within these layers of literary tradition. We spent so much time inspecting the trees, that we never got around to learning how to cultivate an appreciation for the forest.

Nonetheless, I did not let any of this put me off greatly. In each of the two semesters of my second or "middler" year in seminary I took almost all Biblical studies (exegesis) courses, even taking on two extra Biblical courses each semester for extra credit, and auditing three more (even doing much of the required written work for these audited courses)! I couldn't get enough of Biblical studies! Of course I had hell to pay my senior year, in that I had a large group of courses required for graduation still facing me. But I never regretted my middler year loaded up with Biblical studies.

Service as a seminary deacon. I was made a campus deacon the very first fall semester at Princeton. I was a lot older than the rest of the students – and having been a longtime professor I scored some "maturity points" among my fellow students that opened up this deacon spot.

The deacons were supposed to be a source of dorm leadership, helping fellow students with personal problems. I took this task seriously, and found that I spent a great deal of my time counseling fellow students operating under various types of academic or personal stress. I also used that time to help walk some of my fellow students through their reactions to biblical text-criticism. I was really busy during my first or "junior" year in this regard. My dorm room door was always open.

✳ ✳ ✳

LIFE BEYOND THE WORLD OF ACADEMICS

The "Celebration" program. I guess I thought that the message of "no more projects!" I had just received when I was back in Mobile was not intended to apply to Princeton/Trenton. Anyway I had always been such a "projects" person that it was not long before I was pushing a number of "good ideas" to get things moving both on campus and in Trenton.

I had the bright idea of creating a Sunday evening "Celebration" service at John's "First Pres" (First Presbyterian Church), and inviting my fellow seminarians to join in. I lined up music (a number of guitars), got a handful of pastors to agree to participate (John, Scoti, and a couple of others) – plus their wives – and began to line up special speakers or programs to focus the evening around. I pamphleted the Princeton campus, passersby in Trenton (mostly state government workers) on their way to lunch near the church, and the windshields of cars parked at a large shopping mall halfway between Trenton and Princeton.

But no one came – except the pastors and their wives. We all had a good time, singing and just visiting. But it was disappointing. I repeated the advertisement process several times – all with the same results (I did get one seminarian to come once – though I finally sensed that her interests seemed to be more in me than in the program).

A visiting missionary. Once I had a missionary, who ran the medical clinic John and I had visited, come through from El Salvador. I was positive that this would draw out people to our Sunday evening "Celebration." But to my great dismay, still no one came out to the program. I brought this same missionary to the campus to talk about the needs of war-torn El Salvador – thinking that at least this would draw out a number of students. But only a handful turned up. I was embarrassed – and again feeling very frustrated.

Just letting things go. Finally I began to realize that indeed the "no more projects" directive also extended to Princeton! So, once again, I backed down and just decided to go with the flow. The Sunday night thing continued on for quite a while, but basically just as an informal fellowship – and with the same 8 or 10 individuals, basically pastors and their wives. But actually it worked quite fine – as long as it was appreciated for being what it indeed was!

In fact, John, Scoti and I extended the fellowship "thing" among ourselves to informal weekly afternoon get-togethers over a pitcher of beer – just to talk about whatever. There were times I forgot that I was a student in Princeton, I was spending so much time in Trenton. But actually, this helped immensely for me to keep things in perspective.

Trenton State Prison and Triumphant Life Church. I also had developed a Wednesday afternoon and evening routine that I kept up until early the following year, when I could only keep up the Wednesday evening portion of it. I volunteered to serve with the chaplaincy program at the Trenton State Prison, working each Wednesday afternoon in "lockup," the punishment cells for inmates who got themselves in trouble over something or other.* Then I would join Trenton friends, Michael and Carol, for dinner in Trenton before accompanying them to their Wednesday evening worship/ Bible study at their church.

----

*Almost all of the guys I found myself visiting were Black Muslims. All I really did was listen to them and pray with them, for I figured there was no point in doing any kind of Christian ministry in the process. But wouldn't you know that I got a lot of Christmas cards from them that December, a real surprise to me. You never know what your impact can be when you just "show up" for others.

I met the family, actually the wife, Carol, through John – for she was the one directing the clothing program housed in one of First Pres's multiple offices on Hanover Street (the street running behind the church). She and her husband, Michael, were charismatics – and I felt quite at home with them. But Carol proved to be less tolerant of my Presbyterian ways than Emmett had been – always trying to convert me to the true "charismatic" faith. Nonetheless, I enjoyed their company a lot and became a Wednesday evening fixture at Triumphant Life church in Trenton, often even joining the men on Saturday mornings for their prayer/Bible study fellowship.

Cultivating a spiritual life on campus. Back on campus, Knox, the fellow who lived across the hall from me in Brown Hall, and I decided that it would be nice to gather with some of our fellow seminarians in the dorm once a week to sing, share scripture and pray. But surprisingly we found only a handful of seminarians willing to give time to such an enterprise – and only a half hour at that, from 10:00 to 10:30 p.m. on Tuesday nights.

This seemed to me to be such an important part of the life of anyone contemplating Christian ministry – that I always remained amazed at how few of my fellow seminarians were willing to give so little time to something that ought to have been at the heart of all Christian life. Also, daily chapel on campus was attended very poorly, Sunday evening worship on campus brought a turnout of seldom even ten of the 900 students, and early Wednesday morning prayers brought out even fewer – mostly the Koreans among us. Everyone was so concerned about homework and grades that they seldom came out of their shells, except at meals, to breathe the air – or exercise their spirits. Friday nights were the only nights "out", and even then, often rather timidly. Forget Saturday nights: everyone was getting ready for Sunday duties at the churches where they served in internships.

How then was it that I was able to do all these things, things that younger and supposedly more energetic individuals, ones presumably headed for Christian ministry, were just not willing to take on?

My personal computer (which I put to great use at Princeton!) certainly eased the task of writing papers. Certainly also, all those earlier years as a professor, gathering research material for my courses in the library and preparing various writings, made my academic work almost routine. I also knew how to read efficiently for information. I also had a knack for languages, so Hebrew and Greek came to me a lot easier than it did for most of the students.

Consequently, I probably spent half the time studying that my fellow students did – allowing me to fill the rest of the time with ongoing worship, personal devotionals, and various outreach projects.

So maybe it was not very fair of me being "disappointed" with my classmates because they didn't just "naturally" go at things the way I did. They had not yet accumulated the years of experience that I had, experience that I drew on extensively to help push myself through the seminary experience.

National politics during this period. Something that amazed me was the level of disinterest I was feeling about a matter that used to occupy my thoughts front and center: American national politics.

It was the Reagan Era, and I generally liked the guy – quite a bit actually. But I now found myself reading no newspapers and watching no television. Not even the news. Consequently, that realm of life simply fell out of focus for me.

I was, however, quite aware at one point that something spectacular was going on in DC, something about an Iran-Contra scandal that was circling around the Reagan presidency. Indeed, I found my fellow students (who supposedly had no time for anything else other than their studies) glued to the TV in the small meeting room on the first floor (down the hall just a couple dorm rooms from me). My fellow seminarians hooted and hollered, jeered and clapped, and I simply walked on by.

Maybe it was because of my disgust with how the Watergate Scandal had become soap opera a dozen years earlier, and I found myself disliking this kind of media-hyped spectator politics intensely.

I don't really know why. I just was not interested. I had other things to occupy my thoughts.

And things would stay pretty much that way for a number of years.

✳ ✳ ✳

THE HANOVER STREET MINISTRY

Crisis at the "Crisis Ministry." When John and I returned from El Salvador in September of that first summer in New Jersey (1986) and made our respective ways back to Princeton/Trenton, one of the first things that greeted us was a major crisis in what was then called the "Crisis Ministry." This was an enterprise involving two wealthy Princeton churches (Presbyterian and Episcopalian) in partnership with John's Presbyterian church in Trenton. The Crisis Ministry itself was located in one of the buildings owned by First Pres on Hanover Street – along with other storefront ministries, such as the clothing ministry I worked closely with.

The Crisis Ministry was supposed to be an outreach ministry to the many homeless (mostly Black males) in the neighborhood. When I arrived to begin my internship and thus first checked it out, what I saw was polite

Princeton women in the back office trying to provide social services for these homeless – particularly in lining up for them both jobs and apartments.

There was nothing particularly "Christian" about the program, just a typical welfare program. The Director was a "street-smart" (though recently Princeton seminary-trained) Black who was serving as Associate Pastor at the prestigious Nassau Presbyterian Church in Princeton. And the rest of the (all-White) staff came from that same church (which in fact was actually located with Princeton University behind and alongside it!), and the equally prestigious Trinity Episcopal Church of Princeton. First Pres of Trenton's humbler role in the triad was strictly to make the space available for the program.

I didn't much care for the rather rowdy "street" behavior that went on in the unsupervised front portion of the ministry where the guys hung out. It was in such stark contrast to Emmett's operation in Mobile, that was just as open to anyone, but had a distinctly serene quality to the whole thing. Consequently, I had avoided the Crisis Ministry. It seemed to have no need of or desire for my spiritual assistance anyway.

Now on our return to Princeton, the three churches gathered to discuss the fact that the Trenton police wanted the churches to shut the ministry down – or they were going to do so themselves, for the place had become a well-known drug distribution center (with the Associate Pastor/ Director apparently at the heart of the operation).

I was in attendance at the meeting, rather amazed that the meeting was neither opened nor closed in prayer, nor was prayer mentioned when they proposed to get together in a couple of days to come to a final decision about the matter. At one point I spoke briefly about my own experience in Mobile with street ministry – and the importance of maintaining a Christian atmosphere in the ministry, especially given the climate in which they were trying to operate. My comments drew no response – only a contemptuous stare from the Nassau Presbyterian pastor who was presiding over the meeting.

In any case the decision shortly came to a shutting down of the operation. Period. That was the end of the Crisis Ministry.

Humble beginnings of a new street ministry. However I couldn't help but continue to be concerned about the large number of homeless males still hanging out on the streets around the church. As September turned into October and the weather became increasingly chilly, I began to think about them and what they were going to do as winter came upon them. There was a large Rescue Mission not too far away – but it opened up late in the evenings and turned the men back out on the streets early in the mornings.

Something inside of me (the "Voice"?) thought of the idea of opening up Fellowship Hall in the basement of First Pres and having coffee, snacks and Bible study as many mornings of the week as we could make arrangements to have someone there to oversee the process. I suggested the idea to my pastor friends, and most of them thought it was a good idea – except one of them who considered himself "streetwise" and laughed at the idea of Bible study, assuring me that these guys would be a blur rushing for the doors as soon as I opened a Bible.

Nonetheless, I agreed to give the idea a try on Monday and Tuesday mornings (with Scoti helping me get started), John on Wednesday mornings and two of the more evangelical women in the church on Thursdays. If the thing looked like it was going to work, I would also come in earlier on Sundays (again with Scoti's help) to open up then as well.

And so I put the word out on the streets about what we were proposing to do, and showed up with Scoti the first Monday morning – with no particular expectations as to what might happen. Only three guys showed up, but we had a good time – and opened up our Bibles to start a study of the Gospel of John. They seemed perfectly pleased to do that as well! For a couple of weeks we didn't seem to have more than three or four to show up, but then our numbers started growing.

The program takes off. The sexton (janitor) who didn't have a lot to do in the church – and liked it that way – began to complain about the crumbs under the tables in Fellowship hall. So John suggested that we simply move the program into the kitchen. We did – and soon we were totally crowded in there with more than 20 showing up for what was now coffee, peanut butter and jelly sandwiches and Bible study (the Nassau Presbyterian Church did support this effort – at least to the extent of paying for the coffee and sandwich makings, because the pastor of that church and John were good buddies, playing music together often).

We extended the days to include Sundays – and a number of the fellows began to stay for Sunday School and then church – often falling asleep on the back pews under the influence of the food, warmth and soft pew cushions. I knew that some of the church members were scandalized by their behavior (or just mere presence), and that trouble was brewing. But John promised to take care of that part of the program.

Christmas vacation (1986) arrived and I returned to Mobile, to Bill's house and Betsey's company (and also Debby's who ironically had become a friend of Betsey's since I went off to seminary). Our relationships had become quite platonic by then – though still quite intimate. This was also a nice departure from the deadness of seminary life – for I hadn't had a single date in the 6 months I had been up in Princeton. But Christmas came and went and it was time to return to New Jersey.

Banishment to Hanover Street. I returned to the news that the morning breakfast Bible study had been kicked out of the church. A coat on one of the racks had turned up missing one Sunday morning (it was Scoti's wife Mary's coat) and the small group of unhappy parishioners (including the janitor) had finally found their just cause to get the program moved out of the church – even though Mary protested that her coat should never have become the cause for such a move.

But as the Good Lord would have things, it turned out very much for the better. The former Crisis Ministry was reopened to house this ministry – giving us some excellent facilities for an even expanded street ministry – Christian style this time however!

The police watched us very closely for a while – but finally became satisfied that this was quite a different program than what had gone on there before.

In fact it was the men themselves who, once offered the opportunity to have a holy refuge, a place of spiritual sanctuary in their lives, were the real defenders of its integrity. For instance, though they were all smokers, almost to a man, it was them, not me, that instituted the "no smoking" rule in the Ministry – and made sure it stayed that way.

So it was the "First Presbyterian Church . . . Hanover St. Ministry" that I painted on the front window. And thus a street ministry was reborn on that site – in very Christian terms this time.

The Hanover Street Ministry grows. I got another seminarian to cover on Friday mornings – until he graduated mid-year. Then just as I began to ponder how we might fill that slot, another seminarian, Tom (who became a very close friend), stepped forward out of nowhere to take the Friday spot, and Saturdays as well. The ministry was now fully covered.

And it was growing. 50 to 60 guys were turning out, sometimes even close to a hundred, especially on Sunday mornings when they crowded in for Sunday "worship", especially when a Black church in the area offered to do some preaching, and rather substantial breakfasting for those who showed up! Who said it couldn't be done? And done "decently and in order"?

As I reflected on it all – how strange it all seemed. I had tried so hard to get so many good Christian programs going, in Mobile, at Princeton, in Trenton at the church. None of them worked exactly as I had planned; some of them didn't work at all. Now on the other hand, the simple, quite spontaneous decision to open up the church to some of Trenton's homeless had moved forward on its own, actually quite effortlessly.

Trusting God. Why was it so hard for me to understand this? How long was it going to take for me to get over being a Yuppie "micromanager" of life? When was I going to fully trust God "to build the house"? Those were questions that I long struggled with (and still do). I'll have more to say about that later.

Alvin, and Black militancy. I decided to take up residency that next summer (1987) in an apartment located directly above the street ministry. This would allow me to go full-time at the ministry that summer, offering Bible study and a small meal not only in the mornings but also in the evenings.

It was quite a move. Not only did the apartment require a lot of work to get back into some kind of decent shape, life in that neighborhood was noisy, and somewhat dangerous. And I was very much alone in making that move. Indeed, John never once dropped in even to see how things were going for me.

Then in July, John hired a recent seminary grad, Alvin, to add to the ministry. He was Black, and one with a very visible affirmation of his Blackness, complete with dreadlocks and a street manner – a manner that none of my street guys themselves ever saw the need to take on. John had hired him presumably to take up full-time management of the Hanover Street Ministry when I returned to my studies in the fall.

And Alvin (unlike me) was paid to do so. The mental health center in Trenton was so impressed with our church's contacts with the street population that they gave halftime funding to the church for the position. That's how we were able to hire Alvin.

At first Alvin and I hit it off. But gradually I came to realize that Alvin's Princeton-seminary "Christianity" was for him merely a veneer which he used to gain credentials for purposes such as the one at the Hanover Street Ministry. He would espouse any theology, even Islam, if it played into his Black nationalism – his real religion.

And he was amazingly like the "street-wise" associate pastor that the Nassau Presbyterian Church had previously taken on for such street ministry, and who turned that ministry into something quite else – in fact, a grand disaster. I couldn't believe that John did not see this.

Nonetheless, I found things for Alvin to do to justify his paid status. But I just did not see him really "connect" with my street guys. He sort of operated in his own world.

Then when I went off to Mobile at the end of the summer, I returned to Trenton to the news that Alvin had taken it upon himself to bring in an A.A. meeting at the ministry on Sunday nights – not only pushing our Sunday evening Bible fellowship back a half an hour but bringing confusion to my street guys, who didn't work by the clock. Consequently, participation at Sunday evening Bible study dwindled.

Also, Alvin did not want to continue to work with the rest of the team, teaching through the same book of the Bible. Instead he went to Revelation – and began to teach a message of judgement of God against the Whites, who were collectively the Antichrist.

A number of the guys came to me complaining that he was not teaching the Bible but instead a form of Black racism. Further, he was building up a small personal cult of "deacons" – guys who received special favors, including full meals while the others merely ate sandwiches, for becoming part of his special group. I spoke to Alvin about it, then to John – but to little avail. John did however make him cut out the special privileges program.   But otherwise he let Alvin go his own way with his version of Black theology.

When I complained to John about what Alvin's "theology" was doing to the spirit of the ministry, he said he did not agree with Alvin's theology – but nonetheless, saw him as a useful "antithesis" to me, to keep us both on our toes.

But actually, Alvin did not keep me on my toes. I simply did the best I could to just work around him – which was at times difficult, since he was capable of stirring things up with some new piece of racist behavior.

I could never figure out John's fascination for Alvin. All I could see in Alvin was lots of trouble. The rest of the people working at the Hanover Street ministry felt the same way.

And yes, even John finally got tired of Alvin and his behavior. I'm not sure what exactly was the event that precipitated John's firing of Alvin. But away he went. We all breathed a sigh of relief.

Meanwhile, I continued my volunteer work at the ministry (indeed for another 2½ years), working closely with these street guys. They were my friends, who taught me (like my German friends once had) about how other people could make a go of life their own unique way, despite all the obstacles placed in front of them. Consequently, I always valued the relationship I had with these guys deeply.

WOMEN!

Continuing frustration. Funny how my relations with the opposite sex swung from feast to famine as I moved back and forth from Mobile to Princeton. It was either too much or nothing.

Further, as I reflected on the matter, it still seemed very perplexing to me why, after all this time, I couldn't seem to make up my mind about Betsey? Why couldn't I just get focused on her? I knew that I wanted to get married – and have children! And Betsey was most anxious for this too.

Finally, I decided to ask God for a "sign." Now I was in the habit of doing this often, especially when I got to a point where I was faced with a decision that I didn't know how to make – and I must say, it usually worked out quite well as a procedure. So I proposed this to God: if Betsey is the one I am to marry, then show me by having her call me, by Valentine's Day (1987), to tell me that she will be coming out to visit me sometime in the spring (she had loosely mentioned the possibility of this at Christmas when I was back in Mobile).

But the next morning I awoke to the thought: no way! This was not the way I wanted the issue resolved. "I'm calling the deal off, God."

Yet wouldn't you know, the day before Valentine's Day Betsey called me to tell me that she was going to be flying up to Princeton to visit me in March! What was this? God's sense of humor in action?

In any case, Betsey and I had a great visit during her week in Princeton (early spring 1987), touring the countryside, Philadelphia, showing her the Ministry, introducing her to my friends on campus, to John and Scoti, etc. But, I still could make little of my true feelings for her.

As far as my relations with women on campus – there were none, other than very casual friendships. Seminary was famous for being a fishbowl environment, and the men and women seemed too busy or too guarded to get involved with each other.

Seminary feminism. Then there was this thing called "feminism." I, of course, had encountered this phenomenon at the university back in the 1970s – when women faculty began to complain that they were not getting the appointments that they thought they were entitled to. We went through a period of self-study and soul searching – and finally agreed that some adjustments needed to be made. But it never became a really "revolutionary" issue. Things just shifted and took a new course. Most everyone agreed, anyway, that it only made good sense to be fully equitable.

But the feminism I encountered in seminary was of an entirely different nature. It was militant and vigilant – looking for any opportunity to make a show of force. "Inclusiveness" in language was the front line of the battle: "man" was no longer acceptable as a generic term (as in the "Rights of Man"), and was to be eliminated from our language in every respect. Indeed, the only document I had to sign as a condition of entry into the seminary was the agreement that I would follow "inclusiveness" in my written work and in all conversation at the seminary.

But "inclusiveness" went further than that. The use of male language in reference to God was also taboo. Male pronouns were out. So was the word "Father." It got ridiculous. A sentence concerning God might end up sounding like: "So God said to Godself that God was going to redeem God's people." And if you did have to use male terms, they had to be offset in equivalent fashion with female terminology.

My parents, visiting campus and attending an Easter vigil service with me, were stunned as they sat through a seminarian's lengthy ode to the Mother of Heaven, whose breasts nourished the universe with her milk, etc., etc., etc. I told them not to worry about it – one got used to it after a while.

But even then, I found the idea of such wild speculation about the nature of God to somehow be touching on idolatry. We had created a Female Golden Calf for the feminists (and the rest of us) to worship – and somehow that did not sit well with me. But I knew to keep my mouth shut.

I was introduced to this militant dynamic early on at the seminary, when in one of my classes my first semester there I spoke up about how the story of Adam and Eve and Cain and Able reminded me of the historic transition of the hunter-gatherer paleolithic man (Adam and Eve) to the farming and herding neolithic man (Cain and Abel).

My statement was met by shrieks and shouts of outrage by some of the women in class: how dare I use the forbidden word "man."

Wow! I was so, so sorry for having thrown the class into a major uproar with my use of such highly taboo language. I promised that I would never ever commit such a transgression again. So, could the class please calm down and get back on track?

A shameful incident. Another such event on campus comes to my mind about the time when a young pastor from Thailand – who was at Princeton working on a theology degree at the seminary and who obviously did not understand the subtleties of feminist politics there – once led 10:00 chapel worship, and made the outrageous mistake of several times using male terminology in reference to God. The feminists exploded.

By noon that same day, they had already organized a massive effort to collect signatures for a petition of complaint at the cafeteria door, denouncing the chapel personnel for having allowed this to have occurred (were they supposed to have pulled him from the pulpit after the second use of "Him" or "Father"?). Shamefully, I signed the petition – as did most everyone else. Not to do so would have merely drawn attention to oneself as being inadequately enlightened. Besides, I was hungry and wanted to get to lunch. Shame on me!

Cultivating a sexual gap. I mention all of this for two reasons. First is the effect it had on male-female friendships within the student body. When we "juniors" first started out – we clung together for mutual support as we encountered the extreme intellectual rigors of Princeton seminary. We were close – men and women alike – struggling to get through the ordeal.

But by the second or middler year you could see a change in the old relationships. The feminist rhetoric was beginning to have its effect. Men were "oppressors" who had too long kept women down. Only now were the stories of men's sexual abuse of women coming out so that we could see more clearly how bad the male specie was. On and on the testimonies ran, until almost every man on campus felt as if he were part of some kind of scumbag tyranny, and every woman a "victim" of men. Needless to say, a good number of our female friends began to lose their original warmth toward their male colleagues.

Some even proudly announced that they were most glad to have discovered that they were actually lesbian. They detested men, and discovered that they had fondness only for members of their own sex.

That was hardly a surprise, given the intensity of the brain-washing going on at the seminary.

Now this by no means included all the women on campus. In fact, some of the women reacted rather strongly against this feminism, and – unlike the men – could actually speak out publicly against this feminist sexism. At the same time, some of the men became ardent feminists!

In short, feminism succeeded in lining us up into hostile ideological groupings, with the feminists distinctly dominating the dynamic.

Cynthia. The second reason I mention this is because of the effect it came to have on a relationship that did finally develop for me with a woman while I was living in Princeton.

I met Cynthia at a weekend retreat (Palm Sunday 1987) in the Pennsylvania mountains – which I had slipped away to in order to get off campus for a while. Cynthia was an Episcopal priest serving as assistant rector at a church in Ohio. She had been living in Manhattan prior to that – and (a few weeks after we had met) in coming back to New York to visit friends, she stopped in to visit me in Princeton for a couple of days.

I found her attractive – though strangely a little hard around the edges. Gradually it became apparent why.

When spring term ended, and I had a few weeks' vacation at the end of May and early June before my 1987 summer plans went into effect, I decided to head back to Mobile for a brief vacation. I also decided to make a wide swing to Alabama via Ohio, to visit Cynthia. With that, a new relationship was on! Then also, a couple of weeks after my arrival in Mobile Cynthia decided to fly down to meet me in nearby New Orleans and spend some time with me in Mobile, before driving back with me north again via Ohio on my return to Princeton.

This was the summer I was spending in inner-city Trenton, living over the Hanover Street Ministry amidst the neighborhood's drugs, alcohol and prostitution, and was glad for any break from the intensity of the situation. I was always glad to see Cynthia – and got together with her several times over the summer.

But the bloom was wearing off the relationship. She was constantly agitated over some slight or other concerning her status as a priest that she experienced from the male clergy (and some of the women parishioners) around her – even frequently calling me long distance to talk at length about her frustration and bitterness. I listened – but offered no advice, only encouragement to go the course, for God would see her through all this. But we really did not connect well on this most essential issue in her life. It was so all-absorbing to her. She had great difficulty in seeing anything else about her work – or at least if she did, she never shared it with me.

After a while – by the end of the summer – it was apparent that we just were not on the same wavelength. The relationship came to an end one evening in early autumn in one of those long-distance phone calls she made to me about this same problem. We didn't argue or anything. It was just apparent that all of this had drained out whatever was good in the relationship – and that, in the end, there was nothing left between us. We never got in touch again.

I often have wondered if it was the power of the feminist program that made her so tormented a person, or if her feminism was merely a way of playing out some deeper aspects of her personality. But seeing how feminism made such harsh changes among female friends on campus, I suspect that it was the former.

✱ ✱ ✱

KATHLEEN (Fall of 1987)

Where was God's hand in all this? Meanwhile, the "woman issue" was adding considerably to the confusion that I felt had overtaken my life at this point. I so much wanted to get on with my life – especially in the area of a partner in my life's work. And I wanted children – badly (quite a shift from my view on the subject when I was the perfect Yuppie!).

But as with all my "projects," so also my endeavors with the opposite sex always seemed to end up so confused and unsatisfying. I had considered several times that God simply did not want me to remarry. Certainly there was Biblical warrant for a divorced person not to marry again. But if God really wanted me to remain celibate for the rest of my life, why had His Spirit (and I was certain that this was the source) put such a strong desire in my heart to have children?

But admittedly all my efforts to engineer a solution were ending with the same result: failure. Finally, one night I prayed long over this matter – and came to a resolution that if celibacy was what God wanted, then so be it.

A very short time after that great decision, I met Kathleen!

The invitation. My Trenton friend Michael was an officer in the Trenton Full Gospel Businessmen's Fellowship, a charismatic organization that met once a month in a restaurant to worship and share testimonies. I had attended some of the meetings of this organization back in Mobile, through Emmett's invitation, but it was not until Michael invited me that summer of 1987 to a Full Gospel Businessmen's breakfast – with my street guys accompanying me – that I got involved in the Trenton chapter.

It seems that they had had a "prophecy" that revival was about to break out in Trenton, particularly among the city's homeless. Michael announced that he had a friend (me) working with just those same people – and wouldn't it be great if his friend could come out to the monthly meetings – bringing some of his people with him. They agreed. The invitation seemed very much in keeping with the prophecy.

When Michael proposed the idea to me, I knew that the guys would jump at the chance to be bussed out to a nice restaurant and have a great meal. So it was all set up.

The hand of God moves. When the event came to pass in mid-July, I had my hands full keeping an eye on the guys, with all the liquor laid out behind an unattended open bar right there in the meeting room, and with all kinds of potential mischief awaiting them out in the parking lot (hub caps were a source of funding sometimes!) as they moved in and out for smokes.

It was on our second visit (in mid-August) that Michael pointed Kathleen out to me as she whisked by on her way to a seat at the table with her mother and some women friends (yes, there were always a number of women in attendance at this "Businessmen's" gathering). He told me that she was someone he thought I should meet.

No argument there! She was absolutely gorgeous! I don't know how I missed her on the previous visit – except that there were hundreds of people in attendance, and, as I said, I had my hands full the whole time.

As the morning progressed, and as I watched from across the huge room the gentleness and grace by which she worshiped God, I grew intrigued – even entranced. I finally decided to put my name and address on a small paper, with the intention of speaking to her and giving her this information before I had to get back to the Ministry. But just as I was finishing the task, I saw her look my way, cross the room – and then come and sit down next to me!

We struck up a brief conversation – brief because I had to get back to my guys to see what they were doing. But before doing so, I invited her to come down to the ministry of an evening and join us in Bible study. Then we were gone.

She didn't come to the ministry – and then a week later it was time (late-August) for me to head back to Mobile for vacation before starting up the fall term. But before I had left, Michael told me something very important. Kathleen had, a month or so back, submitted a prayer card, and he had been the one assigned to pray for her request.   It was for a Christian man to come into her life! He told me that as he had been praying over that card, I kept coming into his mind. That's why he thought it was so important for me to meet her. I told him about her coming and sitting down next to me. We both thought something was up.

I didn't see her again for a long while.

Praise the Lord for air conditioning! When I got back to New Jersey in late September (1987) Michael greeted me with the news that he had spoken to her at the September meeting about "us." He said that she assured him that she had intended nothing by sitting down next to me at the meeting! It was just that there were no other seats available in the room except those around me and that she had moved there because where she was previously sitting, she was catching a chill from an air conditioning vent directly overhead! Michael ribbed me a bit about all our speculations. But my thoughts ran more along the line: praise the Lord for air conditioning!

Now as I came out to the meeting in October (again, with two huge van loads of my guys) my thoughts returned to my visit in August. I knew that despite the putdown, something was up. Would Kathleen be there? What would happen?

All in God's time (Kairos). We were late getting there, and I was among the last to arrive. Kathleen was there – but at a fully occupied table. However when she spotted me, she got up and came up to me to tell me that she was sorry that there was no space at her table, but that we could maybe sit down together afterwards and talk! And so we did.

Conversation with her was so easy. We talked a while – and then I asked her about why she hadn't come down to the Ministry. She told me that girls do not go into the Trenton inner-city at night alone [of course not, stupid! I don't know why that had never occurred to me!]

Before we said our goodbyes we had agreed that I would indeed pick her up early the next morning (Sunday) bring her down to the Ministry, we would attend church, and then spend some time together in the afternoon before she headed off to a job she had at the McCarter Theatre in Princeton.

It was like we both knew that it was our jobs simply to get to know each other! Something really was up – and we both sensed it.

Well, the rest is history! We hit it off – putting it mildly! I had never been so captivated by a woman in all my life. And she seemed so comfortable with me!

I found out that Kathleen was of almost pure Irish descent, was the middle child among seven (!) siblings, was living in Princeton, and was a teacher at the Princeton Montessori school. I soon met the rest of her family, who lived just outside of Princeton. She was raised Catholic – but, with her mother, had become an Evangelical/charismatic, worshiping at the Faith Fellowship (megachurch) in Edison. Kathleen loved children – and at age 27 (soon to be 28) was wanting to start her own family. And I was all for that too!

Giving it all over to God. But there was one major glitch in our program. Her mother, discovering that I was 46, was horrified! After about two weeks of wonderful chemistry – in which it seemed like this relationship was lining itself up to head off into the sunset, I began to notice a pulling back on Kathleen's part. I didn't understand what was happening – and made no mention of my concern to her. But something was wrong.

I decided at this point simply to leave matters in God's hands. I had, from the very first, considered this relationship to be a matter of God's doing. So I (correctly) took the attitude that if God wanted this relationship to work out, then He – not me – was going to have to fix whatever was wrong!

And so it was, partway through a Saturday evening date [which I was ready to assume would be our last], that Kathleen finally told me what was up. She mentioned the age factor – for which I obviously had no reply. I couldn't change anything about that. Clearly the decision on this matter was up to her. Yet even as she spoke, we knew that she had made up her mind. She was simply going to have to face down whatever criticism awaited her from others about our age difference.

And having resolved that matter – the relationship really did move off into the sunset!

Closing down a longstanding relationship. But even as we dated, there remained one last piece of unfinished business in my life. Betsey had invited me to join her and her extended family who were gathering in Virginia that Thanksgiving. By the time the end of November had rolled around, my relationship with Kathleen was well on track – and I knew that I would be going to Virginia only as a friend and no longer as a potential "significant other" for Betsey.

Betsey and I walked and talked a lot that weekend. We had been on the same road together for a long time, through good times and bad. I told her about Kathleen; she told me about her still uncertain social life. I truly felt a deep affection for her, especially as I knew that this chapter in my life – our lives – was about to come to a close. Indeed, as I said goodbye to her it was with a profound sadness – and yet profound determination to get on with things.

✱ ✱ ✱

ISRAEL (December 1987)

For reasons I can't explain, I was chosen, along with three other Princeton seminarians, to be part of a large group of American seminary students, also selected from a number of other seminaries, given the privilege of visiting Israel for a couple of weeks, for free. The trip was scheduled to take place over the Christmas vacation season.

But it almost got cancelled at the last moment, because of a massive uprising of Palestinians against Israeli authority – the outbreak of what was termed the Intifada. But the trip went ahead as scheduled. However most all other tours were cancelled. Thus we would have Israel almost to ourselves, during one of its normally most busy tourist seasons!

But things were a bit tricky nonetheless. We spent a half-day at the Jordanian-Israeli border (we had actually arrived in the region via Jordan), tightly checked for security. And later, when we made our way to Bethlehem for Christmas Eve services at the Church of the Nativity, our bus convoy was carefully checked and guarded by Israeli soldiers. And soldiers were placed all around the square in front of the church (including on the roofs of surrounding buildings), in order to fend off any Palestinian mischief.

But otherwise, it was a most blissful visit. We went from one Biblical site to another, in Nazareth, along the Sea of Galilee, in and around Jerusalem, the Garden of Gethsemane, the heights of Bethany overlooking Jerusalem, the road to Jericho, and even the Dead Sea – although I did not go on the Dead Sea trip, instead undertaking a return trip on my own to Bethlehem.

It was in Bethlehem that I was asked by a local Christian merchant why it was that American Christians were so against the Palestinians, when so many of the Palestinians were fellow Christians, whose ancestors had been Christians living in that part of the world since Christianity's origins, and now they were leaving their homeland in large numbers because their situation had become so untenable.

I myself had no answer to that question. And it was a matter that truly saddened me. American Christians were so enthusiastic about the Israelis taking full control of the area, not understanding how that Israeli takeover decided the large Christian population of the region to call it quits and leave the area, in essence, turning out the lights of the Christian Gospel in Christianity's birthplace itself. The Jews of Israel had no interest in Christianity.

Some Jews were moving into such highly Christian towns as Bethlehem and Nazareth. But mostly it was Muslims, displaced elsewhere in the old Palestinian territory, that were taking over the abandoned homes and shops of the departing Christians.[*]

Anyway, the height of the whole visit was the Christmas Eve service at the Church of the Nativity in Bethlehem. What was remarkable (besides all the security!) was that a very small number of people, which included our seminary group, had the church to ourselves. It was a very traditional service, taking me back to Crusader times, like worshiping in Paris's Notre Dame Cathedral. It was always both thrilling and humbling to me to know that I was standing where countless generations before me had stood, experiencing pretty much the same sights and sounds that I was now experiencing! For an American, for whom "history" typically meant a century or two back in time, this was a plunge far deeper into history.

And it considerably deepened my appreciation of my Christian faith.

✷ ✷ ✷

MARRIAGE (June 1988)

Kathleen and I announce our engagement. At the beginning of April of the next year (1988) Kathleen invited her parents and me over for dinner in her new condo unit which she had just purchased – right outside of Princeton in one of those "instant cities" that were popping up everywhere in the area. But her parents knew that this was no ordinary dinner invitation. In fact, we wondered how long one of Kathleen's sisters, the very curious Colleen, could hold off from calling that evening to see "how things are going."

---

[*]And I would find out years later that the Christian character of such Palestinian towns as Bethlehem and Nazareth was completely erased, as the Christian population had abandoned their homelands, almost totally so.

Indeed, we got to the point very quickly with her parents. That evening would make it official. Kathleen and I had decided to get married – though the date (June or September) had not yet been decided. We preferred June. But I had a two-month trip to South Africa already scheduled for the summer (July and August) and it seemed crazy for us to get married – and then for me to disappear for two months.

Anyway, her parents were very pleased for us (and yes, Colleen did call soon to see if everyone's suspicions were right!).

We soon decided on the September date and I got us on the Princeton Chapel calendar. Then we looked at the matter of having Kathleen meet my family – and, for that matter, my friends in Mobile. We decided to take a couple of weeks in June after school was out to head West to St. Louis to meet my parents, and then South to Alabama to meet all my friends in Mobile, before returning to New Jersey.

Crisis. Then it happened! I should have guessed it might. I was so totally and passionately in love with Kathleen that I simply let my good senses leave me. But in early June Kathleen sensed – and then it was confirmed – that she was pregnant. My happy world shattered.

We faced up to the music the best we could. Her Mom was actually a great help – greeting the news of Kathleen's pregnancy with jubilation rather than condemnation. As she put it: Look at the bright side of it all. The one thing we both wanted most, children, was now indeed confirmed. Kathleen's pregnancy should be celebrated, not mourned. Also, we might as well go for that June wedding date after all. She was sure that everything could be assembled quickly and with no hitch before the end of the month.

John was rather unperturbed by the news – in fact heartened because he had a scheduling conflict with our September date and wasn't going to be able to officiate at our wedding – but was very available for our June 25th date to marry us. And moreover – he would be glad to perform the ceremony in the venerable old First Presbyterian Church rather than at the Seminary Chapel. Actually it made more sense – and had more meaning to me anyway that we should get married in the church that I had been serving (and had changed my ministerial candidacy to) since I came to New Jersey.

Scoti was stunned by the news. We both knew what a cloud this would throw over my "moral credentials." But as I saw it, because of my divorce, I already had little claim to any such moral credentials anyway – though goodness knows, I didn't need to be making that situation any worse. Whatever. Anyway, Scoti rallied – and stood ready to serve me as Best Man for the wedding (her sister Colleen to be Kathleen's Matron of Honor).

My friend Tom (close comrade-in-arms at the Hanover Street Ministry!), who was about to graduate from seminary and had a pastoring job waiting for him in nearby Philadelphia (where he was from) was more than willing to assist John in the wedding service. So – everything was set.

Into the home stretch. Things moved so quickly in that first week, that everyone encouraged us to go on ahead with our plans to visit St. Louis and Mobile, arriving back only a few days before the wedding. Indeed, everyone really had jumped into the fray to help out, and they all had things well in hand. Thankfully the wedding dress that Kathleen had ordered from London had already come in, so even that vexing detail had worked out astonishingly well. So – we decided to take off.

We drove out to St. Louis where Kathleen met my parents and spent a number of days seeing the sights, eating and just relaxing. Nothing was ever said about our situation, but instead we just had a good time together. We then bid my parents goodbye, knowing that we would be seeing them in a couple of weeks back in Trenton, and headed on to Mobile.

Everyone was excited to meet Kathleen, wondering who it was that finally got me settled down. Martelle had a big reception for us. And Betsey invited us down to her parents' place on the Gulf. It was amazing how smoothly things worked out. Even in this crazy skifoffel, God stayed there right alongside us.

And we arrived back at Trenton in late June, had a great rehearsal, rehearsal dinner, a Saturday afternoon wedding, and an outdoor picnic afterwards at her parents' home, attended by family and friends from all over. It was done, we were now husband and wife. And the next day, Sunday, Kathleen became a member of the First Presbyterian Church of Trenton!

The South African arrangement. One problem remained: my trip to South Africa coming up in a little over a week's time. People began to protest that I couldn't go off leaving a week-old bride behind like that. Well, travel to South Africa cost money – lots of money! Actually on my part, I had received a grant from the seminary that paid for my ticket, and a seminary official had arranged all my stays for the two months I was to be gone. So I was completely taken care of!

But it seems that once the idea of Kathleen joining me in South Africa got put forward, people showed great interest in helping us out financially. We had originally asked for no wedding gifts, as we already had two households of furniture and gadgets as it was – and proposed instead that people make donations to the Hanover Street Ministry (which they did, generously). But once the idea was formed of actually seeing what we could put together to get Kathleen down to South Africa, gifts designated for the trip started pouring in.

And in the end, wouldn't you know it, we had exactly the amount ($1400) needed for her air tickets. As for the rest, Kathleen would simply become included in my own arrangements in South Africa.

But the miracles did not stop there. Getting a visa to South Africa was a lengthy and precarious process. We had friends still in Nairobi not able to advance further toward South Africa because their visas were still held up – and they had been working on this for months. But I had become friends with a consular official, Sommie, working in the South African consulate in New York City. In fact, I was going to be staying with his parents for a short time while I was in Pretoria, and he would be meeting me there! He assured me that Kathleen (whom he also knew at this point) would get her visa in record time!

Still, she didn't even have a passport yet, much less a visa. But even that – even down to getting a parking space on a very crowded street right in front of the office where she had to pick up her passport papers – seemed to get expedited by a mysterious hand. Thus by the time I was put on the plane for South Africa (actually Amsterdam, as the first leg of the journey), she had her passport, it was being hand processed for a visa, she had her air tickets, and would be joining me in Johannesburg in early August (which was the earliest we figured everything would be completely ready) to accompany me during my last month in South Africa.

✳ ✳ ✳

SOUTH AFRICA (Summer of 1988)

Bernard. It was the Sunday before I was due to leave for South Africa, and I was telling my street guys that regretfully the ministry would be shutting down for the next two months during my absence. I didn't want to do this, but I could not come up with an alternative procedure, try as I might.

And literally, just as I was explaining this to my guys, in walked Bernard, trying to be as inconspicuous as possible. But there was no way that would happen. He was one of my street-guy regulars from some time back, but now dressed up in a suit and looking very different from the person I once knew. It was a wonderful sight to see.

I really did not have much success in getting my guys moved off the streets, and had come to live with the fact that I was there simply to bring Christ to them as they presently found themselves, in whatever condition that might be. But here now before me in the form of Bernard was clearly something quite different.

He told us that he was getting ready for church, showering and shaving, when the "Voice" told him to pay a visit to the Hanover Street Ministry. Sure, why not? It had been some time and a very different world ago. But the ministry was a big part of the reason for that new world.* But the Voice repeated itself: "go visit the Hanover Street Ministry." Okay, okay, I'll swing by sometime soon. A third time the Voice hit him: "go visit the Hanover Street Ministry!"

At this point Bernard figured that the Voice wanted him to do it immediately, even before he headed to church. But why was the Voice so insistent on this?

As Bernard explained to all of us gathered at the ministry this most peculiar set of circumstances, I knew immediately what the Voice was up to. So I asked: "Bernard, would you be willing to take over the directing of the Hanover Street Ministry during my absence in South Africa?" Bernard laughed! So that was what this was all about! Obviously he would do so, for clearly God was behind this strange development.

And so the ministry continued during my absence. When I arrived back two months later, I arrived to see the place filled with my guys. Bernard had done quite well. He informed me however that it didn't start out that way. At first the guys (whom he knew quite well) refused to take him seriously. He was, after all, just one of them! But Bernard stayed the course, and little by little the guys started returning, realizing that Bernard was the real thing. And he (and the church he was attending) would continue to be a big help to me in my remaining time at the ministry.

Praise God for such miracles!

A sense of something about to break forth. Anyway, it had been over 20 years since I had written my Georgetown master's thesis on South Africa. And my prediction that things would change little politically over the next generation had held true. Now I had a sense that things were beginning to shift dramatically – but for reasons other than the great armed uprising that the Liberal world had long been waiting for (and encouraging).

True, in the mid-1980s a lot of violence had hit South Africa. But I knew that this was as a result of new developments, not as the cause of

---

*Bernard later told me that it was one Sunday night at the ministry when the Lord hit him hard. "Don't you remember that night?" he asked me. "I was jumping around and screaming." Actually I didn't, probably because wild behavior was not very uncommon at the ministry. Anyway, that was the last night at the ministry for him. He immediately moved on to clean up his life: job, apartment, church, all part of a new existence he was able to undertake. He said that it was a complete miracle, way beyond a person's natural ability to come off the streets. I certainly had to agree with that!

them. Under President Botha, the government had been moving gradually but perceptibly toward a loosening of the apartheid restrictions imposed by his political predecessors. By the mid-1980s an atmosphere of change was evident everywhere – and translated itself easily into a sense of political opportunity among the Blacks ("revolution of rising expectations" we called it). It was this heady mood that caused the sudden outbreak of violence.

Botha responded (as I expected he would) with a clamping down on this behavior through a number of "emergency" laws. The Liberal West greeted his efforts to keep South Africa from blowing apart with cries of outrage – and by imposing a deep boycott on South Africa. To me the boycott appeared hypocritical – for it came actually as things were improving, not when things were their darkest. But I have never been a fond admirer of Liberal virtue.

But what intrigued me was that the reforms continued (though admittedly very guardedly). Now this was indeed something of note! This was a very strong departure from typical Afrikaner (Dutch-speaking White) behavior. Something big was going on in South Africa, though not as the West would understand it. And I proposed to find out what it was – as a senior thesis I was going to undertake at the seminary. And it was this proposal that had drawn the funding to allow me to spend two months in South Africa studying the situation. My old talents as a political risk analyst were being brought back into action!

Checking out my intuitions. Actually, my first couple of weeks in South Africa were very informal. I spent the time just relaxing in and around Pretoria and at a Zulu mission station (KwaSizabantu) in Natal. But this time was very important – for it gave me a chance 1) to see the thoughts and ways of the "new" Afrikaners and 2) to catch my first glimpse at how the White church was involved in promoting new attitudes of racial openness.

Not surprisingly, when the West thought of the "church" in South Africa, it thought of only one institution: the militant church of Nobel prizewinner Desmond Tutu and of Allan Boesak, enshrined in the South African Council of Churches (SACC). This was indeed a heroic institution. But I had my suspicions that it had greater influence within the West than within South Africa itself. True, this made it a very present "in-your-face" voice within South Africa. But I knew that this only served to steel Afrikaner hard-lining rather than soften it, much less break it down.

I found this institution to be of interest to me – but not nearly as interesting as the White church (the Dutch Reformed Church and the Anglo Protestant churches) that was actually beginning to address Afrikaner (and Anglo) racial attitudes. This White church had great influence within the South African political and economic scheme of things. But it was also the institution the West loved to ignore and even despise. Yet I knew that it, and it alone, had the power to bring the country around to a "new thing." And I had a sense that it was doing just that. This is what I wanted to study.

I explored White and Black districts – intrigued at the Afrikaner effort to restrict the flow of rural Blacks into the "White" cities, where typically Blacks headed to the districts such as Soweto and Alexandra. The effort had proven futile and hypocritical. It was futile in that there was as little likelihood of stopping such movement, just as there had been against the Angles and Saxons migrating into Celtic Britain – or as there was presently against the Central and South American Hispanics moving in mass numbers into Anglo California (and elsewhere in America)! It was hypocritical in that the White districts were quite ready to utilize the cheap labor produced by these migrants – which only acted as a greater magnet to the migration! And as with all hypocrisy, it produced enormous human cruelty.

Observing the shift. Nonetheless, the scene was shifting. Downtown Johannesburg was a scene not of apartheid (separateness) but of mixture. Shopping was robust and multiracial. The lunch counters and fast food restaurants where I ate when in town were fully integrated – with all races eating side by side quite unselfconsciously. This was not the image of South Africa that the West loved to hold of the country. In fact the contrast between the popular Western image and the reality of South Africa was shocking.

I spent two more weeks in the Pretoria-Johannesburg area interviewing – and awaiting Kathleen's arrival.

Very interestingly, I was greeted at the SACC offices with a mixture of politeness and suspicion. I had not arrived in South Africa as a participant in one of the many "study teams" that the West (to the huge annoyance of the South African government) sent to South Africa to get the "true story." Thus people at the SACC offices were not sure how to react to me. They did treat me to a presentation of the "true story" of South Africa. But sadly, I got little but well-rehearsed political cant from the SACC. But that in itself was revealing to me. I sensed that the SACC had played little, if any, role in producing these major developments currently unfolding in South Africa. Instead, it seemed content to conduct on-going warfare with the past.

The power of repentance. What was more revealing to me were the interviews I had with the leader of the Dutch Reformed Church and the personal secretary of President Botha. I knew that the DRC had officially "repented" of its previous support of apartheid. I knew that this had come at a great emotional cost to these very pious Afrikaners, involving virtually a crisis of identity. And I knew that one did not do such things unless there were very serious reasons for doing so.

In interviewing both men I listened to a story of true spiritual repentance (the sign of a distinct movement of God in their lives) – the kind of spiritual repentance I knew of from my own crazy personal life. I knew that this spiritual repentance was capable of moving mountains – the kinds of mountains I was seeing moved in South Africa. But sadly, I also knew that the secular West (even the Western church) seemed to find no way to appreciate – much less support – such spiritual development.

These men were dedicated to seeing real change – true integration – come to South Africa. They had a huge political task ahead of them: keeping the country from exploding while they moved it in the direction they now knew it had to go. They had political tempers to deal with everywhere that were poised ready even for a blood bath if necessary. They had to avoid letting power slip into such hands – or South Africa would end up a bloody tribally-torn country like so many others on the continent. I told them I would pray for their success. I meant it.

Kathleen joins me in South Africa. Kathleen's arrival began our "honeymoon" phase. To contribute to this phase of our new marriage, my sister had arranged a week at a timeshare resort along the South African coast. But as it turned out, we were so busy touring that we gave the week to an elderly South African couple.

But the blessings continued nonetheless. For instance, we ourselves were given air tickets by our friend Sommie, so as to be able to make a grand tour of the country, from Johannesburg to Durban to Cape Town and back.

Another lesson about God's hand. Kathleen and I stayed with an Indian family in Durban – a young pastor with a very large church and an even bigger evangelical "crusade" going on. We got to participate in the latter on its very opening night. He had pitched a huge tent on a field in the middle of a very Hindu community, and I wondered just how successful he might be in trying to reach these very dedicated Hindus.

The evening came – and the people came! The tent got filled up (there must have been at least a thousand people packed in there)! The band played praise music quite familiar to me, and the pastor spoke – though only for what seemed like a very few minutes, before he announced an altar call. I was surprised. He hadn't "worked the crowd" with a fiery message. I sat – only for a moment – wondering if anyone would come forward. Then I watched in amazement as the whole crowd pressed forward for prayers (as if there was any room forward anyway). I couldn't believe what I was seeing. Hindus (and Muslims) were well known for their stiff resistance to the gospel message. And yet I was watching masses of Hindus (and probably also some Muslims) respond to the call!

Kathleen and I had dinner with the ministry team afterwards – and I had to ask the question: how did all of that happen? The pastor smiled, and pointed to one of his associates – the latter who explained that this was his first meal in two weeks. He and a team of 200 others had been fasting and praying during that time for the success of this crusade. That – not any fiery "working of the crowd" – was what they understood produced what I saw earlier that evening.

I felt sheepish for having asked such a foolish question, and for having to be reminded that God, not man, brings souls to Christ! That was a lesson I will never forget!

Completing the picture of the "new" South Africa. I then took Kathleen to the KwaSizabantu Mission – in time to attend a multiracial pastors' conference taking place there. Hundreds of pastors had come from around the country to talk about a "new" South Africa, the work of the hand of God. I chose to sit among some of the Afrikaner pastors to get a closer feel for their reactions – and to be able to engage them in discussion about their feelings on the subject. They were in fact very affirmative, and quite hopeful that the miracle of a "reconciled" South Africa was at hand. As a lot of these pastors were from churches in very-White rural South Africa – I knew that indeed big things were going on in the country.

We flew on to Cape Town, stayed among Presbyterians, and again – had confirmed this sense of new things stirring. We visited the townships, met with a wide variety of movers and shakers of events at the Cape – and also remembered just to take in the wonderful natural beauty of the area.

At this point, I had a sense that I had a pretty complete picture of the dynamics of the country – enough to make a senior thesis presentation – and thus it was time to relax and just enjoy the last of our stay. We returned to Johannesburg, I did some final interviews, and then we returned home to the States, weary but transformed by the experience.

In the process, Kathleen and I had really become a team.

✳ ✳ ✳

MY LAST YEAR OF SEMINARY

Kathleen and I returned to our new home in the condo unit just outside Princeton and got ourselves ready for my final year of seminary.

Actually, the year (September 1988 to May 1989) at school went fast. I had a number of required courses I had to take (ugh!)* but was able to include some courses I really did want, such as the one on Dietrich Bonhoeffer and the one on John Calvin.

Allan Boesak. One incident stands out strongly in my memory of that last year: Allan Boesak's evening appearance at the Nassau Presbyterian Church in Princeton in October. He was out of the country when I was in South Africa (as was also Archbishop Tutu) so I hadn't had the opportunity to interview him. But I was very curious about what he saw in the numerous changes taking place in his country. So I was looking forward to this event.

Actually hundreds of people turned out and the church was packed. I recognized a lot of people from the seminary – most of them from among what I styled as the "peace and social justice" group.

Unfortunately, as the talk proceeded, I quickly recognized that we were simply going to be treated that evening to a repetition of the SACC "true story" – the unbearable pain of life in South Africa and the evil dimensions of those who governed the country – a litany which I (and I guess most everybody else there) knew by heart. But then I guess that that was what most people had come for. I was disappointed – for the talk provided no real insight into what SACC leadership was thinking about what was presently and most clearly unfolding within the country.

Then we went to a question and answer period – and as I was pondering whether or not to disturb the evening's peace and social justice ritual with a question about his views on some of the positive recent developments, a man stood up in the balcony to pose just that question. He announced himself as a minister who had returned from the country after a long stay there and had noticed a number of hopeful developments going on within the country – and would Rev. Boesak be willing to elaborate for the benefit of us all about those.

Whew! I was so glad that I was not the poor soul who posed that question, for Boesak lit into him as if this man were some kind of demented soul who had somehow gotten himself ensnared by the propaganda of the White racist government – for "obviously" he knew nothing about what was really going on in South Africa. There was "nothing" in the unfolding situation within South Africa – past, present or future – that pointed to hope. The only hope was for outside help in crushing the fascism that gripped the country.

The crowd went wild! They hooted, they hollered, they set up a rhythmic stamping of their feet in wild support, as if they were in a

---

*Such as the course on Presbyterian Church "polity" (rules and regulations directing Presbyterian churches), rather pointless for me since I had already studied all that – and indeed had passed all my ordination exams qualifying me for the Presbyterian ministry.

basketball gymnasium rather than in a church. This went on and on – with Boesak beaming, and with the people finally rising to their feet in wild approval. After several minutes of this, Kathleen and I quietly made our way up the aisle through the frenzy and out the door into a calmer and more refreshing evening.

I was reminded by this incident how it was that Hitler had so easily mesmerized the masses with his inflammatory (but otherwise rather banal) rhetoric. He gave the masses what they wanted to hear. And that became for him – and the German people – the definition of "Truth", which led both Germany and its leader to social and personal suicide – not to mention the destruction of millions of innocent Europeans in his death camps.

Rachel (January 1989). Christmas and New Year during my last year in seminary was a very special time. Not only did Kathleen celebrate her birthday in mid-December, but we were entering the ninth month of Kathleen's pregnancy. The baby was expected shortly after mid-January. We were excited.

On Sunday the fifteenth (Martin Luther King's birthday) at less than one minute before midnight a baby girl entered independent life and drew her first breath. As with all couples experiencing their first birth – we felt totally unprepared to meet such an awesome event. But it went very quickly – as if it were just going to happen anyway. This is just one of those events that's bigger than even its participants. It was a great lesson in trust.

The next day, as I returned to the hospital following a few hours' sleep – I was very lightheaded, though not just from the lack of sleep. There was such a surreal aspect to finally becoming a father. Rachel (as we had a name ready for a girl) and Kathleen, as I saw them together, seemed to me to embody all of the wonderful qualities of a Madonna and Child painting: beauty, peace, vitality, hope. And I was at one with the universe!

People on campus and at church shared our excitement. I was so glad I heard not a single snide comment from anyone about the discrepancy in months from wedding to birth. This was something that I know weighed heavily upon us. But indeed, people were not only gracious but also truly nurturing of the new parents. It made everything so completely wonderful.

GRADUATION (May 1989)

Liberation Theology ("Jesus with a submachine gun!") strikes back. The last semester of my senior year I got seriously to work on my senior thesis – done under the direction of a young professor that I had worked closely with in Trenton in my first year there on a project to bring some of the city's poor children to Sunday School at the church. I think that was the only reason he agreed to supervise the thesis – for I knew that he was an ardent Liberation Theologian and he himself told me that he was quite certain that nothing short of armed uprising was ever going to change South Africa (not that he knew very much specifically about South Africa).

At first he was very laudatory of my work. I turned in my first 100 pages simply outlining the different racial groups, explaining their different political positions, and laying out the socio-economic situation under apartheid. He told me that it was very well written, and that it gave him the clearest picture he had ever had about the South African situation. But we never got together on the rest of my study: the role of the various political interest groups inside and outside of the country, the very special role of the church, the recent changes in the mood of the country, and my prognosis of something big about to break in the form of a truly multiracial regime in the country – all achieved by "reform" or "spiritual reconciliation" rather than violent revolution.

The title of the thesis "Reconciliation in South Africa" did not sit well with him – but that was nothing in comparison to how he greeted the rest of the thesis. As I turned it in (a total of over 250 pages – the size of many doctoral dissertations!) at the end of the term, we really had never discussed my ideas on where the rest of the thesis was headed. And as he departed for Nicaragua for a week just prior to the end of the term, I really got no playback at all from him on the thesis. But I really hadn't given it a thought, as I had many details to keep track of as I finished off my seminary experience.

But I wasn't prepared for the phone call from the Registrar on the Friday before Tuesday's graduation day – to inform me that she had, just that afternoon, finally received his grade report for my thesis (it was way overdue being turned in – in fact she had to chase him down to get it). But he had assigned an "F" to the project!

But she told me not to worry, she had already taken the initiative to rearrange my course categories in such a way that she had, on her own, reconstructed a senior concentration for me (Biblical studies instead of Christian ethics). Anyway I had so many extra course credits that this 6 hours of "F" would hardly be a ripple in the stream.

On Monday I picked up his written comments on the thesis. He was outraged by my conclusions – feeling that I was merely playing the part of propagandist for the tyrannical Afrikaner regime by taking such a weak position against the real needs of the country for liberation. The "F" was his way of making clear the size of his sense of outrage.

Things move ahead anyway. I think he was quite surprised to see me the next day at commencement exercises. He did not know I had all those extra credits. Ordinarily that "F" would have been sufficient to keep a student from graduating – as he well knew. Also, lacking the seminary's degree, this would have also prevented my ordination. That had been, after all, the purpose of the "F."

Ah, bubble-dwelling intellectuals, you've got to love them!

That next year after my graduation was a heady time for the world – for not only did South Africa turn upside down but so did all of the East European Communist world. Without a shot being fired from the "Free World," Communism collapsed. I could imagine the disappointment of some in the Pentagon who were not going to get a chance to destroy Communism themselves! It was, I imagined, much like the feelings of some of the Liberation Theologians who were not going to get a chance to destroy Apartheid in South Africa!

As I thought about it – though militants in the Pentagon and militants in the Peace-and-Social-Justice movement probably thought of themselves as total opposites – I realized that they had much in common.

What I learned from all this (including watching the scene in Eastern Europe) is that God is Redeemer not only of individuals, but also of nations and civilizations. All of the events of those days seemed to me to have not the hand of Man on them – but of God. Of that the South Africans seemed certain. And this is also what I think I heard coming from Gorbachev. I just don't why that is such a hard concept for some Americans, particularly some Christians in America, to understand!

Commencement. Anyway – graduation itself came on a bright day at the end of May 1989. My sister and her husband flew in from California and my parents from Arizona. Rachel was a special feature of the proceedings – a living symbol of the new things opening up before us. It was a warm time of coming together with some and also saying goodbye to others, people with whom I had spent many close moments. It was also a time of major transition, an event marking a key point along the way of my own personal spiritual pilgrimage.

CHAPTER SIX

A TOUGH CALL TO GARFIELD
December 1990 to December 1997

* * *

SEARCHING FOR A CALL (February to May 1989)

As I moved through my senior year, I still did not have any keen sense of what all this seminary experience had been pointing to in the longer term. I had no better a clue at this point than when I entered almost three years previously.

Trying to make the Hanover Street Ministry a full-time call. My natural inclination was to suppose that I should somehow parley my work at the Hanover Street Ministry into a full-time ministry. It certainly made some sense. The program was well established, well participated in by the people it was designed for, and certainly not unknown within the local Presbytery where I was a candidate. Of course, such a ministry would never become self-sustaining, but would constantly have to depend on outside monetary support for survival.

On this basis I approached Presbytery, but got no support, despite all its talk about developing a focus on "urban ministry" – which ultimately sounded to me like a process for merely underwriting traditional suburban ministry in the areas of Trenton and New Brunswick.

The Princeton churches had once supported a street ministry, which I knew turned disastrous. But unlike their failed Crisis Ministry, the Hanover Street Ministry had prospered in the years I had headed it up. Even the Princeton churches knew this because they had been helping with the funding for the sandwiches and coffee we served at the Ministry.

But I got nowhere here either. The pastor of the Nassau Presbyterian church in Princeton explained that he was not able to support me because of my "evangelical style." He claimed that it reminded him too much of a southern evangelical style he had gladly put behind him years ago.

But since he had never heard me either teach or preach, he actually had no real grounds to make such a judgement. I realized, in fact, that what was behind his opposition was that he never cared for me much personally, ever since my jumping into the Crisis Ministry discussion three years earlier.

In any case, failing to get his support I knew was not only a major financial loss but also a major political loss presbytery-wise.

I solicited other churches in the Presbytery for partial support of the Ministry as a mission project and as a point of contact for their own people in their own outreach efforts. But only one church gave me the promise of some support ($2,000 a year salary contribution).

Sadly, I finally concluded that the project was dead in the water.

College chaplaincy?   While I was struggling to promote the Hanover Street Ministry, I got a phone call from the president of a Presbyterian college in North Dakota. He and the Placement Director at the Seminary had been discussing me as a possibility as chaplain, with academic teaching responsibilities at his college. The idea of this kind of work excited me greatly! But North Dakota? I told him I would think on it. But in fact my only thoughts were a loud, No! It was just too far removed from the world I (and Kathleen) delighted in.

Overseas mission work?   I had prepared a "dossier" (résumé) to be circulated within the Presbyterian church. But it was so obviously and narrowly oriented to inner-city mission work that I got not a single response to it, not for a long, long time.

I met a recruiter on campus from the denomination's Global Missions office and he encouraged me to apply. I did. But nothing happened. I soon learned that the Northern and Southern churches were still in the process of trying to integrate their separate overseas mission programs and therefore were quite slow in moving ahead. Finally, I got a call from a missionary, home from Africa, whose husband was director of the central African office. My Mobile friend Martelle, who had served with them two years (1985-1987) as a "volunteer-in-mission" in Zaire, had told them about me. They were looking for someone who had exactly my credentials to develop a church building program in Zaire. The job involved both church construction and evangelism – naturals for me. The fact that I was also fluent in French was for them the clincher.

I'm afraid that for Kathleen this was a bit too extreme of a jump from her close family life in New Jersey – probably even more extreme to her than my thoughts about North Dakota. True, she had been with me in South Africa, even nearly a week with me at the Zulu mission station. But this did not give her great comfort. Anyway the idea got put on hold, awaiting the national church in getting its missions-programming act together.

* * *

THE LONG WAIT (June 1989 to October 1990)

Habitat for Humanity. As no call had come my way by graduation, I was very glad to be offered a summer internship sponsored by a Princeton group that paid me a small stipend to supervise a multi-house Habitat for Humanity project in Trenton. My duties included working with weekend volunteers (a fairly competent group), the future homeowners who were supposed to add their own "sweat-equity" toward the construction of their own homes (mostly a fairly incompetent or unmotivated group), and a number of youth groups who came into order to have a week's experience with Habitat (not greatly competent, but lots of fun). I also had the task of overseeing materials acquisitions, guiding inspectors through the projects , and a lot of work on my own, siting and laying footing, framing, roofing, insulating, drywalling, trim work, kitchen/bath cabinetry, tile work, etc. I helped with the excavation, block work, floating concrete, and running the electrical and plumbing services, though we had professionals as volunteers to oversee those specialty tasks. I loved it!

A little extra "twist" I brought to all this was the morning devotionals I led every morning (even when alone). To me, it was important to remind ourselves that this was not a secular building project, but a definite part of Christian living. I found that the prayers, short Biblical messages and opportunities to reflect simply on what we were experiencing in the inner city, helped all of us – especially the youth – connect ourselves to the work in a very special way.

Construction/Carpentry. Then, just as the summer internship was running out, what I used to recognize as *Fortuna*, but now knew personally as a very loving God, came to my rescue as usual – at the very last minute! Kathleen and I were attending a picnic with her family and their friends where I met a young Englishman, Peter, who was doing a lot of construction work in the Princeton area and who asked me if I would be willing to come to work with him while I awaited my "call." I was more than glad to do so.

So, after having taken a month's vacation with Kathleen and little Rachel to St. Louis and Mobile, I began my new life as a construction worker. Thankfully I had the summer to get my 48-year-old muscles somewhat into shape, for the work was very heavy and I was having to keep up with younger men in their 20s (including Kathleen's younger brothers John and Brian, and occasionally her youngest brother Craig).

At first the work was purely dirty and unexciting. We were tearing out the whole first floor interior of a huge office complex. As I, on my way to the dumpsters, pushed the huge dollies filled with plaster dust and floor sweepings past the secretaries who were outside taking smoking breaks, I could feel their sneers. I was filthy from head to foot.

What a comedown for someone with a PhD, a former professor, and a seminarian who had just graduated from Princeton!

Actually, I realized that this was exactly what I needed to have happen to me at this point in my life. I had of course worked in the inner city, and knew hard, smelly and menial work. But I had always been able to return quickly to a life of dignity at the end of the day, for "who I was" was still "professor" or "Princeton student." Now I simply was "construction worker." I learned quickly to accept my position with humor and a sense of dignity about my work.

Eventually we began rebuilding the first-floor offices of this business complex, and the work became both interesting and challenging. And when we were through, we had created something of rather considerable beauty.

From there, the job went to some very fancy work for some Princeton homes (Princeton University administrators usually), for instance a huge greenhouse for a wife of one of those officials, a woman intending to make her orchid-growing talents a true business (I was put in charge of the extensive tile-work involved in that project). There was also a huge project of building an "addition" to a home (the "addition" being much larger than most houses), a project involving five garages, a health spa, a fabulous game room and exercise room that was fitted out with the latest of everything. And we did a project that involved 25-foot-high vaulted ceilings, balconies, huge decks, about five of us working closely together to do all the work from beginning to end ourselves.

The work was always changing, always challenging, always stimulating even when it was 20 degrees below outside and we were installing aluminum trusses on scaffolds with the snow tumbling down on us! But I loved it.

I have the instincts of an architect. Every vocational aptitude test I have ever taken since high school always returns the same result. First preference: Architecture. I love design – especially when it is closely connected with the creation of something very tangible.

Trying to stay true to my sense of Christian call. In the meantime, a year went by this way and I received virtually no inquiries from any Presbyterian church in that time. The mission position in Zaire was still open though still awaiting some kind of resolution of things at national headquarters – and was even chasing us a bit. But I knew that Kathleen was too frightened or worried for us to be able to say "yes" to this should it ever get squared away. Still I was getting very concerned that nothing was moving for me in terms of a call.

I continued to serve at the Hanover Street Ministry on weekends. That was still going as strong as ever, and it remained for me my sole opportunity to perform Christian service. We were, of course, regular worshipers at the First Presbyterian Church in Trenton. But we had not been asked to take on any special functions within the church, perhaps because they figured I still had my hands full with the Hanover Street Ministry (which I did).

Still, I felt so part-time – and even minimally so at that – about my Christian life. I had not left the university to do carpentry work, as much as I enjoyed it. I had pledged my life fully to God's service. I had given up my university tenure, had cashed in my 15 years of accumulated teacher's pension credits to help pay for seminary education, and had sold my house to pay for the rest. I had thrown everything I had into this endeavor. And now, as time moved along, I felt that the original purpose of everything I had lived for over the last five years was dropping out of sight – and possibly even dropping out of God's sight. Or so it certainly felt.

I would awaken many nights in the middle of the night and go out and sit on the couch and pray, sometimes tearfully. I just couldn't figure out why God, who had previously been in such easy communication with me about so many simple daily matters in my life, now seemed so "silent."

I was one who expected to live in the midst of recurring miracles. And yet it seemed that the miracles had dried up in the last year. True – I knew that my construction job came as a result of a miracle. True – I knew that my marriage to Kathleen and the birth of Rachel counted as major miracles which I was still enjoying as such. But there was nothing "new" in the realm of miracles that had occurred in a whole year. I had not felt God "moving" anew in my life in a long time.

✳ ✳ ✳

THE CALL TO GARFIELD (October to December 1990)

A "sign" in the night. In October of 1990 I was beginning to finish up a major building project and nothing new was lining up. It looked like I might be totally out of work by Thanksgiving.

One evening I was doing my "thing" on the couch, praying or just pleading with God, when a deep sense of peace came over me. When I headed back to bed I woke Kathleen to tell her that I had a strange feeling that God was about to answer our prayers.

Saturday, when I returned home from my morning at the Hanover Street Ministry, Kathleen greeted me with the news that someone from Garfield (up in northern New Jersey) had called to see if I was still looking for a church. Kathleen was not wild about the area, having grown up in

New Jersey and being aware of how different things were in that part of the state, just opposite New York City. But I knew immediately that this was what I had awakened to tell Kathleen about.

Having that sense of things made my phone conversation with the head of the pulpit committee, Dot, come easy to me. I told them that if they wanted to see me in action, to really understand what I was all about, they should first come down to visit me at Hanover Street. She agreed. The following Saturday they drove down to Trenton to meet me in the Ministry.

Interviewing. Things went well. Some of them were obviously moved by the sight of "tough" street guys responding so sweetly to the teaching and the prayers (they were a bit nervous about being around streetwise Blacks). We talked afterward and I laid out for them my very evangelical vision of Christian ministry. That seemed to work well for them. I was impressed with their reception to the vision!

They came down shortly after that to hear me in the pulpit (I hadn't been in the pulpit for almost 2 years). The sermon was about 35 minutes in length. But that had been pretty typical for me whenever I was in the pulpit. A comment was made by Dot that "we would have to work on that." But otherwise things went well.

Garfield. Soon after that I was up in the neighborhood, conducting a funeral for an aunt of mine, with my parents (visiting from St. Louis) and Kathleen and Rachel in tow. We swung by Garfield to have a look.

My heart sank. Garfield was a formerly blue-collar industrial town whose industries had moved out.   A huge former chemical plant sat abandoned only a block away from the church. The Passaic River, which bordered the town two blocks away, was lined with used car lots and auto repair shops. That seemed to be the base of the present Garfield economy, such as I could detect one. The rows of two-story houses (built around World War One) were closely built with no driveways and only narrow walkways between them. There were few trees along the streets, and a maze of telephone wires were strung overhead everywhere. Cars lined the streets with hardly any spaces available for parking (I could not see where people coming to church would ever park). There was something of an-Hispanic flavor to the neighborhood (it became even more pronounced over the following years), for the music which blared forth from passing cars announced that fact. The pastor's manse was next door to the church, only a few feet away, with a small backyard running behind the church. At least the manse had its own driveway and garage located behind the other side of the church – the only driveway around. What privilege!

Well, what could I say? I felt that God had spoken, so there was likely to be little argument with Him about this call which I knew would be forthcoming. It certainly was not what I wanted. And I did not have that sense of "peace" that had greeted me years earlier when I entered inner-city Trenton. But I knew that this was where I would be serving. Ah well.

Words of warning from the Committee on Ministry. As part of the interview process, I was required to meet with a very important committee of the Palisades Presbytery under whose jurisdiction the Garfield church found itself. The Presbyterian system does not have bishops that churches are accountable to. Instead a Presbyterian church is supervised by a regional conference made up of the local churches (typically about 50 or so churches making up a presbytery), each church represented at presbytery by its own pastor, and one or two (or more) of its elders, depending on church size. And it is this presbytery that performs the supervisory roles typical of a bishop.

Anyway I had to be interviewed by the presbytery's majorly significant Committee on Ministry (COM) before I could be cleared to receive a pulpit call from Garfield.

During this interview I was asked if I was aware of the precarious financial position of the Garfield church. I really was not. I was told that Garfield had been receiving Presbytery subsidies to pay the salary of the previous pastor and COM was inclined not to continue this practice. I pointed to Garfield's financial reserves of $35,000. The COM chairman told me that typically a small church built up such reserves during a pulpit vacancy, not having to pay a regular pastor. With a regular pastor in place these monies would be drawn down very quickly. If indeed there was a shortfall of regular income to the tune of say $1000 a month, it would be around 3 years when the church found itself in financial straits again (the estimation was right on target almost to the month!). The COM had come very close to not letting Garfield issue a full-time pastoral call, but instead only a part-time call. They thought I should be aware of that before I said "yes" to the situation there.

I, at that time, felt however that I could accomplish most anything I set my mind to, especially since it was quite clear in my mind that Garfield was where God wanted me to be. I listened politely to their well-intended advice. But I knew I would say "yes" to an invitation from Garfield no matter what.

Anyway, I preached my candidating sermon before the full Garfield congregation in late November, and after the service, the congregation voted me in as their new pastor.

Appearing before Presbytery. My last hurdle to leap would now be the vote of Presbytery in admitting me to full membership as a newly ordained pastor. I had to submit to an "examination" by the full gathering of the presbytery (all the pastors and a select number of elders from each of the churches in the presbytery), an examination centering on my Statement of Faith, which carefully outlined my particular Christian beliefs.

I knew that there would be raised eyebrows over my use in my Statement of Faith of male language in reference to God. But I felt that it was time to announce myself as one who believed that the church ought not to experiment with or reinvent the identity of God as given in scripture, specifically by our Lord himself, just because it pacified certain strongly vocal political interests in the contemporary church. I had hated having been muzzled by the feminists on seminary campus and I was determined that I was not going into the ministry under that same sense of compromised faith and personal oppression. It was a risky move, and I was well aware of the fact.

And of course wouldn't you know that on the evening in late November that I appeared before Presbytery I was suffering from a horrible cold, was doped up a bit on antihistamines, and just generally was very, very tired from all the last minute hustle to get me into the pulpit before Christmas.

My Statement of Faith was indeed a red flag. As soon as I finished reading it, a woman immediately jumped up and with sobs in her voice mentioned how it was just such statements as this that had once made her feel "cutoff" from the Christian faith (I learned later that she had been raised Catholic). From there it went downhill. After what seemed like hours (it might have been 15 or 20 minutes) of examination I was ushered outside while Presbytery went into consideration about my being received into their membership (and thus being ordainable). I spent a full 30 to 40 minutes outside while debate raged back and forth about me. As I learned later, this had not happened in a long, long time. Usually the whole thing from reading of the statement of faith to final vote on a person might take 10 minutes, 15 minutes at the most. For me the ordeal lasted for nearly an hour. Finally I was called back into the meeting. I had been voted into the presbytery.

And I didn't just sort of slip in unnoticed. I would be recognized from then on as the "conservative" voice of the presbytery.

Actually where I stood on the social-political spectrum depended on where other people stood who were evaluating me. Palisades Presbytery was one of the most Liberal of the denomination's presbyteries and could always be counted on to take the "Left" side of any given issue.

But God had a strange way of making this whole thing work out – very wonderfully so. But I'll have more to say about that later.

Ordained and installed (December 1990). I officially took up my duties in Garfield the first Sunday of December. And on December 16th, I was formally ordained and installed as a Presbyterian Minister of the Word and Sacrament.

The Peace and Social Justice Presbyterians, and the Kuwait Crisis. It was very soon after my ordination, in fact the very next meeting of Presbytery in February of 1991, that I got to see once more how "Liberal" the world I had just stepped into happened to be.

I had been following events developing with Iraqi dictator Saddam Hussein when his troops invaded his neighbor, Kuwait, that August. President Bush (Sr.) had been trying to get former US ally Saddam to understand that this action was unacceptable and that he would have to back his troops out of Kuwait. But once committed to this action, Saddam realized he would lose considerable power at home in Iraq if he now retreated from Kuwait. He would withdraw only if other nations also first withdrew their own occupation of land that was not theirs (pointing to the state of Israel). Also, fear began to grow that Saddam might expand his move into a relatively defenseless Saudi Arabia, also next door.

Thus President Bush, backed up by wide global support (the United Nations, for instance) and especially support from the Arab World, moved American troops into the Saudi Arabian region right next to Kuwait, and there began to assemble a multinational force. Finally in January of 1991, this coalition force, led extensively by the US, began aerial attacks on the Iraqi troops in Kuwait.

When we had that February Presbytery meeting, the exchange of bombs back and forth between the two contending parties was now in full. We were at war. Therefore, at the end of the presbytery meeting, we were given candles, so that we could march by candlelight through the area. We were to do this in protest against yet another round of American "imperialism", supposedly the heart of the dynamic (as the protesting Liberals were viewing the matter).

I had not much choice but to join them, my status with the presbytery being already so marginal. But as I joined the procession, I felt as if I was back in Princeton, protesting about the "outrageous" behavior of that Thai pastor who had violated the "inclusive" standards of the seminary in his male-chauvinist usage of male terminology in his sermon.

In short, I hated what I was doing. And I realized that these fellow Presbyterians had absolutely no idea whatsoever of the stupidity of this procession. Bush was doing exactly what should have been expected of the leading world superpower, who was simply trying to keep things from spinning out of control in the vital oil-producing region of the world. This was not imperialism. This was American diplomacy doing exactly what everyone (except these "peace and social justice" warriors) expected.

Anyway, as it turned out, Bush's coalition was very successful in returning things to the way they were prior to the war, Bush showing no intentions of going any further against Iraq. His Secretary of Defense Dick Cheney later explained to the press that to have tried to move in and take over Iraqi politics would have been to fall into a quagmire, and that America had no business doing something that foolish. Ironically, these were wise words that he himself would later ignore as US vice president under Bush Jr.'s presidency!

And as for the presbytery, nothing further was said on this matter.

✳ ✳ ✳

TENSIONS AT CHURCH (1991 to 1993)

The "family church." Garfield classified itself as a small "family" church. I soon came to learn what that actually meant: namely, a handful of families ran the church! But it took me a while to get this figured out. I also learned that the pulpit committee that had called me to Garfield was not representative of this family structure. Those ruling families were too busy, too important, to engage in such mere committee work. Furthermore, I was to learn that what the Garfield Pulpit Committee put forth in its Church Information Form (CIF – the church's job description it had used in advertising for a new pastor) as the basic mission of the church, and what the "families" expected the church to be about, were two quite different matters.

Being new to pulpit ministry, it took me a while to understand that this was not untypical for the way small churches are run. The pastor is there not as a teacher or program director. The pastor is understood as being there essentially to serve as the family "chaplain," that is, called to the church to serve the particular needs and perform the necessary rituals that undergird the life of certain leading families.

The debate over sermon length and content. Now to me, the pulpit was understood as being a teaching platform – a platform for the teaching of Scripture. My sermons turned out to be expositions of Scripture, 30 to 35 minutes in length, designed to highlight God's Word and will for his people. But I soon learned that despite the affirmations of the Pulpit Committee when I queried them about this, the strong biblical preaching I was accustomed to offering was not what the "families" wanted from the pulpit.

The comments were quick to come in that this was all too much. According to the "families," everyone knew that no one preached more than 15 to 18 minutes. Someone suggested that if I would cut out all of my scriptural references in my sermons, I would probably have a decent 18-to-20-minute sermon!

Others were more aggressive in their criticism. I was told that if preachers couldn't get said in 18 to 20 minutes what they needed to say, then they obviously had no grip on the material. Besides, I was told, people's attention spans could not hold for a presentation any longer than that. Furthermore, they had dinners to get to and they were unwilling that anything should delay that most-important part of their Sunday schedule. Church attendance was only one, rather brief, portion of their long-standing Sunday rituals, which no one was going to reshape – not me or anyone else!

My response – that I was aware of many powerful churches, big churches, growth churches, whose worship was often over two hours in length and whose sermons were sometimes over an hour – was unwanted information. The "families" simply did not want to hear about it. Their minds were made up. That's how things were. That's how things would stay in this church.

The battle over changes. It was not long before complaints started going forth to Presbytery that I was "changing things." The line of complaints was how I had added 15 to 20 minutes to the worship service. I soon was receiving visits from fellow pastors who took it upon themselves to give me professional counsel: give up on the sermon strategy. It really was not necessary – only upsetting good people.

Actually, the changes that came during my first years at the church were much more substantial than this matter of the length of Sunday morning worship. In fairly short order after my arrival in Garfield I added to the activities of the church a weekly Bible study, a men's group, a daylong retreat in a nearby mountain campsite, participation of a growing youth group in a weeklong summer camp, and participation of a number of our members in the Tres Dias renewal "weekend" retreat. These were soon followed up by a prison ministry program and a couple of church picnics each year.

Involvement in these new activities was consistently by the same group: about 15 to 20 of the newer and more "evangelical" members (and their children) of the church, some of whom had been on the pulpit committee. No member of the "families" bothered to participate in any of these new activities.

The real change taking place in the church was the empowerment of these newer members in the life of the church. As they became more active, including coming on Session (the church's ruling board) and taking a sincere interest in introducing new ideas into the church, the "families" found their monopoly on church life profoundly challenged. New initiatives by the "newcomers" (some of whom had been there for 10 years!) left the families feeling that control was slipping from their hands. This was what was really bothering the "families." I had come in and upset the whole status quo by playing to the spiritual agendas of the "nonfamily" evangelicals.

There really was no answer to the demands of the "families," except to scuttle everything that had been added to the previously well-defined life of the church, retaining only 60 minutes of Sunday worship, the choir, the women's association, and a small Sunday School program for the children and even smaller youth program. Anything beyond that was of a questionable status – one which never failed to draw the ire of the "families," when things started to show life.

My second year at Garfield: We hit a low point. By the middle of my second year in Garfield (1992) tensions were running high. Monthly session meetings constantly centered on the changes that had accompanied my arrival in Garfield. At one point I brought to a session meeting the CIF and read its contents, in an attempt to point out that what I was doing was exactly what the church had said it was looking for in a pastor.

But I got the response from one member of the "families" that the CIF was merely a set of ideal Christian principles – not something that was to be taken at face value in terms of the running of the church!!!

I realized at this point that there was no logic of mine that would reach the thinking of this group.

Just general difficulties in making Garfield feel like "home." For the life of me, I couldn't figure out why God had brought me to Garfield. I was miserable.

My misery even extended to the very "alien" feel that the town of Garfield itself had for me. I was living in a place that I found very difficult for me to call "home." I hated the physical ugliness of Garfield, its cramped living conditions, its constant noise (morning, noon and night!).

The situation was such that even the "families" did not live in town, but in surrounding communities of a more comfortable nature. The "families" converged on the church of a Sunday morning simply to revisit old friendships, and practice long-standing religious rituals – before heading back to their comfortable worlds. They didn't even stick around to attend fellowship-hour after worship, an activity that the local "newcomers" looked forward to – for the way it added some grace to their Garfield lives.

I had done what I could to relieve some of the starkness of the immediate Garfield surroundings by planting approximately 100 rose bushes, several hundred tulips and daffodils, and even more marigolds, petunias, impatiens and other annual flowers around the manse (pastor's home) and the church. I also put in a vegetable garden, which added to the sense of "life" in this depressed area. This helped some – though not enough to make me feel pleased to be there.

What am I doing here? By 1993 (the third year of my ministry at Garfield) profound self-doubt had set in on me. I had never set out for myself the idea of becoming a parish pastor. I had answered the call to Garfield only because that seemed to me to be what God had called me to do. I certainly had not sought this call myself.

I was miserable. Despite the encouragement of the evangelicals in the congregation who assured me that I was the best thing that had ever happened to Garfield, each Sunday morning was something I dreaded because I knew that I faced a number of people who thought (and said so openly and loudly) that I was the worst thing that had ever happened to Garfield. Trying to preach a message before a group of people who were adamant in their opposition to me was one of the most demeaning experiences imaginable. And I got to do this every week!

Asthma sets in. It was at this time that I began to develop the symptoms of asthma – the first time I had ever experienced anything like this in my life. I couldn't understand why a winter cold I caught at the end of my second year in Garfield would not go away, but was slowly sinking down into my chest. It was finally diagnosed as asthma.

The doctors wanted to put me on permanent medication. But I decided that I needed to do something else permanently, especially as I came to understand how asthma is stress-related.

I needed to get out of Garfield. But where was I to go? I wanted to go back into teaching. But I wanted to teach the gospel – and what college or university would let me do that? Also, I enjoyed very much working with my evangelical parishioners. In fact it was the delight of my life (well, in addition to my family which was also the delight of my life!).

I did not know where to turn or how to move forward. I always knew that unless God moved me it would all be pointless. But I also must admit that I was very unhappy with God for bringing me to Garfield. I was sure that there was some kind of message from him in all this Garfield mess. But frankly I didn't find anything very thrilling about such a message. Anyway, I wasn't even sure what the message was.

Also, I really felt abandoned by God. It had been several years now since I had heard a single "word" from God (other than his permanent Word in Scripture). I was surely living in one of those "long, dark nights of the soul."

Further crisis of confidence. In February of 1993 my parents asked me if I had been following the events centering around the announcement of my old college/early graduate school sweetheart, Kim, as a Clinton nominee for U.S. Attorney General. Actually, I had not, for I neither subscribed to a local paper nor watched TV very much as a rule. That was the first I had heard of the matter.

Eventually I picked up a little on the story, one that ended quite sadly for Kim, whom I was sure wanted that job very much, though she would end up as a senior US District Judge of the New York Southern District Court (New York City).

But the story had a very interesting side effect on me at this point in my personal journey. Though Kim had not landed the position, the mere nomination reminded me of how far Kim had moved along in life and how insignificant my own life seemed to be by contrast. How far I had plunged downward, from a life that once promised so much, to a life that seemed as antlike as I had ever feared human life could be, since that day I gazed down from the Empire State Building and had that chilling feeling about how unimportant a single life could be. I had actually achieved that great unimportance!

My depression at that point was all too obvious. Then one morning after church, during fellowship hour (which only the evangelicals ever attended), a surprise Valentine's Party was held for me and a whole battery of cards and notes was given to me by these beloved parishioners reminding me that I had been vital to their personal spiritual journeys, rescuing them from impending divorce, drugs, alcohol or just a general spiritual deadness that marked their lives. To them I had acquitted my life quite admirably, and I needed to bow my head in shame before no one.

Admittedly that party helped lift my spirits some – though it still did not remove the deeper self-doubt I had about myself as a pastor or anything else which might truly matter to the world. I didn't want to diminish the importance that these dear parishioners placed on my role in their lives. But in all honesty, I really wasn't convinced that I was making much of a contribution to the world by my work in Garfield. Indeed, I still had no idea of how or where I ought to be making my contribution to larger life.

The search for an understanding. I was so desperate for something to clue me in, that I decided if God was not going to shed any light on my life, then I would seek it for myself. I laid my plight before the Presbytery's Executive Presbyter, Barbara Worthington. She in turn suggested that I undergo a testing program in Princeton that the church used regularly to give guidance to its pastors concerning their call. So, in March of 1993 I journeyed to Princeton to undergo this two-day testing/counseling program.

The test itself involved a number of vocational, aptitude and personality tests, and, unknown to me, an IQ test. Test results revealed that in terms of the range of broad professional interests, I ranked very high in religious activity, only just behind art. But in terms of specific occupational profiles, I ranked as a minister at the low end of "moderately similar (college professor being the highest at "very similar"). So how was I to understand the very high religious interest and rather low ranking (15th) as minister? The answer was revealed in another test that differentiated religious occupations.

In this test I ranked highest as:

> Spiritual Guide 91 (very high) ["helping people to develop a
>   deeper or more mature faith"]
> Evangelist 84 (high)
> Scholar 81 (moderately high)
> Teacher 75 (moderately high)

Closer to the median rank were:

> Preacher 66
> Priest 65 ["conducting worship services & performing sacred rites
>   and rituals"]
> Counselor 62 ["bringing comfort and encouragement to lonely,
>   troubled and sick persons"]
> Administrator 57
> Reformer 56 [social justice activist]
> Musician 54

In other words, I was lowest (with only an average aptitude for these roles) in those areas that are most commonly associated with parish ministry (preacher, priest, counselor, administrator) the professional pastor. I was much higher in the areas of scholarship and teaching. Well, I knew that.

But highest of all religious roles were evangelist and spiritual guide. This was no surprise either, for my life's work, even as a secular teacher, had/has always been centered on helping people catch what I call the higher vision of life. I left the university when I discovered that this higher vision had something to do with God – God in Jesus Christ. I wanted to follow that out at all costs. And I wanted to bring that discovery (the Good News of/in Jesus Christ) to those around me.

The problem is, as I discovered in Garfield, that there are not a lot of people in the church very interested in this process. As one venerable session member put it: "I made my peace with God in the trenches of World War Two. I do not need anyone telling me how to get closer to God!" But interestingly I discovered that there are a lot of people outside the church who are very hungry for just this sort of thing. The only problem is that the church (or at least mainline Protestantism) seems unable (or unwilling) to get to them.

One test I did not realize I was taking was an IQ test. I scored at 145 (+/- 3). I was told by the counselor that this pointed to great potential, for both good and bad in my life. I needed to be mentally challenged or could face the possibility of more frustration and stress.

The need to take action. Putting it all together, I was told that I was at a turning point in my life. I needed to find positive outlets for all my interests, my energy, and my thoughts. If I did not, clinical depression might become the outcome for me.

In any case, as I surveyed these results, as I considered my first 2+ years in the parish ministry, and as I considered my persistent asthma and stress, I decided that I needed to do what I had to do. My health, my spirit, my life, my family all depended on it.

✳ ✳ ✳

ON A VERY POSITIVE NOTE: THE FAMILY TAKES SHAPE

Mind you, life was not all confrontation, stress, confusion and disappointment during those first years in Garfield. We did not live during this time without any of God's blessings. We would not have kept going at all during this very hard time if we had not been keenly aware that something of God's favor was still with us. And that favor showed up in the joy of our family life.

Career or family? An issue that had long bothered me ever since I had moved on from my Yuppie existence was what it was that I was going to let define me. During the 1970s and very early 1980s I had been such a professional, such a careerist. That's one of the reasons I had given such little thought about family. In fact, during those years I actually was glad not to have to be burdened with the larger responsibilities of family life.

But since the serious change of directions in my life in the mid-1980s

I had come to have quite a different appreciation of family. For that matter I had come to have a different appreciation of community and social life in general.

Kathleen came into my life with a strong set of family values already in place. She had been raised in a very close Irish-Catholic home and was still very close to her sisters and brothers, all of whom still lived in the central Jersey area. Kathleen's primary reference system in life was family. Kathleen wanted to become a "mom," period. We both understood and appreciated this determination on her part when we got married. And when Rachel came along, we both understood how things were going to be.

Once upon a time there would have been no argument about the determination of a woman to be an at-home mom. But those times had disappeared with the empty-nesting of the generation before us. The emphasis was now for women to think in career terms (not as the family homemaker) in exactly the same way that men were to think in career terms (not as the family breadwinner). Everything else in life would just somehow have to work itself around this "careerism" as the grounding of our personal being. Indeed, for much of our culture, who you were was defined largely in terms of the career path you were on. Do not read "job." Job and career are not the same thing.

This decision that Kathleen would be an "at-home mom" meant much less family income for us. But actually, we were not financially strapped by this decision! But sadly, it also meant a lot of loneliness for Kathleen because there were no other at-home moms in the entire Garfield congregation.

Kathleen's place in the scheme of things. When we came to Garfield in late 1990, Kathleen was several months pregnant with Paul. This brought out all the "hovering" instincts of the women of the congregation. I must admit, we enjoyed this attention.

In fact, Kathleen and the family were always a very important counterbalancing part of my ministry in Garfield. I was, for better or worse (as people viewed these things) always the one actively engaged in promoting new things with the church. This brought a lot of enthusiasm. It also brought a lot of opposition.

But Kathleen stayed out of church affairs. She was always in worship with Rachel and then later, Rachel, Paul and Elizabeth. But she didn't get into any of the "politics." She was always gracious about the attention that people like to give the "pastor's wife." But she did not let this draw her into church politics. Consequently, everyone found her easy to love. And that helped to soften the hearts of some of my "opposition" – a little bit anyway.

Paul is born (May 1, 1991). Paul was born in the early part of my

Garfield ministry on a very sunny morning on the first day of May, 1991 (50 years after I was born in 1941!). He was about 10 days overdue so we were very watchful during those days. But Kathleen woke with only the first sensations at about 7:30 that morning that this might be the day. We called some friends to come in and watch Rachel, and an hour later were on our way to the hospital. As with Rachel, birthing Paul was fast and relatively easy for Kathleen (Kathleen was made to have babies!!!). An hour after she was checked in and situated, Paul was born. We had not asked when Kathleen's sonograms were taken whether we were expecting a boy or a girl. Somehow nonetheless we sensed that this would be a boy. Anyway, we had a name ready only for a boy. We named him after our fathers: Paul Henry (Paul: my father; Henry: Kathleen's father). We now had a matched set of a daughter and a son.

Rachel was delighted with her brother – who seemed to her like a most wonderful doll. She had a hard time keeping her hands off of him and not smothering him with her affection (we had that same problem with all our little ones!)

And I couldn't help but thanking God for having brought me so far from my aloofness to small children as a Yuppie to the point where they (along with Kathleen) were the most important things in my life. In them I found great contentment and a heart full of praise for God.

Elizabeth is born (January 20 1993). Kathleen was soon pregnant again. The due date in early 1993 was exactly the same as for Rachel, January 17th! (Rachel had come two days early however). Actually, it was on January 20th that Kathleen knew that the time had come. Again, it was a fast and relatively easy delivery. We got to the hospital at about 9:00 p.m. and an hour later a little girl was born.

That was convenient, as we really had only a girl's name fixed in our minds, Elizabeth Jeannine Hodges. And once again we had waited until birth to find out whether it was a girl or boy that God was bringing us – though also once again, a sense of things told us that it was going to be a girl. "Elizabeth" was a family name on Kathleen's side (an aunt and a grandmother), though I myself had long loved the name. "Jeannine" was Kathleen's mother's name.

So now we were a family of 5!

PRESSING FORWARD IN GARFIELD

Trying (unsuccessfully) to move on. In the spring of 1993, after taking this battery of vocational tests, I resolved to put together a Presbyterian Personal Information Form or PIF (personal dossier or resumé) to see if I couldn't find a position in a church elsewhere. But somehow looking over the "Opportunity Lists" that the denomination circulated seemed to leave me cold. Everything just seemed more of the same. I really wanted to teach – but could not figure where it was that I would go to teach the kinds of subjects I wanted to teach. A secular classroom held no interest to me. And from what I could tell of the church-related colleges, they hardly differed from the secular colleges in their course offerings. Nor did I see how I would fit into the specialized world of the seminaries.

I did interview with a number of churches over the next several years, one in Chicago, one in Florida, one on Long Island, one in California. But, for one reason or another, nothing came of any of the efforts.

Trying to settle in a bit in Garfield while I wait for God to move.
Remembering that it was God that had called me to this position and that it was God that would move me on (when he was ready) I began to focus a bit more on the issue of what I was going to have to do to make my stay in Garfield work a little better for me.

Basically through a lot of prayer and soul-searching I realized that I simply had to take rather clear positions on certain issues and go with whatever consequences thus arose. I was simply going to have to trust God and leave to him the problem of human reactions.

As for trying to cut back on my Sunday style – there was little hope that much was going to change there. I tried to cut sermons short – but succeeded merely in disappointing the evangelicals who felt that I was no longer giving them the "meat" that they were hungering for. Soon I was back to my usual 35-minute exegetical study as a Sunday sermon.

Likewise the extensive prayer time, complete with hands on for healing, remained part of our regular Sunday routine. Despite the fact that one cantankerous member of the old guard always walked out in disgust during these "unPresbyterian" prayers, I continued to pray this way for the rest of my stay in Garfield.

Likewise, we continued to use "joys and concerns" time for members of the congregation to get up and not only spell out prayer needs but also state their thanksgiving for prayers answered or for work that the Lord was doing in their lives. This too disgusted some of the old guard, who would get up and complain loudly during this time period about how horribly things were going, especially when (on the few occasions this actually occurred) somebody new had wandered into the church. This was a not-too-subtle way to guarantee that they would not return, that there would be no "new blood" to further change the structure and character that the old guard expected in their Sunday morning ritual.

Nonetheless, we stayed the course of opening up worship to the worshipers for their own testimonies and spiritual needs.

A deep change in Session membership. In November of 1993, the church went through something of a "revolution", one originally designed to bring me down – but which in fact had quite the opposite effect.

It erupted when an all-female Hispanic family (the mother was on the search committee that called me, but who had eventually taken sides with the "families") moved from the area, weakening the choir, causing two other choir members to decide to no longer continue their services. At the very same time, three of the "family" members resigned from Session (although one of them had not been attending for the previous five or six months). And Dot, the woman who had headed up the search committee (who had also come to ally with the "families"), now also transferred her membership to a church nearer her home. All of this was done to underline the point that I was ruining the church.

The presbytery's Committee on Ministry and its Congregational Strategy Committee was called in to attend the session meeting that month, where the families presented what they presumed would be the death blow to my ministry. However, what they were unaware of was not only did the Garfield church already have a record with the presbytery as being a church that had always given its pastors a hard time, but also that such church drama was tragically not a very exceptional matter.

In other words, both committees knew that they were simply dealing with typical church politics. The trick was to see what could be done before the Garfield congregation self-destructed over this matter. Instead of calling for my resignation, the committees suggested that the church undertake a serious rewriting of its mission statement, to give both sides in the contest a chance to work together.

But that was not what the "families" wanted to hear. They were interested in no such review of things. They simply wanted things to return to the way they had been 30 years earlier during their "good-old-days" at the church. Consequently, the old guard simply went into retreat.

But it did allow my support group to bring new faces onto Session, in replacement of those that had just quit. And the choir reconstituted itself.

Indeed in all this, the church reached something of a major turning point. Even the draining of the finances came to an end, as giving increased (not however on the part of the "families"). So yes, something of a "revolution" had just occurred at the church – just not the one that the "families" had hoped for!

Trying to reach the youth through confirmation class. Toward the end of my first year in Garfield I learned one of the hard realities of life in the mainline church. I was excited about the dozen youth that were attending regularly – with some apparent enthusiasm – my confirmation class. But what I did not realize was that for most of them, completing that course would be a sort of "graduation" event – and that having "completed" confirmation and thus Sunday School, their parents would no longer be returning them to church. So instead of building a new youth program on the momentum of the confirmation class, we found the next fall that we had only a handful of these youth still around to work with.

Logos. A parent of one of the remaining youth, Janice (who also was a session member), came to me with the concern that if we didn't get something going, we were likely to lose her daughter from all participation. Fortunately, she had heard of a youth program called Logos, was highly impressed by it, and asked me to take a look at it. It looked good to me. It offered a training seminar to introduce the program to inquirers – an intensive retreat type of program of several days duration, which however took place during the week. Thus it was that she and I and another person, Craig, a newcomer to the church and a father of two of our younger children, took time off to attend the training seminar. It was a wonderful experience, a spiritual experience even, and we came back enthusiastic.

The enthusiasm was not to last long however. Janice brought the matter to Session to get its approval, which we both thought would be just a formality. But this was in my second year in Garfield. The proposal was met explosively by some of the "family" members of Session! "How could we even think of undertaking any new programs, when we had hardly begun to digest the changes already underway?" Janice was shocked; but so was I. Considering the fact that those who were doing the protesting had no children of their own in the church, that the program was entirely self-supporting and would cost the church nothing – their opposition made absolutely no sense to us. But the voices of opposition were not to be moved on this matter. Thus the idea simply got tabled – at least for a while.

The Creation Festival. Meanwhile I moved ahead with the youth on another front. In June (1992), Craig and another young man of the congregation in his 20s (Rich) and I took about 8 of our youth on a weeklong retreat in the mountains of Pennsylvania. Here 40,000 youth and adults gathered to live in self-provided tents, fighting flies and surviving the early summer heat (mixed with frequent freezing downpours) in order to participate in what can best be described as one big ongoing Christian rock concert (with teaching and preaching interspersed) including D.C. Talk, the Newsboys,

Amy Grant, and a whole host of other Christian rock groups. We all loved it. We prepared our own meals over a kerosene stove, stood in very long lines for the few available showers (until the men decided to brave the freezing water from the more readily available water spigots to do bucket-baths in our swimming trunks) and came home from it all to sleep for days!

Logos: success! The following year (1993), we decided to raise the idea of Logos again. And we found us a very capable leader: the whole group of us committed to the project! And this time when the Logos proposal was put before Session, thankfully this time it was approved.

The "group" got to work putting this very complex midweek, full-evening program together (game-time, meal-time, choir-time, Bible-study-time). Then we signed up about a dozen young people for the program – most of them high schoolers! Now we were back in business with a youth program!

The youth were faithful in their attendance – enthusiastic really. We ate together, played together, and sang together – a real achievement for some high schoolers. But best of all was the Bible studies. We had three sections: junior high, freshman/sophomore and junior/senior high school. I led the junior highs. In the meantime adults gathered elsewhere in the church building for midweek Bible study, led by one of our elders. We would all gather at the end of the evening for prayer, dessert, and last-minute conversations. Wednesday evenings at the church were thus very exciting.

Disappointment. But sadly when the next fall came around, the two most charismatic of our youth, both seniors the year before, were no longer with us. Further, for reasons we could not fully explain, many of the others now had jobs or had become active in high school sports programs. The others, seeing that the leaders of the previous year were no longer with us, lost interest immediately. When we were able to sign up only 3 youths (with 8 adults committed to staffing the program) we decided to call it all off.

We were surprised – shocked really – for all summer long we had been expecting to come back in the fall with an even larger Logos program – not a smaller program. We really never did know what to make of this shift in fortunes.

The director of our Sunday School program, Richard, and I were mystified. Neither of us had a clue as to what to do. Instead, we decided simply to carry on as we had before, remain as dedicated as ever to Biblical teaching in our Sunday School work and leave the rest to God.

Slow recovery. For two more years things just dragged on – sometimes it seemed pathetically. Then gradually, very gradually, new children began to show up for Sunday School. Our music program began to sound a little better with more voices and we started to get three or four, then five, even six at times, coming out to one or another of our three age-grouped classes. We started having communion in Sunday School on the days we had it in church (3rd Sunday of the month), to the delight of the kids. Finally, we knew that we were back in business with a Sunday School program!

By the fall of 1996 we had 15 to 18 children attending Sunday School regularly. And we definitely had the makings of a very young youth choir – which I put to work from time to time in regular worship. The Sunday before Thanksgiving of 1996, the sermon I preached was actually an extended children's sermon in which I retold to a group of about 20 youth seated around me the story of the Pilgrims and their arrival in America. The Sunday before Christmas the youth even put on a wonderful Christmas pageant ("The Little Drummer Boy"). And almost needless to say, they were there to help in the Palm Sunday and Easter festivities next spring (1997).

Through having to depend on them to give new life to our diminishing congregation, we made them feel as if they were an integral part of the church. And why not? They were! Maybe this was what God wanted all of us to learn through this episode of growth, decline and growth again of our youth program. He wanted them to be an integral part of the spiritual development of the church.

✳ ✳ ✳

REACHING OUT BEYOND OURSELVES

The Chuck Colson Prison Ministry. I had long valued prison ministry for its power to train hesitant Presbyterians in the art of evangelism. Prison ministry offered Presbyterians an opportunity to undertake an unfamiliar venture without having first to become an expert in it – exposing them to the wonderful discovery of how much the Holy Spirit is able to accomplish for them in the face of their own inadequacies!

Thus it was that in my second year at Garfield I invited one of the staffers of the New Jersey Chuck Colson Prison Fellowship to come to our church and lead about 15 of us on a 5-week training program that qualified us for service as jail or prison "facilitators" (meaning staff or team) for weekend seminars. It was quite involved. But all but one of us stayed the course and ultimately received our certification. We were ready to start doing prison ministry. I was excited. I knew that this would make a big difference in the lives of those of the congregation that got involved.

A weekend of actual prison ministry was scheduled for April (1993) at the Middlesex jail (Middlesex Adult Correctional Facility) – and I put us on the list to attend. Even though it was an hour's drive to the south of us (but the car trips were always enjoyable anyway) the facility was clean, the guards friendly, the program very well organized and the seminar leaders warm, deeply faithful and quite humorous as well. Our experience with the inmates was just as warm and friendly – and there were tears at the Sunday evening closing, with promises that we would be back in a couple of months for the next weekend seminar.

And we did come back – again, again and again – for the rest of my stay in Garfield. And the Garfield participation grew to ten or twelve for each visit.

Testimony time at church on the Sundays following a weekend seminar was always filled with stories of something or other wonderful that happened during the visit.

However, not everyone in the congregation was so enthralled with all this. One member of the "families" once commented afterward to one of the parishioners who had spoken up during testimony time that if he enjoyed this so much why didn't he just rob a bank – and then he could be with these jailbirds all the time. Hah, hah! Except that when he repeated the comment a few minutes later to the same person, the humor was missing.

The Loaves and Fishes Food Pantry. When I came to Garfield, there was almost no contact among the town's various churches. The pastor of a small Lutheran (Slovakian) church nearby and I got together for a few lunches in the first years. And I attended one of their church picnics. But nothing much more happened – until 1995 when the mayor of the town called the dozen or so pastors together for a brunch meeting, the purpose of which was never entirely clear to me. The outfall of this meeting was the decision by the Lutheran pastor and myself to try to revive the long-defunct Garfield Ministerium. But in our early efforts, we really only got one more local pastor interested. But he happened to be the pastor (priest) of the largest (Italian) Catholic church in the area (actually just over the hill in neighboring Lodi)!

We three pastors got together several times over lunch to talk about what we might do to make the Christian presence a bit more unified and more "obvious" in this supposedly largely Catholic, but actually very secular town. A food pantry seemed most immediately doable along these lines. And the Catholics had exactly the place to put the pantry: a vacant convent building.

With that matter settled, we sent out the word that we needed food for our new Loaves and Fishes Food Pantry – and gathered volunteers from the three main churches involved, about 40 of us, to begin organizing our rapidly growing food stocks. We found ourselves inundated with food – and with parishioners from other churches in town (their pastors themselves were slow to get involved) who wanted to help out. Also, the postal workers made a huge Saturday morning collection of food for us – as did the Boy Scouts.

The most wonderful thing about all of this was being "the church in action" – Christians of all denominational colors working side by side to try to help lift up people in town who were struggling to make ends meet. Whether Catholics or Protestants, we discovered that we all seemed to have a very similar spirit – very evangelical. We not only worked together, but prayed together and helped each other out. Very quickly I become very close to those taking the most active role in the Food Pantry.

We didn't merely pass out food to families, but we prayed with them or just took the time to listen to their stories. Some of them were our own parishioners – others were from other parishes. Many were unchurched. But just as with the prison ministry – we served only one church, one Christ, one God.

The New Jersey Senate Committee on Urban Policy and Planning. One other area beyond my service to the parish ministry had opened up for me during my Garfield days: working with a newly created New Jersey Senate Committee, given charge to come up with a comprehensive plan for the state to work with its various metropolitan districts in encouraging urban self-redevelopment (1994-1995).

This had all started with my involvement in the New Jersey Kairos Prison Ministry, an activity I pursued on my own, quite early in my Garfield years. I had enjoyed my participation in the program in my last days in Mobile, so I sought out and soon joined the program in New Jersey. And I soon also found myself on the board of directors of the New Jersey Kairos program.

It was in the course of this involvement that I developed a special friendship with a fellow teammate, who served as the head of the New Jersey Republican Party conference (a bureaucratic rather than elective position). This friendship in turn led him to introduce me around to larger New Jersey political circles.

Indeed, he saw to it that I was invited to the Presidential Prayer Breakfast held in Washington in February of 1995, where he introduced me to a number of key political officials. He was also aware that I had once been a friend of Newt Gingrich, who just the previous year had produced something of a Republican political revolution, which swept the Republicans to power in Congress. With Newt also attending this same breakfast, he thus made it his business to go up to Newt at the close of the event and tell him that a friend of his was attending the conference, to see what his response would be when he mentioned my name. He said that Newt lit up, and asked that we meet before things cleared out. But by the time he was able to get back to me in the midst of the mass confusion that accompanied the closing of the event, I had to get started back to Garfield (I had a passenger to take back as well). We could maybe meet at some future date. But that opportunity never seemed to present itself.

However, although politics still interested me (in a cultural-spiritual sense) it was not about to become my new focus. Anyway, at the time I was very busy trying to help the Presbytery move down a science and theology road.

However I did fulfill a request made to me to put together a proposal – ultimately a 17-page report presented to the Senate committee in January of 1995 – on ways for the Republicans to push into the world of urban reform, a world that the Democrats seemed to believe that they alone had the right answers for, as well as the only valid experience in the matter. Yes, true enough. The welfare system – the same one that I came to realize had crippled the institution of the Black family and had sent so many Black males into the streets – was indeed their product.

But I had my own version of how to go at the problem, less programmatic and more personal, based on my own extensive personal experience in this matter. And that's what my proposal was all about: ways to effect true interpersonal (non-programmatic) social reform.

Anyway, my report was well received, some publicity eventually came my way, though ultimately nothing life-changing seemed to result from my effort. And so things went for me!

Deeper involvement at the presbytery level. Considering my catastrophic startup as the '"conservative" of the presbytery, it was odd that very early in my presence there, I found myself called upon to jump into presbytery activities. I was asked to co-chair the committee that planned the annual fall clergy retreat for the Presbytery – the other chair being someone I had known fairly well during my seminary days. Anyway, this was my introduction to the professional circle of parish clergy.

And of course not only did I plan – but also participate in the three-day event, held in the full bloom of the beautiful fall colors (mid-October) of the mountains of upstate New York. And thus it was that I was discovered during those days to be in fact a kindred spirit with a number of the pastors of the presbytery, especially among the younger set.

The pastors' Wednesday breakfast group. As a follow-up to that first retreat, I was asked to join a recently assembled weekly breakfast group of about eight Presbyterian pastors, all men, most of them of the more evangelical sort. What a group it was – exciting, alive. We had no particular agenda – except to form a bond that would undergird our respective ministries. What I learned from them was incalculable. Furthermore, I cannot imagine how I would have survived the kinds of pressures that I worked under in Garfield without their support.

At first I thought of myself as being something of a misfit. I was pastoring the most marginal of the churches in the presbytery. At the same time, two of the group were pastoring the biggest, most prestigious churches in the Presbytery. My problems were not their problems – or so I thought. But soon I came to understand that we all faced many of the same challenges, no matter what the outward appearances might happen to be.

Anyway, we not only formed a bond among ourselves but we began to make our own mark on Presbytery. This came at a time when our Executive Presbyter, Barbara, was beginning to soften the shrill style, knock off the edges of some of the ideological harshness that I felt was driving presbytery meetings during my first year there. And also, the breakfast group itself constituted a rather influential portion of Presbytery's membership (myself definitely not included!) and thus brought to Presbytery a more evangelical tone – though by no means a conservative one, for we were a definite mix on the conservative-liberal spectrum.

Our harmony helped to increase Presbytery's harmony – as we faced the kinds of issues that seemed to want to tear the church apart. Although the members of the group by no means agreed among themselves about the ordination of homosexual issue – the hot issue of the day – our own ability to differ on this issue and yet keep our close fraternal bond intact itself became instructive for the presbytery.

For the rest of my seven years in Garfield, I would look forward, each Wednesday morning, to my 7:00 to 8:30 breakfast time with these fellow soldiers in the Lord's army.

The presbytery's Spiritual Development and Theology Unit. In the second year of my arrival in Garfield, the presbytery itself underwent a very deep restructuring. In the reorganization of the presbytery, some new "units" (large committees) were created, one of which was the Spiritual Development and Theology Unit. Still holding the reputation of being a conservative evangelical – yet also having gained a reputation for possessing a certain depth of theological understanding – I was asked to become a member of this unit. This was quite an honor, for only three ministers would be brought on board this committee (along with 3 non-minister or "elder" members of the presbytery) – and there were a large number of ministers that had candidated heavily for the position. Ironically, I had not, having a tendency to not be very impressed with committee work. But in agreeing to the appointment, I actually came upon an exciting new venture of moving Presbytery beyond being just a large administrative apparatus for presbytery business.*

And thus it was that I took up the challenge of the unit's very new, and largely uncharted, mandate. It was up to us, the members of this unit, to decide what "spiritual development and theology" was to become, what its role in the presbytery was to be.

As such I worked with the planning team for the annual clergy retreat, actually serving as chairman of that responsibility. The intention was that these three-day retreats would focus themselves around these issues of spiritual development and theology. And so it was that each year we invited in teachers, authors, etc. who formed the centerpiece of the retreat.

Richard Tarnas. In my third year with the unit (1995), I organized, in addition to these annual retreats, a very special seminar on behalf of the Unit, one that brought in from California Richard Tarnas, best-selling author of *The Passion of the Western Mind*.

I was very familiar with his work, a wonderful distilling of the broad features of the intellectual-cultural history of Western culture, for I had been teaching a course in the Garfield church that focused on this very subject, and used his book as our primary text.

I had taken up this interest (bringing it humbly to my own support group in Garfield!) because I was quite concerned about how deep or far-reaching our rejection of our own intellectual legacy had become within our American culture. In the now-rising Boomer world, almost everything that smacked of tradition was being viewed as "oppressive" and to be purged from our contemporary self-understanding. With such "reductionism," we were supposedly going to build a much more enlightened culture – from scratch it would appear.

I knew this was indeed not a sign of our enlightenment but instead a sign of our cultural confusion. And it was coming on at a time when I knew our Western heritage was being challenged by a number of other cultures that had no such hesitations about themselves.

This was a dangerous development for Western culture – as history

---

*Interestingly, the chairman of this unit had been the president of Hanover College back in the days when I was there. I asked him about my Bible professor, the one who committed suicide. His only reply was that he had been a man with many personal problems. Well, that much was obvious!

itself bears witness. As the famous British historian Arnold Toynbee put it, it is not by economic or political decline that civilizations collapse; it is through moral and spiritual decline that they collapse. Our mood of social deconstructionism to me pointed exactly to this kind of moral and spiritual decline.

Anyway, I was (and obviously still am) not one inclined to stand by and watch it happen. Though I might not save Western civilization by my efforts – I wanted at least to give a try at saving the few Western souls that I could, by bucking the trend, by bringing back to light the wonderful elements of our cultural heritage. I would do it at home. I would do it from the pulpit. I would do it wherever and whenever I could.

And I was thus strongly inclined to challenge the presbytery to take a look at this issue as part of its own commitment to spiritual development and theology.

So – I invited Richard Tarnas to come out and meet with us and walk us through the high points of our own legacy – in the hopes of stirring a sense of loyalty and renewed commitment to the basic moral and spiritual values that have undergirded Western (Greek, Roman, Jewish and ultimately Christian) society for the past 2500 years or so.

I was very delighted when, in the fall of 1994, Rick Tarnas agreed, in coming East the following April, to lead an all-day seminar built basically around his book. I gave the event a lot of publicity in Presbytery – challenging my fellow pastors and elders to come out and catch a vision of our great intellectual heritage. I advertised the event in *The New York Times* (the New Jersey edition) and in a number of other regional papers. I put out flyers in every bookstore in the area: an author who hit *The New York Times* bestseller list would be coming our way.

I naturally made the decision to host the gathering at our Garfield church. I did this simply because a number of my own church people were excited about this event and were willing to come out to do the kind of work that hosting such an event required. They cleaned and cooked – and got the church ready for this big event.

I met Tarnas the night before the "big day" and found him to be an easygoing, open person – in fact a true delight. We found that we shared a lot of views in common, especially about the "basics." But having read his book, I suspected that this would be the case.

Deep disappointment. The day arrived – and disappointment hit deep. We had prepared enough food for about 200 people. Instead, only about 20 showed up, most of them from the Garfield church. Only two other pastors from the Presbytery came out for this event.

How sad it was really. Rick was dazzling – as outstanding in personal presentation as he was on paper. And only a handful of people were there to receive his wisdom.

I was told by one of the pastors who attended that the problem was that I had chosen to hold the event in Garfield. That was the kiss of death for such an event. I listened closely to this advice – a little late though.

Nonetheless, the people from the church who had worked so hard gathered with Rick for a picnic afterwards. There the conversation continued to flow, exciting, humorous, insightful. When I returned Rick that evening to his hotel in Manhattan we parted as friends.

My trip to Santa Clara (June 1995). A couple of weeks after Rick returned to California, I received a call from him. There was a world conference of the International Transpersonal Association that was going to be held in Santa Clara in about a month's time. It would feature such people as Huston Smith, Brian Swimme, Matthew Fox, Stanislav Grof, Rupert Sheldrake and many others, including himself, that would be leading panels over this five-day affair. He had arranged with the Board of Directors a scholarship or fee waiver ($250) for me if I was interested in flying out for the event. Was I interested?

Yes, of course I was. I had read the works of most of those he had mentioned and though I did not necessarily agree with them in their philosophy, I knew that I would be very interested in meeting them first-hand. In fact, I knew that this would put me in the middle of a very fast-moving "Boomer" philosophers' circle that I wanted to know more about. Ever the social/cultural analyst, I've always been very interested in anything that opened up another slice of our developing culture to my viewing.

I spoke to my Executive Presbyter, Barbara, (who was herself from California) about what she thought of the idea. You see, by this time she had asked me to actually chair the Spiritual Development and Theology Unit! Indeed she recognized in me some kind of potential that truly needed an outlet larger than simply pastoring the Garfield Church (she was the one who suggested and had the presbytery pay for my professional testing in Princeton back in 1993, and had taken careful note of the results).

She agreed with me that I would find myself in the midst of the cutting edge of the "new science" and "postmodern" philosophy circle – and that it would be most enlightening, especially given my desire to get a better fix on what is happening to our culture. She thought it was a great idea. So did I.

Thus complements of Barbara's efforts, I received money from the Presbytery for my flight out to California (red-eye special). Once there I rented a car, and found lodging at the home of my sister's boyfriend (Joe) south of San Francisco – just a 20-minute drive to the conference center.

It was amazing how it all worked out – so quickly, so easily.

The conference itself was, "interesting." An obvious "New Age" spirit hovered over the whole thing. It was heavily "Boomer" in age – mid-40s to late-40s seem to be the average age profile. It was a bit reminiscent of some of the hippie gatherings that used to take place near my Washington D.C. apartment back in the late 1960s, except that the flower children were starting to get wrinkles, receding hairlines, and a bit of gray and were a little bit paunchier.

The focus was on "spirituality." There was Daoist spirituality, Zen Buddhist spirituality, Hindu spirituality, Sufi Muslim spirituality, Jewish Kabbalah spirituality. Every kind of spirituality was present – except Christian spirituality. Rick Tarnas in his historical study of Western culture spoke very favorably about the Christian underpinning of our Western culture. But apart from that, the few times that any time anything Christian was mentioned, it was done so with contempt.

I was deeply saddened by this – for Christian spirituality has long been at the heart of Western spirituality. True, there have been some awful things done in history by the Christian religious establishment. But Christianity itself, the spiritual legacy of Jesus Christ, is the finest spiritual vision under the sun.

When I saw that Matthew Fox was leading a panel on Sunday morning, I was delighted that finally we would hear about this great Christian spiritual legacy. After all, Matthew Fox had once been a Catholic priest, had recently been re-ordained as an Episcopal priest, so surely he was there in the name of Jesus Christ. Wrong...! Much to my chagrin, what he talked about was the seven Hindu Chakras and how they integrate the essence of God with our own holistic being. As I left his talk, I wondered why he even bothered being an Episcopalian. Didn't Episcopalians believe in Jesus Christ? Of course they did. I know the great depth of Christian faith of many Episcopalians. But I was disappointed at the lost opportunity for a Christian official within the group to present the very spiritual gospel of Jesus Christ to this huge gathering.

That Sunday afternoon I took a flight from San Francisco to LA to visit my sister, Gina. Her boyfriend Joe was there ahead of me (they would typically get together each weekend, in LA or San Francisco, or the California desert or Mexico). I was still deep in thought about what I had experienced in Santa Clara. It all seemed so alien to me. California seemed alien. But seeing my sister was great.

I stayed on in LA for two more days. There was nothing to do during the day while my sister was at work. But she had a copy of *The Celestine Prophecy* (which she hadn't yet read!) that someone had given her. I myself had not yet read this massive bestseller – and sat down and quickly read through it. Then I reread it, taking careful notes this time.

This seemed to go right along with the rest of my California experience. I made up my mind then that it was time for someone to bring Christian spirituality forward into this huge swell of interest in spirituality. I would attempt it if no one else would.

I reach out to local "New Age" Boomers. With the coming of summer, I had more time to do some reading. I busied myself looking into the New Age Movement, the broad name for what I had basically experienced in California. I was trying to get a feel for its general shape and content, a sense of what some of the major contributors to the movement were saying. It was not an easy task because the whole thing was very amorphous. Structures were very ad hoc or impermanent – if there was any real structure there at all. Everyone was sort of a spiritual entrepreneur, with this or that idea to promote. It was highly eclectic, everything being borrowed from whatever seems the most "exotic", meaning non-Western – and especially non-Christian.

Then I noticed that a local Barnes and Noble Bookstore had a spirituality group that met in the store monthly. They were studying *The Celestine Prophecy* – the way other people studied the Bible. I decided to come out to their next gathering just to see what it was all about.

It was a large group – thirty or more – of the same age profile as had been at the conference in Santa Clara. The discussion centered on everyone's spiritual experiences, things that pointed to the presence of some kind of a higher power or consciousness (there was a careful avoidance of the use of the word "God.") The discussion often turned around the experience of feeling especially "spiritually-connected" to a particular set of events – or other people: "coincidences" that were much more than coincidences, much in the way I once was so appreciative of the work of *Fortuna* in my own life. Sometimes the talk reached to the idea of having connections (Hindu-style) with our previous selves (incarnations). But mostly it was a discussion that if you inserted a word here or there that referred to God or to Jesus, it would largely have been in keeping with the Biblical studies I led at church.

With this as a positive note in my mind, I jumped into the conversation – bringing Christian language into play. There was a bit of a stunned look on the faces of some. A few more comments and the group suspected that they had a Christian in their midst! Indeed, by the end of the evening they all knew that they in fact had a Christian minister in their midst.

Overall reactions were mixed. Some warmed up – and hesitantly followed up my lead. It seems that there were other Christians in the group, or people who had been raised Christian and still had some loyalties to that early inheritance. A few were even practicing Christians, including the group leader, Debby, who was a Sunday School teacher at a Presbyterian Church pastored by one of my Wednesday breakfast buddies. I guess these covert Christians had shied away from being "Christian" in their language in this discussion group in order not to be "offensive" to others, a principle that I obviously had just violated!

Others were made a bit nervous by this Christian language. There were a number of ex-Catholics in the group who had a definite negative attitude toward Christianity. There was also a Jewish individual who was very negative – but who had a generally negative attitude about everything. But there was also an older Jewish couple participating who were quite intrigued by what I had to say. In any case I silently decided that I would be back the following month. I wanted to see how my presence worked out over the longer run.

Actually in the next couple of months I sort of "fit in" as the Christian voice – if there was some question as to what Christianity had to say about this or that. People got used to my presence and those who at first were a bit defensive about it warmed up (the negative personality being the exception – although there was nothing personal about his continuing negativity!). Some of my own parishioners came out under my encouragement to become part of the conversation. But most of them found it less important to be there than I did, and soon it was just me that was coming out.

In the meantime this group spun off a smaller share group that met in the home of one of the participants. Only about a dozen attended this meeting. It too met only once a month. I became a regular member – and would remain so until I left Garfield two years later.

We became very close. Not only was my Christian witness accepted – but it definitely added certain dimensions to the discussions. And we all drew close as friends. As a share group, we held each other up in our celebrations – and in our hurts. They became a very tender source of support when my father died. They were a major source of encouragement when things were getting more and more unsustainable in Garfield. They even at one point put together a major food purchase for Kathleen and me when finances were crumbling at the church.

I didn't convert anybody to Jesus Christ during those conversations. But I made Jesus a part of our company. That included also the Jewish couple – who were intrigued with my explanations of Jesus' Jewishness. I made Jesus accessible to them in a way that surprised and delighted them. Maybe that was all I was supposed to do. In turn, their warm reception – at a time when I didn't always get that from some of my own parishioners – was a reminder to me of why I had left home, job with tenure, friends, everything to follow out the call of Christ in my life. I had not left to bring "church" to the world. I had left in order to bring Christ to the world.

This relationship with these "New Agers" was indeed for me a great blessing. I had Rick Tarnas to thank for getting me started down this road!

Science and theology studies. Over that same summer (1995) that I took up reading about the New Age Movement I also undertook to focus other parts of my reading on this matter of science and religion. One of the first pieces I picked up was Fritjof Capra's *The Tao of Physics*. I also looked at several works of the holistic psychologist Stanislav Grof, the holistic sociologists Dana Zohar and Margaret Wheatley, holistic healers Larry Dossey and Deepak Chopra. Needless to say, I was intrigued at the idea of a "new science"' arising – not through the abstraction or taking apart of reality, but through an integrative approach that looked at the nature of things as they worked together to produce a comprehensive "reality" – one that even included the participation of the scientific observer.

This of course led me deeply down the road of study of quantum mechanics: Bohr, Schrödinger, Heisenberg. Years before I had read books by and about Stephen Hawking. I now returned to those to look at how they did/didn't correspond to this "new science." And that in turn led me to look at works by the scientific metaphysicists, with Paul Davies turning out to be one of my favorites. And I also encountered Chaos Theory along the way – which opened up yet even another vista into this "new science."

Since ultimately I was motivated by a desire to understand how Christian doctrines and teachings interfaced with these developments in the "new" science, I turned to the works of Polkinghorne, Torrence, Barbour – especially the scientist and Episcopal priest Polkinghorne who was a prolific writer on this issue. I became very excited as I read – for I realized that here were some thoughts that were very important for the church to be aware of, ideas I wish I had known about when as a young man I was having such a struggle with the "reasonableness" of my Christian faith.

At some point in my readings, knowing that the best way to learn is to teach, I made the decision to put together yet another course at the church on this subject of science and theology. I advertised it at Presbytery for those who might be interested in the subject.

Once again, the turnout was entirely from my own congregation. But by then I was used to these things not taking on big ways and was quite content to study this subject with a handful of the Garfield faithful. We had a lot to talk about, to try to come to an understanding about, to reflect on how the truths of the new science related to the truths of our Christian faith (understanding that there can be by definition but one Truth). It proved to be very exciting material to study.

I decided on another tack in my strategy to get Presbytery to take a look at this issue as an evangelistic matter. As chair of the Spiritual Development and Theology Unit I had a lot of leeway about inviting key individuals to address Presbytery on the subject. So in 1996 I invited the head of the Presbyterian Association for Science, Technology and the Christian Faith (PASTCF) to come to the area to deliver a seminar on the subject – at the upscale Ramsey church this time rather than at the down-at-the-heels Garfield (I had learned my lesson with Tarnas) – and to address Presbytery the next day. There was a nice turnout of about 20 (mostly pastors) for the all-day seminar – and a nice reception before Presbytery the next day. Finally, science and theology as an issue had caught on in the Presbytery.

The following summer (August 1997) I had the opportunity to study the subject at Syracuse during a week-long seminar entitled "Rediscovering Cosmos." Here were gathered a large number of major writers on the subject of science and theology, including Kitty Ferguson who had written a couple of my very favorite books, one a biography on Stephen Hawking and another entitled *The Fire in the Equations* which was a wonderful survey of the whole subject of theology and the new science. Seeing that she was from New Jersey – and not far away at that, I asked her if she could be available to come and speak before a gathering of pastors (on the same model as the previous years' seminar at Ramsey). She was. She first came to speak to the whole of Presbytery in September. Then in October we held a full-day seminar in Ramsey. The turnout was again very good with about 2 dozen (again, mostly pastors) turning out for the event.

In the meantime, I undertook, with two other colleagues, to put together a presentation for our annual clergy retreat in October entitled "Chaos Theory and the Christian Faith." For two months prior to the event the three of us got together to plan out a strategy for presenting chaos theory in such a way that we could relate our own spiritual experiences to the dynamics of this theory.

This was easy for me because by that time my own Christian life was in total chaos – with my situation in Garfield becoming financially untenable. I was really living by faith in the midst of chaos and my actual situation fit right into the subject.

I was also aware that despite the chaotic appearances of my situation, it really wasn't just "breakdown" but in fact was merely the first stages of the growth of an entirely new, beautiful life pattern (even though I couldn't see it at the time – and even though I didn't know I was only a few weeks away from the beginning of the unfolding of such a new pattern of life centered on Dunellen)

Anyway, when the event finally came into being at our annual retreat site in the mountains of Holmes, NY, I myself needed to receive, to feel, to understand existentially, the weight of that idea of Truth amidst Chaos.

I knew it to be so in my rational mind. But I was hurting emotionally. Overall, just discussing the issue turned out to be for me a painful event. But it helped get me ready for what was lying just ahead.

NCD (New Church Development) possibilities. Meanwhile, I had never let up in my effort to move on from my situation in Garfield.

In early 1996 I was sent by the presbytery (again, with Barbara's considerable support) to Atlanta to undergo training, the Presbyterian Church's first effort at creating NCD work as a "programmatized" venture! Once the seminar got underway, I found myself in easy agreement with fellow participants (pastors from around the country, mostly much younger than me) that this was all just clever marketing analysis, that treated Presbyterianism as a religious product rather than as a spiritual experience. It all seemed a bit of a waste of time (and presbytery money).

Nonetheless, my friend Scoti had always insisted that starting up a new church was the only approach to pastoring I should give serious consideration to, for I was so "out of the box" that only a church that I myself had started up from scratch would truly be a match for my pastor-teacher skills. Others in the Presbytery thought so too. I had very clearly a strong entrepreneurial spirit and the kind of stamina that could stay with the demands of NCD work.

And thus after my return from Atlanta I got busy putting together the first stages of an NCD proposal for the Palisades Presbytery. We were particularly interested in trying to plant a Presbyterian church in the midst of newly reviving (or "regentrifying") Hoboken, just across the Hudson River from Manhattan. But the only problem was that there really was no presbytery money available for the huge investment required. We all knew it. We then thought about trying new church development at a movie theater (on Sunday mornings these tended to be closed, and thus available). But even this would require developmental money the presbytery simply did not have.

Thus it was that I applied for NCD positions in other presbyteries – but seemed to get nowhere with them either.

✳ ✳ ✳

EDUCATING OUR CHILDREN

Pre-schooling. Meanwhile, as our children started getting older, Kathleen and I were confronted with an important issue of our own as a family. How were we going to see to the education of our children on a pastor's salary?

The first up in facing this issue was our daughter Rachel. As a former Montessori teacher, Kathleen was highly appreciative of the benefits of some formal pre-school learning and wanted to enroll Rachel in a Montessori program. She finally found one she liked in nearby Maywood, one that would involve Rachel three afternoons a week at the school. Kathleen's mother agreed to help us with some of the tuition costs. So at age three, Rachel started out her first formal schooling.

Two years later we were able, through some wonderfully favorable circumstances that broke for us (well understood by us as God's intervention on our behalf), to get Paul enrolled in a special half-day public education program (also in Maywood) at age three. Both thus got an excellent early start on the formal learning process.

Christian schooling. In the meantime, an aunt of mine quite unexpectedly left us some money for the nurture, health and education of Rachel and Paul. When Rachel was ready to enter Kindergarten, we began to put this money to use in covering half of her school expenses at an wonderful private school in Garfield run by an Assembly of God church – known for its academic excellence, its ability to make the learning process exciting for the children, and its commitment to Christian values. Being a pastor, I was given a special price break on the tuition so that the costs ended up being not that heavy for Kathleen and me.

This was a wonderful "gift" for us at a time when we were struggling to understand our placement in Garfield. I remember coming home from having registered Rachel at the school, with a song of praise to God ringing in my heart – and a very new attitude toward Garfield! This helped us immensely to finally feel a bit "at home" there.

A couple of years after that, Elizabeth started at the same Montessori school where Rachel had been – and Paul joined Rachel at the church-school in Garfield. The Montessori school gave us a 50% scholarship for Elizabeth and the church-school charged only 50% more for Paul to join Rachel at school. In fact, all this education ended up costing us a monthly $133 for Elizabeth and $300 together for Rachel and Paul. We were indeed being well taken care of in meeting our family needs by the Divine Provider.

What a blessing this all seemed. When we first began to look at the educational situation how hopeless it appeared. But in fact how wonderful it all turned out. We were blessed by wonderful teachers and wonderful learning environments for our children. Not surprisingly, our children came to love learning.

This all served as a constant reminder that God will indeed take care of us if we will just trust Him. Kathleen and I were/are very aware of this care and have always celebrated it.

Travel. One of the things that meant so much to me growing up was the time I spent with my sister and parents exploring some part of the world, or at least America (but also southeastern Canada), which was indeed my "world" at the time. So I naturally had a predilection for family travel as something special. Also, shaped by the preferences of my own youth, travel for our family tended to be built heavily around historical places of interest.

Early on during our Garfield years, my sister, Gina, offered us a week in Williamsburg, Virginia, as part of her time-share exchange privilege. Rachel and Paul loved Williamsburg, Paul making the clip-clop sound of the horses as some of his first words (he was not quite two at the time and only slowly developing his language skills). We loved it so much that we negotiated a return a couple of years later, and ended up purchasing a double-unit time-share of our own at Williamsburg's Powhatan Plantation – scheduled annually for the very pleasant month of May. Thus regular visits to Williamsburg, and nearby Jamestown and Yorktown, became a key part of the Hodges family development.

Also, we found quite affordable a tiny September vacation home in Cape Cod owned by another Presbyterian pastor. And the sandy shores of Lewis Bay were only a block away. The kids loved it. Thus a week or two at Cape Cod also became part of our regular family experience.

And possessing the Powhatan time-share, we were able to exchange one of our weeks' privileges for stays elsewhere, from the mountains of central Virginia, to the shores at Hilton Head, but most frequently to Quebec City. The beauty of the walled city and the French language spoken in Quebec made the visit even more intriguing to the kids.

Regular travel thus came to be understood by our kids as one of life's fundamentals.

✳ ✳ ✳

MY FATHER DIES ON HIS 82nd BIRTHDAY (March 1996)

Growing up with my father. My recollections of my father when I was growing up was that he was gentle (though quite firm when Sis or I were disobedient, which thankfully was not often!), soft-spoken – and lofty. His adoration of my mother was total. I never heard a raised voice pass between them, much less anything that even remotely qualified as a disagreement. Father lived for mother first and then us kids next. That was the understood priority of things in our family. I never questioned it as a concept of what family life was ultimately all about.

My father's world was orderly – in keeping with his chemical engineering career. While his world was not distant, neither was it intimate, at least not in the way that at the time most people understood such a relationship should be. We did not play any sports together or do father-son events together. Indeed, the time he joined me at a weekend Boy Scout campout was so exceptional for him that I never forgot it.

Yet I understood through just the way we went at life on a daily basis how much my sister and I were loved by our parents. For instance, dinner times (unfailingly started at 5:30 on a daily basis) were very special, a time of family closeness, built especially around conversations that reached out into our world and brought that world to my sister and me in a special way. And Sundays were not only time of worship together at the Presbyterian Church in town, but also a very special Sunday meal afterwards (in which my father usually played the role of head chef!), and then an evening together again at church (Sis and myself at Westminster Fellowship youth meetings and my parents attending Mariners' Fellowship for adults at the same time) followed by some special event at home upon our return, my favorite being the making of sticky and deliciously syrupy popcorn balls!

And then there were our two-week trips together in our car, across different regions of the country (also Canada), which started up when I was in the 6th grade. They brought the family together in a kind of closeness that was deeply special for me. And they also left a deep impact on me, in particular in shaping my love of travel (my sister Gina responded the same way!)

My deep admiration for my father as I stepped into manhood. I always viewed my father as a very noble individual. But it was while I was in graduate school in Washington, DC, that this sense took on a concrete meaning. As already mentioned, my father had been tapped by Monsanto Chemical Company in the late 1950s to formulate and head up a new program in anti-pollution technology and corporate policy. For several years during this period he attended courses at Washington University in St. Louis to earn a Master's degree in the newly created field of Pollution Control. By the early 1960s he was helping Monsanto take the lead in this area – and was appointed by the Illinois Governor to the Illinois Pollution Control Board as their main technical member. By the mid-1960s, as the pollution problem came forward as a great national issue, my father found himself called to Washington for consultation on some pending piece of Congressional legislation. I was impressed.

Being part of the Washington D.C. scene myself in the 1960s, I understood the importance of Dad's appearances in Washington. Also it gave us a chance to get together occasionally for lunch and just talk about things. I realized that it was also my hope that one day I should be so important a person in our country that I too would be invited to Washington to impart my knowledge to the nation's policy makers. In this, Dad was clearly my role model – very much so.

Our relationship as I myself became a professional. I would say that this then pretty much remained the nature of my relationship with my father during my twenties and thirties – even into my early and mid-forties.

He and Mom were transferred to Belgium in early 1977 (living in Belgium was one thing in which my parents followed my lead however!) – and for the next few years they settled comfortably into Belgian life. My dad's job was to help the Belgian government clear up the Antwerp harbor, and the Schelde River that flowed (via a tiny corner of the neighboring Netherlands) to the North Atlantic. The Dutch would not let the Belgians expand their vital harbor at Antwerp without first making the Schelde River "drink-water pure." That was my father's responsibility: to help the Belgians advance towards that goal.

And as mentioned earlier, their home outside Antwerp served as a useful gathering point for Martha and me – and our friends that traveled with us in Europe during those several summers. My parents were gracious and generous hosts. They were, as always, awesome.

From Belgium my father eventually took his retirement. And then he and Mom traveled around the world on their way back to the States – taking an entire year to do so! Again – awesome. And once back in the States they remained always on the move. Most of the time I had no good idea of where they were located: in Illinois, in Arizona (where they had two more homes, one in Phoenix and one in Flagstaff), or off somewhere in the U.S. or the world.

We would try to get together at Christmas and maybe one other time during the year – though never more than a few days with each visit. My parents would usually combine a visit to Alabama and later to New Jersey to see me and my family with a similar visit with some of the many friends they had made over the years. It seems that we got no particular priority in the scheme of things – no more nor no less time was spent with us than with any of the many other people they would visit on such a swing through the region.

The later years of our relationship. Our relationship continued on its usual path during the years when I was installed as a pastor in Garfield and my parents were in their later 70s.

However, I began to realize that my father was taking a deep interest in a bible-study group in Arizona that he had put together with some other men, and this group was becoming of increasing importance to him. This was sort of a new thing in the Hodges family. I had grown up with a "reasoned faith," not a biblical faith. It seemed intriguing now to see my father in his later years starting to take a deep interest in this matter. It showed up wonderfully in the discussions we now found ourselves having about the Christian faith – and what it meant at a deeper level than just good moral common sense.

This was the first time in my life that Dad and I had really ever talked about personal things (my mom and dad had always left personal things for me and my sister to work out on our own.) This was the first time that he truly seemed interested in what I had to contribute. He had always been proud of my work – but not until late did he take an active interest in the details of my work.

His declining health. My father had always been the one with this or that minor health problem – even from the days of my youth. But Dad never complained about anything. Actually however, he was in pretty good shape despite the "this-or-thats" which came on from time to time and which he managed to get past amazingly quietly.

As he entered his eighties he was still going strong – though not as strong as Mom, who though almost two years older than him showed absolutely no signs of aging (she would die some fifteen years later of no particular cause, just days short of her 99th birthday). They were still going to Europe each summer for a couple of months at a time, each living out of a small suitcase that they toted behind them as they trouped to England, Belgium, Scandinavia, Italy, Poland, Russia, Finland (they had a strong preference for northern Europe, though also a longstanding love affair with Italy). Mom could outwalk many people thirty years her junior. Dad, I suspect, had a bit of a time keeping up with her. But he would do anything for her – even keep up as best he could. But the "this-and-thats" of his health were coming on a bit faster and I knew he was slowing down a bit.

In early February of 1996 (on my parents' wedding anniversary) Dad went into the hospital because of colon blockage – thinking it would be a same-day-surgery matter (he had undergone this procedure some years earlier). But the surgery didn't seem to correct the blockage. So about a week later the surgical team went back to redo the operation. This too did not seem to improve matters any – but left my father extremely weakened. He was having an even more difficult time recovering. Weeks went by and he was still in the hospital.

It was now March and my sister and I were getting worried about his failure to recover. I made up my mind to fly out to Arizona to try to cheer him up – though Sis and I were afraid that my unexplained arrival might cause him alarm. But it just so happened that his 82nd birthday was coming up on the 18th, so it was decided that this would be a sufficiently appropriate reason for me to make my way out to Tempe.

When I arrived a few days before his birthday I was surprised that it was my sister who met me at the airport, because she was not due to arrive from California until the following day. She greeted me with the news that even as we spoke the doctors were attempting a third operation on my father. I knew that this was sort of an all or nothing shot. The doctor thought that a third try might work – though it might also leave him so debilitated that he would not long survive the attempt. All Friday night I prayed for him – knowing as certainly as an experienced pastor knows how these things can go. On Saturday he was awake, though weak and unable to speak. Sunday by midday he seemed to be gathering strength, better than the doctor had seen in a long time (though from my point of view he was still extremely weak). But late in the afternoon his condition worsened. That night I expected a call from the hospital. But on Monday, his birthday, we awoke to the news that things were about the same – which actually was not good news.

By noon the doctors were trying various procedures to keep his blood pressure from dropping away to nothing. I knew that my Father's body was trying to shut down. Sadly the medication only seemed to be convulsing my father, giving him a frenzied aspect that deeply tormented me. By noon the main doctor was advising that we stop the procedures and let things take whatever course they would by nature. I called my sister, who late the day before had returned to work in California, to ask her what her thoughts on the matter were. She was very close to Dad – and it was very hard for her to say the words. But she knew it had to be. She had in fact already said her goodbyes the day before. So anyway, we gave the doctors the go-ahead to disconnect Dad from all the attachments.

His death (his 82nd birthday). A gentle peace came over Dad – who could communicate only with his eyes. For about an hour Mom and I sat with him in this quiet calm. I read from the Psalms. But finally I admitted to being exhausted. I needed to get a little rest, even for just a half hour. Their house was only a block away from the hospital so I decided I would walk back. But I was home only for a few minutes when I got a call from Mom, asking me simply to return to the hospital. I asked no questions. I knew what that meant.

When I walked into the room I found that I had the strangest disinterest in his body, which now just seemed like something thrown aside. Instead my thoughts rose up – high above me. Where are you Dad? Are you with God? Are you still with us in this room, spiritually at least?

Since I could not bring myself to approach his body, I asked a nurse to come in and cover my father. She did not understand what I was asking for and just sort of tucked him in with a blanket. I just let the matter drop. But I really did not want my thoughts about my father distracted by something (a body) that to me clearly had no further connection to my father who now lived on in eternity.

This was my first chance to really come face to face not just with my well thought through theology on death – but my actual gut deep response to the death of someone as dear to me as my father. I now knew that I really did believe what I had been encouraging others to believe. I knew that I really did believe in that after-life, that spiritual state of being in God's company. It was no longer an abstract theological matter for me, for it involved someone that I loved deeply.

The memorial service. There was a strange finality about my father's earthly existence as my mother and I left the hospital. There would be no funeral – for Dad's body had been left to the hospital for whatever uses med students studying there it would have for it. That was fine with me.

I realize that funerals are not for the deceased – who rest in God's care – but are for the living, to help them cope with death as they are best able. To me all the emotions poured out over a body lying in a coffin have long seem misplaced. I understand that most people need to express their grief through all these (very expensive) shows of tribute that go with the typical funeral service. But to me personally, a death is a time for remembering how God gives life and takes it away – that all life comes from God and all life ultimately returns to him. Death is a time for remembering that earthly life is but a portion (a small portion at that) of the larger handling of our eternal being by God.

A funeral is to me an opportunity for people to say their goodbyes, to give account of their continuing love for the one who died, to find a way of saying thanks for the part that the beloved played in their lives, to give honor as honor is due to the life and now the memory of the beloved. But it's also a time to remind people of the basics of human existence – and of the wonder and mystery of how that existence, through our faith in Jesus, ends in such a sublime fellowship with God.

But you do not need the presence of a body to do any of that. Thus it was that instead of a funeral we had a memorial service. There was a huge turnout of the retirement community and the church that Mom and Dad belonged to. The choir sang, many, many people offered testimonies declaring how my Dad had made such a huge difference to their lives. My sister, who returned to Arizona for the service, read a poem she wrote – and I read from the Psalms. And thus it came to a conclusion.

Some enduring thoughts. I still feel the "presence" of my father. And sensing that presence, I have felt a new kind of kinship with a wider realm of the departed saints. I feel connected with greater things – much, much more than I had previously. It's hard to describe what this really is all about. It's just something that's there, just like my father is "there." Anyway, I now view death not as the great divider – but as the great translator of our being.

∗ ∗ ∗

MINISTRY TO THE (POLISH) HOMELESS

Matthew (September 1996). In late September (1996) a new area of ministry opened up for me in Garfield. After my father's death in the spring, my mother decided to sell our Collinsville home (the one I had grown up in) in order to live permanently in Phoenix. Thus it was that in late September I headed out to Collinsville to pick up my boyhood furniture and some other household items. My first morning back in Garfield, as I was setting out the trash for pickup, Kathleen spoke up: "Some of the parishioners are complaining about couch cushions lying at the bottom of an unused stairwell. Obviously someone has been sleeping there. There's probably a big mess to clean up."

Indeed, I knew that alcoholics used our facilities regularly to sleep off a drunk – for I was forever cleaning out empty wine and vodka bottles from under the hedges around the church, and nasty clothes which they constantly left for me to get rid of. (I was not only the pastor, I was also the secretary and the sexton or janitor at the church!)

But as I came up on the scene, I was more than a little surprised to find someone still sleeping on the cushions. As I gazed down upon this person, with the slight bite of a cool late September wind nipping at me, I had but one thought. This can't be. This person will never make it through the winter if he has to live like this. Every winter we would lose 2 or 3 (Polish) homeless along the Passaic River (two blocks away) where they huddled among the trees, weeds and trash trying to survive. I knew that the police kept close watch on the abandoned chemical plants along the river – so they didn't even have that as a refuge.

Now I didn't make any kind of decision about "saving" the homeless of Garfield. Years of working at the Hanover Street Ministry with Trenton's homeless showed me the folly of thinking that I could do anything like that. But I made the decision on the spot to do something – even just a little something – to help out. I talked a little bit with the man, Matthew, though with his lack of English and mine of Polish, communication was elemental.

The beginning of the "Commerce Street Ministry." I talked with Session about my desire to open up Fellowship Hall three mornings a week: Tuesday, Thursday and Saturday mornings, from about 7 to 9 for coffee, sandwiches and Bible study (the Hanover Street formula). The response was very affirmative.

I then put the word out through the various N.A. (Narcotics Anonymous) and A.A. groups that met in our church (we housed 6 such meetings) – one of which was Polish. In fact the Polish group was very excited about the idea, some of the people even putting in money toward the purchase of food/coffee supplies. I made up neon green posters announcing in both English and Polish the start up of the "Commerce Street Ministry" (named for one of the corner streets where the church was located) effective October 1 – and posted them wherever I felt that they might catch the eye of the drifting homeless population.

Start up was very slow. Only a few would show up – sometimes none at all during the first month. But by the end of October, with the weather turning cooler, the numbers began to grow (slowly) – four or five, sometimes six, would come in. I found that oatmeal and raisin cereal was much more popular with them than peanut butter (which they disliked) and jelly sandwiches, so I switched my breakfast offering accordingly. I covered expenses through receipts for funerals (I was rather popular with a number of funeral homes in town!) which I otherwise would have turned over to the church. In fact I did a number of funerals in December so that I was able to buy about a dozen pairs of snow boots to give out – and about a dozen Polish Bibles for us to use in our study.

People I was working with in the Food Pantry turned out to be supporters of the ministry. The director of the Food Pantry had a thousand dollars worth of grocery certificates to give out, and so passed about $150 worth on to me. Richard (our Sunday School Director – and what some affectionately termed our "Associate Pastor" though he was only a lay leader) and I used that money for Christmas packages of socks, razors, shaving cream, tooth brushes and paste, and candy bars to give out to the guys (mostly about 20 or so males, and a few women from time to time).

We also served a huge Thanksgiving meal at the ministry on Thanksgiving Day, complements of the mayor, Louis, who purchased the turkeys, and Adam, a young Albanian Muslim restaurant owner in town who wanted to show his thanks to his adoptive country and to God by preparing the meals. We prepared for 20, with 15 showing up – and had a marvelously good time (one showed up later that evening and had a meal with our family!)

I also put on a Christmas meal on Christmas Day, though only a handful of guys showed up (I was told the rest were still sleeping off a major Christmas Eve drunk).

The shoes didn't last too long – but got traded for drinks, though I noticed that there was some shoe trading around within the group as well! One of my guys came out to our 11:00 p.m. Christmas eve service tipsy – and shoeless (even sockless). I was out of shoes, and very busy trying to get the candlelight service ready. But an elderly parishioner dashed back to his home and came up with a pair for the man. Our Polish guy worshiped with us that night in tears.

A couple of them did freeze to death along the river – though none of them happened to be from any that I knew (though the guys knew them well). One was a Polish woman in her 30s.

The 20 or so I knew personally didn't always come out every morning we were open, though some were regulars. During the height of winter (though thankfully it was a quite mild winter by comparison to most) daily attendance averaged around 8 to 10, sometimes more, sometimes less. Then as winter passed and the spring came on (though colder than usual – just as the winter was warmer than usual) we dropped back to about 5 or 6 in attendance. Some were getting jobs, as construction work picked back up for the spring (though there was relatively little building going on in this overbuilt part of the world).

The ministry matures. I always looked forward to Tuesday, Thursday and Saturday mornings. I didn't have any special agenda: I set out the coffee and fixed the oatmeal – no big deals. And when we seemed settled, we opened up the Bibles, someone read in Polish and, if I had in attendance one of my guys who spoke a little bit of English and could translate for me, I gave them a very brief commentary on the text. We passed out lots of clothing (again, compliments of my friends at the Food Pantry who constantly brought around clothing for me to give out) and otherwise just relaxed. I tried to give them this "hassle free" time to get their mornings started – and they obviously appreciated it.

I couldn't do much to help them out about sleeping arrangements. There were so many legal problems related to opening up one or another of the abandoned buildings in town that what I had hoped would prove to be a simple solution just did not come to pass. I myself had an old metal storage shed in our back yard in which two or three spent the nights staying out of the wind and away from the police. But it was hardly an adequate solution – either for them or my children, who keep a lot of their things in there.

But my family from the very beginning understood the seriousness of their plight – and my children were more than happy to help these people out even in their own little way of letting them sleep in their shed.

Shutting down the ministry.   When the spring came and numbers dropped off in participation, I realized that my work was coming to a close: we had gotten them through the worst of the winter that had so alarmed me. By June participation was so small and irregular that I finally called off the ministry until the fall.

But by that fall, my tenure in Garfield was obviously coming to a close and I just couldn't see getting something restarted that I was soon going to have to abandon. Nonetheless, several of the men from the church (myself included) did prepare a huge Thanksgiving meal to which about a dozen of the old Polish street group came. But by that time I knew when and where I would be moving on to. But at least it gave me a chance to say my goodbyes to them.

✳ ✳ ✳

CLOSING THE GARFIELD CALL
(August-December 1997)

We finally stem the financial outflow (1994).   From a very low point for me in 1992-1993, things seemed to have been turning around in 1994. In May of that year we held a very intensive stewardship campaign to reverse the steady drain on the church's reserves ($1,000 month since the day of my arrival in late 1990). The reserves were down to almost zero and something dramatic had to be done. So we did the dramatic. We challenged the church members to become tithers. The appeal fell on totally deaf ears from the "families", who had not/would not increase their giving even a penny in all the years I was in Garfield, even though it was they that were always so critical about the financial condition of the church. But the appeal did touch the hearts of the more evangelical members – and almost all of them pushed forward in their giving, a number of families stepping up to the 10% tithe mark. As a result of this change in the giving pattern, we finally were able to balance our costs with our income, something that hadn't been achieved apparently in 15 or 20 years.

But: the departures of a number of our evangelical families.   But the new spirit of giving was also a sign of the new sense of health among the "newer" members, the evangelicals. The down side of this new spirit was the readiness of these newer members to push on with their lives – meaning, leaving Garfield for greener pastures. That fall one of the mainstays of the evangelical circle and one of our biggest tithers, announced that he and his family would be moving back to Iowa sometime before Christmas. This would be a real blow to us for this was a family with young children, the husband was a member of Session and a regular in our youth ministry and prison ministry.

Soon thereafter came another announcement, again from a family with youth, the husband serving on Session, and both husband and wife active in our prison ministry and the Tres Dias renewal movement – and very generous givers. They would be moving about an hour west of Garfield to an area recently brought under development.

Both of these couples I had helped to bring back from the brink of divorce. And now with their lives patched up, they were ready to move on.

Then the following year (1995) another older, retired couple announced that they would be moving to Pennsylvania where they had bought a house. This was one of the old "families", but a couple that however had been very strong supporters of my ministry, both very active in the prison ministry, Session and prayer circle. The husband had been something of a spiritual director for me – a real help during the darkest hours of my ministry in Garfield. This couple was also very lavish in their financial support of the Garfield ministry, but thankfully would continue to be so, even from a distance, for the rest of my days in Garfield.

Things start to cave in. At this point you could feel our spirits sag. Thankfully we had not lost all our tithers, and some that moved away continued to send money to support the ministry. But definitely the wind was taken out of our sails just as we were beginning to make some headway. It wasn't just the financial loss we were feeling, though certainly that was a big piece. But the departure of these particular individuals took the very heart out of our evangelical fellowship.

In 1996 we had to appeal to Presbytery for financial support. My pension/health plan had not been paid in a while. We were meeting our other expenses. But I could not afford to jeopardize my standing with the Board of Pensions (which also paid for our medical insurance).

In early 1997 we had to go to Presbytery again, for an additional $5,000. Each time we begged for support we had to go before the Presbytery's Committee on Ministry for our appeal. This time they announced that this would be the last of the money they would be giving us. Furthermore, they recommended that the church admit that it could no longer afford to pay a full time pastor, and downscale my call to a half time position. We told them that we still hoped for miracles.

From February through June or July we managed to barely keep up with our financial obligations. But that summer, we had to face up to the fact that we all were getting stretched to the limit. What was left of the evangelicals could not go any further in covering the shortfall. The only recourse left was to reclassify my status to half time. That would cover the church's basic costs and leave the church with a little bit to maneuver on. We again called on the Committee on Ministry and told them we were ready to make the shift. We were throwing in the towel.

Now what are the Hodges to do? Of course there was no thought as to what the Hodges family was supposed to do about having its income cut in half (that amazingly never came up in the discussions about the church's situation). There was no talk of how we might make up the difference financially for the running of our household. That was because there was no such plan. No one had any idea at all as to how that could be done.

In any case in August of 1997 I underwent a halving of my cash salary (though we still had full use of the manse). I was now "half time" though nothing really changed with respect to my pastoral duties – which had never been that heavy anyway in such a small church.

Something that briefly looked hopeful as a salary supplement was a halftime position as new chaplain at nearby Bloomfield College. But as I followed discussions during the summer of 1997 about the possibility of such a position actually opening up, I realized that nothing was going to happen soon on that issue. The position had not been agreed on by the College administration, and there was not enough money available to pay for such a position even if it should get approved in the next year or two.

In the meantime, love gifts started coming in from various sources. One church in the Presbytery gave me a $1000 check to help out. My old buddy Courtney, back in Indiana, sent along $500. Some of the members of the church started giving us supplemental money. We found that by cutting back on everything to just the essentials we could get by. In fact, oddly enough, we started putting a bit into savings – for when the money didn't come in like that. But that moment never arrived. Like Elijah with his little jar of oil, we always seemed to have just enough to survive, but little more than that.

While all this was going on, I found myself very busy during August, September and October with my studies, and with various seminars I was sponsoring on science and theology.

John is born (September 21, 1997). Meanwhile, while all this chaos was deepening, another member was added to the Hodges family roster.

Our approximate 2 year spacing between our children looked at one point as if it were going to be repeated yet another time – except that toward the end of the second month of pregnancy Kathleen sensed that something was not developing right, and a sonogram confirmed it. Though her body had been triggered for a pregnancy, the egg had not really developed.

Another two years went by and again Kathleen found that she was pregnant. We were much more watchful this time – until sonograms announced that everything was proceeding quite normally. It was good to see Kathleen pregnant again; she seemed like such a living symbol of life and its unbounded hope. But anyway, this would be our fourth. This would be quite enough for the Hodges.

Kathleen woke up on a bright Sunday morning sensing that the time was close. Sunday morning – hmmm! I was more concerned at this point at getting a neighbor over to the house to take care of the children so that we could get away to the hospital than I was about what would happen to Sunday worship arrangements. In any case by the time we had the kids settled at home and Kathleen in the car with all her gear, it was approaching 9:00 a.m. As we backed out of the driveway, the first of the Sunday School teachers were arriving. We waved goodbye to them as they looked on in bewilderment!!!

The hospital was about 20 minutes away (Valley Hospital in Ridgewood, where Paul and Elizabeth were born) and we arrived and were quickly escorted to a delivery room. By this time, it was noted on her medical records that Kathleen was a fast deliverer. At around 10:00 we were settled in. The doctor arrived – a young woman who was a new member of Kathleen's obstetrics group – and things indeed moved quickly.

At 11:41 a.m. John Miles Hodges was born, 8 lbs, 11 ozs. He was very responsive and had excellent color. But there was something in the way he was breathing that gave caution to the doctors, so he was put in infant-ICU for observation. But two days later he went home with Kathleen, adjudged to be in tip-top condition.

He was built with a bigger frame than Rachel and Paul had been at birth – more like his sister Elizabeth. Indeed, he would soon find himself drawing the nickname "Bubba" from an amazing number of people who just instinctively wanted to assign him that title. So did I. Kathleen didn't like the name – but it kept popping up with people (but he soon would become quite lean in physique!).

Once again Rachel had a new doll to play with – though now at 8 years of age she could actually be of real use with her domestic instincts. Paul was pleased he had a brother to play with – though it would be quite some time before he could do so. I wondered as I watched Paul's excitement if the six years difference would prove to be too much. Elizabeth rather looked on John as the pet she had always wanted. We had to watch her, for she was a bit rough with the baby – having learned to play tough with an older sister and brother.

CHAPTER SEVEN

THE INTERIM PASTOR
January 1998 to December 2001

✳ ✳ ✳

DUNELLEN (January1998-January 2000)

The decision to look into interim pastoring. In October, I attended a week's session of interim-pastor training. But why now interim pastoring? First of all, my preference would have indeed been "new church development." And certainly the Palisades Presbytery (especially Barbara) had done everything possible to support me in such an endeavor. But the financial costs involved greatly exceeded the presbytery's own resources.

Then suggestions began to rise that I would make a great "church doctor", that is, interim pastor. Transitions in churches from one pastor to a new pastor tended to be traumatic times of adjustment for a congregation (as I myself knew full well on a very personal basis). Very often these transitions occur not just because a pastor decides to retire. They, in fact most frequently, happen because of a decision of a pastor to move on to a new congregation, for various reasons.

And such transitions tend to be a bit like a death in the family, or a divorce. It leaves behind wounds for the next pastor to deal with, making life very difficult for that new pastor. Besides coming on the scene with his or her own ways of doing Christian ministry (a jolt to a community already used to doing things religiously in this or that particular way) there are hurt feelings to be dealt with. This then requires a very special kind of pastoring, well beyond the normal definition of pastoring.

It has been discovered that the best way to handle such transitions is to bring in an individual who purposely is there only to help a congregation make the emotional adjustments needed to ready the congregation for a new pastor. Everyone understands that the interim pastor will not be that actual pastor, but certainly will lead (in a very special way) during this brief (typically a year or two) time of adjustment.

But it's not only a time of adjustment. It's a time of self assessment, of introspection as to how the congregation sees itself, its priorities, its needs as its faces the future. These matters must be made as clear as possible to a congregation, before it begins the process of a new pastoral search. Because it must know as much about itself, as it knows about the makeup of the pastor it seeks.

Thus it was that I agreed to possibly go down this new road of interim pastoring.

The call from Dunellen. Barbara's husband, John, happened to be the Interim Executive Presbyter of Elizabeth Presbytery (fairly close by in central New Jersey), and she put him in touch with me. It just so happened at that moment that one of the churches in his presbytery was in need of someone who could get it through just such a traumatic time of transition. Both the senior and associate pastors had just left the church, one week apart! They had not gotten along, the associate pastor having long served the congregation in the role as mere associate, and was deeply disappointed when the church called a younger man rather than himself to lead them when the former lead pastor retired. Tensions built over the years between the two (and their respective followings) to the point that the younger lead pastor was finally able to announce to the congregation that he had just accepted the call to a new church, only days after the associate pastor had turned in his resignation, in his desire to simply retire from the ministry.

Thus John passed on my dossier to the church committee that was now looking for an interim pastor. The Dunellen congregation being the most "evangelical" of the churches in the presbytery, he believed that I would be a "natural fit" in that worshiping community.

However, a short time later I received a phone call from the head of that committee, Ned. He basically was calling to thank me for my dossier, but to let me know up front that the committee already had two people in mind for the interim position and probably would not be considering me. He was very matter of fact, but nice, about it all. We just fell to chatting about things. I wasn't particularly bothered by the call – as I really had not given the Dunellen matter any serious thought before he called.

Then a couple of weeks later, just as I was about to head off to the interim-training seminar I got a call back from the same man. He told me that the situation in Dunellen had taken some new turns and now the committee was indeed interested in interviewing me. I told him that I would be glad to do so after my return from the seminar. We agreed to get together in early November.

During the seminar held at Stony Point, NY, this phone call was somewhat in the back of my mind – though only just slightly.

Now a week or so after my return I found myself on the way to an interview in Dunellen, not sure what to make of the matter.

The interview itself went completely smoothly. I enjoyed it very much

– but had learned not to read too much into anything. , except that upon my return to Garfield a call had already been put through to Kathleen. It seems that within a few minutes of my departure they came to a unanimous decision that I was the one for the job. So I gave them a call – told them I was interested. And that was that.

They wanted me to start as soon as possible. In one way I wanted to get on with my life. I had every good reason to leave the next day for Dunellen – and a whole new world (and full-time pay). But I realized that we were getting close to the Christmas season – and I really felt that I needed to stay through to the end of the year to bring my life to a proper close in Garfield. And so it was: the family and I would be moving to Dunellen in time for me to take up my duties there on January 1st, 1998.

Saying goodbye to Garfield. When I informed the Garfield session of what was up, I was not expecting the stunned reaction. I couldn't imagine that they hadn't figured out that the Hodges family just could not go on like this forever.

Anyway, despite the millions of reasons why it had to be, the decision did not come as easily as I thought it would. Our kids didn't understand things from our perspective. Garfield was all they knew of life. The only friends they had ever known were in their Garfield world. I didn't think it was much they were leaving. But they didn't know that. Garfield was everything to them.

It had been a very tough seven years. I was exhausted – physically, emotionally and spiritually.

Anyway, we finished out a fairly normal Christmas season during which my widowed mother paid us her annual Christmas visit, and during which we packed, and packed. It was a strange Christmas for me. Life was both highly disrupted and yet very good – full of promise. I knew that a major chapter in my life was coming to a close. And I was anxious to get on to the next chapter.

Dunellen – and the First Presbyterian Church. Dunellen is a tiny town (1 mile square) located just to the west of Plainfield. It is an old middle class town with nice-sized homes set back from tree lined streets. The First Presbyterian Church sits behind a small park facing the main north south street, Washington Avenue. Intersecting Washington Avenue is Dunellen Avenue, where are situated both the church and the 2 manses owned by the church. Dunellen Avenue is a broad, quiet, tree lined street, with large turn of the century (or earlier) homes facing out on it. I fell instantly in love with the area. It reminded me very much of Georgia Avenue in the Oakleigh Garden District of Mobile – which I once loved dearly.

The church is a complex of buildings attached to the sanctuary, which seemed as I was being escorted through it all to be a veritable labyrinth of rooms. The sanctuary is painted white and is light and airy with warm hues from the stained-glass windows.

When I arrived at Dunellen, they were debating about going to one worship service – for their membership had dropped from a high in the late 1960s of almost 2000 members down to the present size (officially) of 577 members. But for me, at over 500 members it was still a very big church. Anyway, we would continue the two-services policy.

Also, as just explained, they had had two pastors leading the congregation. That was another decision they had made: to have only a single pastor (to avoid future conflict, the likes of which they had been dragged through?) and instead of hiring an associate pastor, to hire a number of part time parish workers instead. That nonetheless left the solo pastor with a lot of responsibilities that parish workers could not pick up on, such as weddings, funerals, a multitude of worship services, meetings, etc.

But anyway, I was glad to be busy again – even if the pace at times seemed totally hectic.

"What are your plans?" I was very pleased to have received this invitation to serve as the Interim Pastor of this church – even though it meant that it would be only for a relatively brief period of time. But I felt that finally God had called me forward from a long stalled life.

When I was presented to the new Elizabeth Presbytery to transfer my pastoral credentials there, among those at the presbytery meeting was an acquaintance from my days in seminary. I know he was trying to "promote" me a bit before the others – but what he had to say on my behalf seemed a bit ironic as he spoke up.

His comments went something like this:

Miles, we're very pleased to have you join us as an interim pastor. Your talents are quite extensive and we're fortunate have you as a part of our presbytery. But really, Miles, you ought to be coming among us on a more permanent basis – with a regular call to a church, one where your talents can really take hold. Do you have plans along those lines? Indeed, Miles, what are your plans?

Of course I was so glad to be moving on from Garfield that I wasn't thinking much beyond the opportunity that Dunellen offered me – even if it was only as an interim pastor. But more than that – I remember thinking: plans?

With a sort of grin taking over my countenance, I spoke up exactly in that manner:

> *"Plans? When was the last time I had 'plans'? I used to be a*
> *person of great plans. As a Yuppie, I had great five year plans*
> *and ten year plans for life. But since I gave my life in service*
> *to the Lord, plans are one of the many things I have had to*
> *give up. In working for the Lord, I have found that my plans*
> *are pointless – as I end up doing pretty much what God wants*
> *me doing, when he wants me doing it, anyway. I have learned*
> *more recently simply to look to the day – and let the Lord worry*
> *about tomorrow."*

And I was serious – for that had indeed been a definite part of the "deal" I
had worked out with God.

The SCC. In the few months that had elapsed between the departure of
the two previous pastors and my arrival, a committee called the Session
Communications Committee (SCC) had been put into place to provide
leadership for worship and other day-to-day matters facing the church. I
asked the four members of the SCC to stay in place as a weekly advisory
group to help me become acquainted with the church and its ways. And
as the rest of the "staff" was also almost as new on the job as I was, I
was going to have to depend on the SCC to familiarize me with procedures
around the church. For the next 9 months this committee (eventually
joined by the other staff members) served as an invaluable sounding board
for church policies.

Becoming their pastor. There were a number of funerals in that first
month, including a venerable saint who had long served previous pastors
as the Clerk of Session. Another funeral that month was of a four-month-
old child that a number of us had prayed over with the oil of anointing – and
that we had thought was making miraculous recovery – when suddenly
he died. These funerals involved the church in important spiritual rites of
passage that called on all my pastoral strengths. But thankfully the Spirit
was with me.

What surprised me the most was that the divisions that I was told
to expect, between the factions that had lined themselves up behind the
previous contending pastors, just never really surfaced – not on Session,
and not even within the congregation. I'm not sure why. These loyalties
had been quite strong. But maybe everyone knew that it was simply time
to move on.

In short, I just sort of fell easily into the role of pastor – and the church seemed quite welcoming of me in that role. For me, having spent seven years doing battle with contending power groups in the Garfield church, this was itself very healing. It's as if God knew what the Dunellen church and I both needed. Well, of course!

The worship issue (again!). There was, of course, one issue awaiting me in Dunellen – the issue that would follow me wherever the Lord directed me as a pastor: the matter of the structure and timing of worship.

The sermon tapes I had submitted to the committee that called me to Dunellen were of typical teaching sermons (I didn't have "favorite" sermons, but usually just sent on the tapes of the most recent sermons I had preached) which probably ran 30 to 40 minutes or so in length – though I was not sure since I had ceased timing my sermons long before. But the issue was passed over quickly in the original interview. They had liked the sermons very much and hadn't given any thought to their length.

In part the inevitable length-of-sermon issue was eased at Dunellen by the fact that the well beloved "emeritus" pastor of 30 years at the church (who had retired eight years earlier) preached sermons that had to fill a half-hour radio time slot – so his sermons obviously ran certainly longer than the normal Presbyterian 18-to-20-minute limitation. Also, the immediately previous pastor tended to preach for about 25 minutes – but managed to keep the overall dimensions of worship "in bounds" by cutting verses from hymns and eliminating such things as children's sermons when baptisms or communions were also to take place (with the two sacraments presumably never taking place on the same Sunday). So services previously had run maybe an hour and ten minutes at the most.

Upon my arrival in Dunellen worship immediately went extensively past that time frame.

But the issue was not just a matter of the sermon length. I always invited elders to participate in worship in various capacities – and most notably in the harvesting of the joys and concerns of the congregation in preparation for Sunday morning prayers (which they then led). Without the pastor running a tight rein on congregational participation, these joys and concerns could get to be numerous, especially as the congregation came to understand that it was okay to speak up during worship about something on their hearts. Not surprisingly, joys, concerns and prayers of the people often ran to over ten minutes – instead of just the 2 or 3 minutes of typical Presbyterian prayer time.

Also, I encouraged the choir to contribute their own music more than once in the service. Besides, we alternated each week between standard Presbyterian hymnody (three hymns) and the newer praise medley by which we called the congregation to worship with a number (at least 5) of praise songs – plus two hymns elsewhere in the service.

Also, I took the children's sermon very seriously. I introduced the major points of the regular sermon to the children in the children's sermon so that they could also be a part of the message that I felt God was bringing the church that particular Sunday. It also helped introduce the regular sermon. Thus I did not eliminate the children's sermon because it conflicted with communion or baptism.

And finally – I love to pray. I reserved the leading of the opening prayer of adoration and confession for myself as part of my contribution to worship (the other parts being the sermon and the sacraments). And these prayers were moved by a keen desire to bring the people to a sense of standing before Almighty God – placing mortal flesh before Pure Holiness – and moving the worshippers to a spirit of both profound repentance and equally profound forgiveness. Anyway, the opening prayers and assurance of pardon might have lasted as long as 4, 5, 6 minutes – which to a worshipper used to that ritual lasting no more than a couple of minutes, such 4 to 6 minutes might have seemed like an eternity.

The reaction. All in all, services got lengthened to around an hour and 30 minutes – and with communion, sometimes even longer. Needless to say, it was not long before mutterings could be heard from the older Presbyterians who were certain that no one ever worshipped that long!

The reaction was not all negative. In fact quite the contrary. On the part of many, the response was highly enthusiastic. And on the part of the large majority at least, the reaction was "give it a try." Mostly everyone enjoyed worship – except those who opposed the change as a matter of principle.

Preaching. My preaching in Dunellen remained pretty much as it always had been: heavily scriptural with a lot of spiritual struggle to gain a hearing of what I perceived as God's message to us through the scriptural work. My preparation style remained consistent with what it had been in Garfield: sitting with the scripture all week and then overnight Saturday, on the couch and with the light on all night, making the last struggle to gain that divine hearing. I would prepare a final draft of the sermon in the wee hours of Sunday morning and then reduce that down to an outline on a half-sheet of paper – which once I started preaching I tended to work without anyway. The whole process was designed to make me the message – everything that I was and thought as I came to the pulpit.

Actually "coming to the pulpit" had not been something I had done for years when I came to Dunellen – for I had taken up the practice in Garfield of preaching from the center aisle. But I was asked to preach from the pulpit, as the previous pastor had also preached from the center aisle, which some of the members complained about. I agreed to do so – even though the pulpit was backed up almost to the chancel wall – so that you had to preach even past the choir to the congregation. It felt very remote from there. But since there were bigger issues centering on my preaching, I figured that this was something that we didn't need to add to the list of issues.

At first my preaching was topical – as I laid out during the first few months the basics of the gospel: God's perfect creation, human sin and the fall, God's loving efforts to heal the breach with the Law, the Prophets and finally his own Son. I preached a Jesus, fully-human and put under the same temptations and struggles as the rest of us humans, yet fully divine, without sin, and the embodiment of the Way, Truth and Life which is the only Way to restored unity with the Father.

Eventually I took up my Garfield practice of preaching the *lectio continua*, that is, preaching through a whole book of the bible, chapter by chapter, verse by verse. I started with Paul's letter to the Ephesians – which took us from the late Spring to the mid Fall. Then I took up the Gospel of John – with an Advent/Christmas break preaching from the Advent and Christmas passages of the Gospel of Luke. This continued on through May of the next year, when I returned to more topical preaching around the subject of the meaning and content of "faith."

Biblical teaching. As I am by nature a teacher, one of the things I took up immediately upon my arrival in Dunellen was Bible study – starting off with a course on Paul's letter to the Romans, and then after completing the Romans study, moving on to a study of the Gospel of Mark. Although all of this was very familiar material to me, as it was to some of those attending the class, we all enjoyed the process of letting God's Spirit bring us to an ever-deeper appreciation of God's Word to us through such Scripture.

Teaching Western Civilization's grand development. By the summer I was also ready to introduce the material I had been developing in Garfield – and which first appeared in various stages of completion on my first personal homepage or website that I set up around that time (1998). It was made up basically of a survey of the historical development of the Great Ideas of our Western culture. The primary focus was on our Western "cosmology" – our view of the universe and our understanding of our place within it. As such, it included a lot of material relating to the matter of science and theology.

In our Dunellen study group, we started up with a lengthy study of the ancient Greeks, especially Plato and Aristotle, who are, in many ways, basic models for much of subsequent Western intellectual theory. We discussed the Roman and Jewish contributions – and then focused on Christ and the early Church as the culminating amalgam for Western thought. We discussed the impact on Christianity of its "establishment" as the official Roman religion (I call this the "Romanization of Christianity"), the material decline of Rome, the onslaught of the Germans and Arabs, the survival of the Roman church, and the "Dark Ages," including both Charlemagne and the coming of the Vikings. We discussed at length the impact of the crusades, the emergence of the High Middle Ages, the Italian and Northern European Renaissance, and the weakening of "Medieval Christendom."

By the fall we were studying closely the rise of the new scientific cosmology under Copernicus, Galileo and Kepler, the challenge of the established church during the Reformation, and the new intellectual individualism which began to emerge within Western culture during this time. Then we looked at the early "Enlightenment" – such revolutionary thinkers as Descartes, Spinoza, Leibniz, Hobbes – but especially Newton and Locke. By the Christmas season we were studying the later Enlightenment and Christian thinkers: Berkeley, Rousseau, Hume, Kant. We also studied the Christian "Great Awakening" in the mid-1700s of Whitfield, Wesley, Freylinghuizen, Edwards and others. Things slowed up a bit after the New Year with a number of special activities coming on. But we did manage to look comparatively at the American and French Revolutions, Napoleon, and then the philosopher Hegel – before we shut down for Lent. Following Lent, we discussed the 19th-century extension of the materialist vision of life (Darwin and Marx) and then turned to the discoveries in physics in the 19th and early 20th century (relativity and quantum theory) that began to call this vision into question. We finally brought the teaching series to a close in exploring the emergence of a "new science" – with the possibilities it holds out for a truce in the battle between science and Christianity!

Amazingly, I managed to hold the attention of a dozen or so participants, who followed this whole series from start to finish, and who told me how much this "introduction to Western thought" had meant to them, especially in the way it added greater strength to their own Christian faiths!

And that – after all – had clearly been my purpose, from beginning to end. And I was very pleased to have been of such service to these friends of mine.

Outreach: "Praise in the Park" (September 1998). I'm not sure exactly how the matter came up. I have long had a dream or a vision of leading a church revival – under a blue and yellow striped tent, with lots of music, a message of repentance and renewal, and lots of prayer.

The Dunellen church itself knows the meaning of renewal – having hosted a renewal weekend several years back. But at some point in the early summer, we got into discussion within the SCC about holding some kind of a revival outside in the park just across the street from the church. The idea was immediately taken up by Session and soon a committee of three elders and myself found ourselves making plans for just such an event, to be called "Praise in the Park."

We figured that September was as early as we dared hold it – and the best month overall for weather purposes. But the park was reserved two weekends in mid-September for the Dunellen Art Show – and we would be starting up our Sunday School program in late September. This really left us only Labor Day weekend to work with. We decided to go for it!

We got permission to use the park on Saturday, September 5th. We hired a professional sound crew, contracted the services of a Christian recording artist to put on the main musical event, had a huge banner made up and placed across Washington Avenue at the park, lined up radio and newspaper announcements and even had me interviewed on a Christian radio talk-show (about 20 minutes) concerning the event – and other unanticipated matters! The church itself swung behind the event by putting together display tables for the multitude of programs the church operated or supported. We had Christian clowns, arts and crafts tables, and skits for the kids. And we lined up some of our own musical talent so that we would run live music end-on-end through the whole event. We bought tons of hot dogs, hamburgers, soda, ice cream – even a cotton candy machine – all offered free to those who came to the event (our Boy Scout troop volunteered to serve the food).

The day arrived – and the weather was an absolutely perfect early Fall day – mild and dazzlingly clear. Noon rolled around and we were ready. And the church was a perfect host – to the thousand or so who came out to see what this "Praise in the Park" put on by the First Presbyterian Church was all about. The music, played from the huge gazebo at the center of the park, was outstanding – not only by the recording artist – but by our own local soloists and choirs. In fact our Spanish-English and youth-adult mix was perfect.

Then at 4:00 we went into the worship portion. A lot of people left as we moved into this phase – but a lot of people stayed. From the gazebo we went into a worship of praise music. Then Silvio Del Campo (our Hispanic minister) and I presented an Hispanic-English message. And we concluded our worship with prayer – and with an invitation for people who wanted personal prayer to join our prayer teams where we would be glad to pray with them for whatever moved their hearts. Wonderfully, five or six long prayer lines formed to receive prayers with the oil-of-anointing. And thus we completed the day's activities with a powerful prayer ministry.

Assessing the event. All in all, it was a great success – though we knew beforehand that it was going to be a perfect success, just because of the privilege of putting the event on at all. We had made up our minds leading into the event that if only 5 guests came out that would be just fine – because the church itself had rallied to the call and that alone was cause enough for rejoicing.

Nonetheless – we had wonderful feedback from the locals about the event – and the continual question: "Will you do this again next year; I want to bring some friends." The answer was a big: "Yes, God willing."

But overall – the best part of the event was what it did for our congregation. We knew we were evangelical. But now the town knew that as well – and that's how we wanted to be known. We wanted to be known as a people on fire for our Lord Jesus Christ – ready to greet the immediate world around us in his name. We were not a closed circle of pious Christians – we were ambassadors of Jesus Christ to the world around us.

Our children's reaction to the move. Dunellen was such a pleasant physical and emotional improvement for me over Garfield that it really hadn't occurred to me that my children might view the move in a different light. My older, now-6-year-old, son Paul was for the longest time deeply nostalgic for Garfield. It was not that he had so many friends at his former school. The boy he was closest to had moved a year before we did, and Paul really had not formed up another friendship in Garfield in that next year. But something about Garfield, even the house, which was the only one he had known so far, seemed to be very dear to him. Elizabeth, our younger, just 4-year-old daughter, was quick to make a whole new set of friends at her new preschool at the Dunellen church and seemed not to miss Garfield at all. Our older, just 9-year-old daughter, Rachel, was both excited about the move – and sad to leave behind a couple of very dear friends, one of whom was like a sister to her.

Getting them slotted into the new life. Upon our arrival in January of 1998, Rachel and Paul were entered into the 3rd and 1st grades of the Redeemer Lutheran School in nearby Westfield. The public school in Dunellen was quite good, we were told. But still, we wanted our children to be educated with the idea that truth and knowledge were not matters divorced from the sovereignty and loving presence of God. The Lutheran school was an excellent one and thus we felt very good about that part of the move.

But it was not really until the summer when our children got involved in outside activities. Rachel, Paul and Elizabeth took swimming lessons at the municipal pool in next-door Middlesex, and Rachel and Elizabeth took a dance course at the church during the summer. In the fall Paul joined the Dunellen recreation department's soccer program and Rachel and Elizabeth continued their dance classes. Also Paul and Rachel resumed piano lessons in earnest in the fall – and so finally we felt that we had returned them to the level of involvement that they had left behind in Garfield.

They of course had friends at the church – though seeing them only on Sundays, they were not, at first, able to form as deep a relationship with them as they would have wanted. But with the passing of time, that changed, as indeed they truly came to make new friends there. Again, Rachel found a young lady at church her age to be like a sister to her. And even after we moved on in completing the "interimship," they stayed in touch.

Social life in general. Life in Dunellen was everything that Garfield was not. We had a huge number of friends, ones that could be as active as us in just enjoying the social offerings of the area, especially excellent restaurants, where we gathered often for just some time together, with no particular agenda other than just enjoying each other's company.

And it was a short distance from Princeton, where Kathleen's family lived, and thus visits were frequent, including their coming our way – often. Indeed, the annual Thanksgiving family gatherings of 1998 and 1999 were held in our large manse.

Thus it was that Dunellen became "home" immediately, in a way that life in Garfield never seemed to be able to attain.

I was not particularly active in presbytery, partly because I had my hands full with preaching, local visitations, and especially those very well attended Bible and history classes I conducted at the church. And partly this was the case because I knew I would soon be moving on.

The larger world. Clinton was US president at the time, and I rather liked his work, especially since the mid-1990s when Newt pushed Clinton to the "center" of American politics, by way of Newt's political goals outlined clearly in his book *Contract with America* – and the consequent 1994 Republican sweep of Congress.

Perhaps it was also Clinton's years at Georgetown (he was there the same time I was, though I don't recall ever having run into him back then), for Clinton's primary interests were more international than domestic. And in terms of foreign policy, he was indeed a classic Georgetown "Realist." This was something very important in my eyes, because with the fall of the Soviet Union, we were the only superpower to help support a peaceful world. It was a huge responsibility, one that I thought Clinton conducted very successfully.

Thus I watched his efforts to continue a very positive relationship with a post-Communist Russia. He also appeared not to be interested in dragging America into some great democratic crusade abroad, or "nation-building" as it was termed at the time. I was also very impressed with his willingness to quickly back out of a UN-requested intervention in Somalia, when it became apparent that the locals were not going to be supportive of such an effort. And I watched him undertake a very carefully measured response in Haiti, getting the country back under its democratically-elected president that the Haitian military had recently overthrown. And I especially liked a similarly measured response (with very strong allied backing) to the ethnic cleansing tearing multi-ethnic Bosnia apart. And I got to see that same response again a few years later when he returned American forces to the area to again put down ethnic cleansing, at that point taking place in Kosovo.

The significance of that Kosovo intervention in fact would become monumental to the Hodges family, though at the time, I had no way of knowing any of this!

Overall – and despite the scandal surrounding Clinton's behavior with a young (and ambitious) female White House intern – I thought he had been an excellent president. As far as the scandal itself, I did not know whether to laugh or cry. It was now my Republican friend Newt that had taken up the weapon of impeachment, for clearly mere political purposes. This was something that now – with two earlier Democratic Party impeachment efforts having recently taken place – seemed to be less and less an emergency measure and now just another regularly employed tactic in the American political playbook, a development that horrified me.

And it was all so hypocritical, as I knew full well that this was sadly rather common behavior in status-hungry DC, where sex, along with money and public attention, drove the political program, often Alpha women as well as Alpha men! Indeed, I was hardly surprised to find out that even as he was leading the assault on Clinton for his behavior, Newt was having another affair, this time behind the back of his second wife, with a woman who would eventually become his third wife, but thankfully one who in future years (after Newt abandoned the Congressional platform), would be part of his move into a serious Christian faith.

I was not one with any right to judge anyone else on this matter, for I myself had gone down a very rocky path before I found it leading me back to God and Jesus Christ.

But still, all this gave me much to think about. I guess I was back in the business of social analysis again!

The New Geneva vision is born. Indeed I was! Even though I knew better than trying to design my own grand plans for my future (much less the future of the world around me), I was by every instinct a social planner, materially as well as culturally and spiritually.

I had assembled various components in building a new desktop computer, complete with a relatively large monitor and all the latest (late-1990s) hardware and software, and found myself much engaged at the computer, putting together a new website (newgenevacenter.org). There I uploaded the masses of historical, cultural and scientific material that I had been collecting in all of my previous church and presbytery courses. But I also posted there the architectural design for a large 25-acre campus, complete with carefully designed buildings, sports fields, dorms and staff housing, where people (presumably mostly Presbyterians) could come for a brief (or extended) stay – to explore more deeply the cultural-spiritual world around us, past as well as present.

And I called this place "New Geneva", honoring the Geneva where I had once lived and studied, but also the place where centuries ago John Calvin had very purposely set up a "Reformed" Christian community, one attempting to live more closely according to Scriptural standards, rather than along the lines of the highly evolved ecclesiastical (and political) ways of the old Roman (Catholic) church of his days.

It was to Calvin's Geneva that reformers had come – from all around Europe – to study and participate in this project of his. This included those who came from England and returned as Puritans, and those who came from Scotland and returned as Presbyterians (for that matter also, those who came from France and returned as Huguenots!).

I wasn't trying to be another Calvin. But I understood what he was trying to do for the Christian community, bring it back to 1st-century Christian standards. And that was my driving motif as well. The church needed to get back to basics, and do its evangelical work within a world that had wandered far from God and his Word. And I thought that New Geneva would be a perfect setting for a similar effort to help develop the wisdom and commitment needed by Christians, to bring the church back to those same Genevan standards.

Anyway, that was the big project I was still working on as I finished my days in Dunellen.

ON TO POTTSVILLE (PENNSYLVANIA) - January 2000

The call to Pottsville. In December (1999) I received a call from a woman, Sue, in Pennsylvania, wanting to know if I would be interested in an interim position at their Presbyterian church in Pottsville. I said yes, but made it very clear to her that if I came, she should expect a very rigorous program of change to come their way. That was, after all, one of the main tactics of the interim pastor, to change as much as possible so as to get a congregation adjusted to the idea of "change," something that always accompanied the arrival of a new full-time pastor. When I hung up, I was really not expecting to hear from her again. But I really was not troubled by it, which was strange, because within a few weeks a new pastor would be taking my place in Dunellen, and I had as yet no alternative plans!

But I did indeed hear again from Sue, who told me that they wanted to interview me. And driving the two hours to Pottsville, I had the strange feeling as I passed the various sites along the way that I would be seeing a lot more of these in the days ahead. I met with the committee, they were pleased with the interview, and yes, I had a new job.

The church had no manse, and after much scrambling around hunting for housing with Sue, we located a rental in nearby Schuylkill Haven, in an old coal miner's home attached to another home, each only 15' across the front. We knew it would be cramped, but doable.

In early January we had a wonderful going-away party in Dunellen, and a few days later, amidst a very cold Pennsylvania freeze, we found ourselves headed to Pottsville (a huge moving van bringing all our furnishings soon after.)

Undertaking changes in the church. Again, being an interim, I knew that I had a lot of leeway in moving ahead with the preaching instincts I had. Actually, comparative little was said about the extended worship time that accompanied my arrival. True, a number of the parishioners were shocked when I put a 12' drop-down projection screen right there next to the pulpit, in their huge and beautifully adorned sanctuary (even Tiffany stained-glass windows dating back to the late 1800s). But most all of them made the adjustments, finding that they liked the verses of the hymns projected there from my laptop computer via a projector located out among the pews, and the way I also projected outlines, bible verses and related illustrations in accompaniment with my sermons.

I guess the unhappy ones figured that they could take the screen down after my departure. But it's still there, 20 years later!

I also had them get rid of the forbidding dungeon-like front doors to the church, and put more welcoming clear glass doors there instead. But even more, I gathered a huge team of enthusiastic workers, and we did a repainting and re-carpeting of the narthex (the greeting hall just inside the church) and a thorough makeover of the huge fellowship hall downstairs, not only repainting it from top to bottom, but also fitting it out with a fantastic sound system (thanks to a grant I drummed up from the presbytery), a multi-level stage, a screen of its own, deeply cushioned chairs for everyone to sit on, and air conditioning.

There were complaints at first when I moved summer services out of the extremely hot sanctuary (huge fans in the back helping hardly at all) and took them down into the air-conditioned fellowship hall. But the complaints were actually few, and quickly went away once the adjustment was made. And they are still meeting there in the summers!

And so things went. Indeed, as in Dunellen, we found our times there to be warm and welcoming. Ah, how easy interim work happened to be!

Schooling for the kids. At this point, our kids were fairly understanding that the world would not come to an end if they found themselves having to move on to new lands, new vistas, new people. They made the adjustment to Pennsylvania easily, and actually in good spirits. We quickly found schooling for them at nearby Cressona Christian School, where Rachel would spend 5th and 6th grade, Paul 3rd and 4th grade and Elizabeth 1st and 2nd grade. And John would eventually start pre-school at another church program in Pottsville.

They quickly found friends, both at church and at school, and fit into their new world quite nicely. Indeed, Jacob, the 2-year-old son of Sue and her husband Rob, would become like a brother to our 2-year-old John. And that close relationship would never change over the years, and still hold true even today!

Getting more involved in a larger pastoral world around me. Unlike Dunellen, here in Pennsylvania I decided to connect myself as extensively as possible to the surrounding pastoral world. I don't know why. Perhaps it was because I supposed that I would be moving on soon, and did not want that to prevent the kind of pastoral companionship that was so valuable to me in Garfield, but was not taken up in Dunellen.

Unfortunately, I found that the most logical starting point, the Pottsville ministerium (local denominational pastors) was not particularly interesting, though I hung in there for quite a while. Where I did find things interesting was a simple informal gathering of a few evangelical pastors, involving a planned event involving a visit to Pottsville of a blind man who had written how he completed the challenging Appalachian Trail, able to do so on the basis of his strong Christian faith. There I met Bill, pastor of the non-denominational Lighthouse Church that he himself had started up, and became very close with him as a pastoral colleague. I also met a pastor, Harold, and his chief pastoral associate, Darnell, both of them directing a mostly Black congregation, and formed up a strong personal bond with both – though especially with the associate, Darnell. He was blind, but musically highly talented. In fact, it was Darnell that would teach flute to our daughter Rachel, and, some years later, trumpet to our son John.

✳ ✳ ✳

THE NEW GENEVA PROJECT

The New Geneva idea takes hold. I also became very involved with the Lehigh Presbytery, even soon chairing a special projects committee, thanks to the Executive Presbyter, Harvey Johnson, who took note of my background of presbytery work in my Garfield days.

But he was particularly interested in my New Geneva idea. As he put the matter simply, why not here, in the Lehigh Presbytery? The presbytery is in possession of 16 acres of undeveloped land just south of Bethlehem, and it would provide a perfect setting for just such a project.

With that invitation, I began to assemble a team of four fellow pastors. The group included my old friend Tom, who came up from Philadelphia to get involved in the project, along with a young and rising pastoral friend of his, Scott, plus two other pastors who were in the area, themselves sort of between pastoral calls: Sue, a recent pastoral associate at the prestigious Bethlehem First Presbyterian Church, and Peter, someone I had known quite well in my seminary days in Princeton – whose father had himself once pastored that same huge Bethlehem church.

And the team included Bob (or Rob), husband of Sue, both of whom had become very close friends to Kathleen and me by this point. In fact it was Bob who was leading the team of Pottsville volunteer workers that had joined me in "upgrading" the church. It was Bob that even financed a good part of the expenses involved (the air conditioning of the fellowship hall, for instance). He was a very successful businessman, and I wanted him to serve as president of the New Geneva corporation, overseeing the business portion of the project. He was even willing to step back from his huge car dealership (turning over responsibilities to a young man he was training) in order to devote himself to this Christian calling.

In short, it was quite a team.

I redesigned the architectural structure of this project to fit the actual acreage and its layout alongside a gently sloping hill. And we worked – and prayed a lot for God's favor in this endeavor – for over a year. Then we were ready to call the first meeting of potential financial supporters, when the whole thing came crashing down.

The New Geneva project is shut down (July). It seems that many of these potential backers were members of that all-important Bethlehem Presbyterian church, and the Bethlehem church officers must have panicked when they realized where a good portion of our financial support was destined to come from. That church itself was about $500,000 in debt that year, due to the closing of the Bethlehem Steel Corporation, and was afraid that support for our project would drain off their own financial support.

What really hurt was that it was Executive Presbyter Johnson who informed us, only three days before the scheduled financial gathering, that we had to cease and desist. He used the claim that we had not gone through proper channels, and would have to back off on our startup. What was he talking about? He knew what we were doing every step of the way, and had been a big source of support for the project. And yes I had worked carefully to get the support of the various presbytery committees that would necessarily be involved in this big project.

So I know that this had nothing to do with "proper presbytery procedures", especially when we were told that we were going to have to meet with the Bethlehem church if there was to be any possibility of us moving forward on the New Geneva project.

So Peter and I met with the Session of that church, surprised to see one of those elders present a man who had been working closely with us, and who remained silent during that two-hour discussion we had with their session.

We were accused of starting up a new church, in a region that they considered to be their territory. We assured them that this was to be a study center, not a church. Well, you guys intend to hold worship there, right? Yes. Well then it qualifies as a church.

As the discussion dragged on, it became apparent that no matter what we said, they had already made up their minds. They would block our New Geneva project.

But how could one single church do that? The hard reality was that despite the fact that there were 50 or so churches in the Presbytery, the Bethlehem church alone provided as much as a quarter of the funding that the presbytery depended on for its operations. And that, not our failure to follow proper procedures, was what pressured Johnson to stop our project.

We go our separate ways. One thing was very clear to us. If God had truly been behind this project, nothing, not even the First Presbyterian Church of Bethlehem could have stopped its creation. Thus it was clear, very clear, that this was not what God had in mind for us to be doing.

Within a short time, Bob went back to his car business and my pastor friends moved on to calls elsewhere. Sue actually started up her own church nearby, an evangelical church (Presbyterian, but with no visible Presbyterian attributes) which she called "The Barn." Actually it slowly but surely did quite well! Scott started up a small Christian drop-in center in a huge shopping mall outside of Philadelphia. Peter took a call to a church in Ohio, which became over the years something of a huge church. And Tom took a call teaching medical ethics at the Philadelphia Medical College.

CHAPTER EIGHT

TEACHING AT THE KING'S ACADEMY
August 2001 to June 2019

✳ ✳ ✳

THE CALL TO THE KING'S ACADEMY (TKA) - August 2001

However, at this point I had no idea of what it was that I was to do next. I had poured heart and soul into the New Geneva project, and had absolutely nothing else lined up for myself at that point. Indeed, the Pottsville Presbyterian Church had already extended a pastoral call (actually to someone I knew in seminary), though she would not be taking up that call until some many months hence. Thus I still had a job, at least until just after Christmas.

So here I was again, looking for a job!

The phone call to and interview with Barbara. It was at this point that one of my parishioners spoke up. She had visited a newly-opened Christian school about a half-hour to the south of where we were living, thinking of enrolling one of her sons there. It had come across her mind that I would be a real gift to the school as one of its teachers, if I was interested. Would I please call the founder and head of the new school (another Barbara!)?

And so I found myself making that call, and hearing Barbara's response: "Oh yes, we are indeed in need of someone with your background, to teach history to our junior-high and high-schoolers." But then she went on to say that the salary was unfortunately very low, only $25,000 (only a little over a half of what I was making as a pastor) – with no health benefits or pension payments offered in compensation either. Furthermore, they could offer (for the first year anyway) only 5/8ths of the $25,000 salary, as I would be teaching only in the mornings, the 5 courses prior to lunch (I would not be needed for the 3 afternoon classes).

Wow, how was a family of six supposed to live off that salary (my rent alone was over $500 a month)? But the "Voice" made it very clear to me that I was to accept this offer, that this would be my next move in life.

And so I took up the challenge, very aware that if this were of God, He and He alone would make this work. And on that basis I found myself

215

heading to an formerly abandoned elementary-level school house that had recently come into the hands of this small group of Christian teachers and supporters.   And I arrived to see before me an old brick country school, with newly-installed modular classrooms situated to the side of the building, the small complex surrounded by corn fields!

And the woman I met was a most gracious, warm individual who was excited about the possibility of me joining the team.   Barbara was, many years earlier, a former Catholic nun, then for many years a non-denominational (or evangelical Protestant) teacher at another Christian school, one that had folded several years earlier.   And she had recently taken up the challenge to put this new school together, under the sense that this was distinctly what God wanted her to do.   It was just entering into its third year of operation, and I would be teaching in one of the adjoining modular units – ones that a local school district had just passed on to The King's Academy (TKA) for service as TKA's junior high and high school classrooms.

But there was something of an important side-benefit in it: I would be able to enroll my four kids there at 1/10th of the tuition cost, and I would get to be their teacher one day.   Actually, I would even be teaching Rachel that fall as she entered the 7th grade.   And as for the rest, particularly in the need to meet our living expenses, God would just have to take care of that for us!

And indeed He did.   We found out that the local Schuylkill Haven School Board would pay us $7,000 to bus our kids.   They were required to do so because TKA was just inside the 10-mile southernmost school district boundary line – requiring busing services from the school district.   It was cheaper to pay us than to have their own buses take our kids to school.   Thus it helped greatly to meet our most basic living expenses, at least during that first year.   We would lose that privilege the next year when there were more students from our school district attending TKA and the school district thus provided its own bus.   But at that point I was making the full $25,000.   Tight, but doable (barely)!

But that's how God took care of things for us!   And we were always well aware of this.

My first class days, and 9/11.   Of course my interest in history is always framed by my instincts as a political scientist: to look into what history teaches us – that is, shows us – by way of real past experience – the truths of social-political and even cultural behavior.   And this historical "laboratory" that I work from is not merely American history, but in fact the history of all the major civilizations of the world – ancient as well as modern.

In that first week or so of classes I was explaining to my students about the various challenges America faces, not only at home but from abroad. I told them that the days of "Fortress America" – where we could safely operate from behind the huge protective walls of the Atlantic and Pacific Oceans – were over. We had to be prepared, like the rest of the world, to deal with foreign challenges right here, even in America itself.

As an example, I mentioned how the Muslims hated everything America stood for, and had tried to bring down the New York Twin Towers (1993), very visible symbols of American economic and cultural greatness. I was quite certain that they would try again someday. I made that point on the Friday of that first full week of classes. I repeated the same message in another class or two the following Monday. And on Tuesday, September 11th, those Twin Towers indeed came down!

The students were not only deeply horrified by the terrible events of that day (as we all were), they were shocked that I had just given notice rather prophetically of just such an event to come our way.

But being thusly "prophetic" brought me only pain, for there was nothing positive in being "insightful" on this matter. I mourned with the rest of the country, and much of the world. And I was saddened ever further knowing full well that there would be huge sections of the Muslim world celebrating this great victory over evil, over "Satanic" America. This was true Muslim "jihad", bringing down Satan's evil servants (Americans and other Westerners).

I was made even sadder when the news reached me that two of my Dunellen parishioners, including the church treasurer that I knew quite well, went down with the towers.

But that Sunday, I presented at the Pottsville church (which I would continue to pastor through the rest of the year) internet pictures on the huge sanctuary screen, showing the world in mourning with America, and that most of the world was with us in this time of great grief, indeed, that God himself was with us. Now we had to do the right thing to honor those who died.

But what would the "right thing" be? I had my own ideas on the matter: hunting down and ending Osama bin Laden's al-Qaeda (actually al-Qa'ida) organization, which I suspected was behind this horrible event, that, or one of its affiliate organizations, such as Ayman al-Zawahiri's Egyptian Islamic Jihad.

The only "plus" side of this tragedy was that my students would henceforth take quite seriously the ideas that I would put before them. And I had lots of those!

✳ ✳ ✳

LIFE AT THE KING'S ACADEMY

Course structuring. There were, naturally, a number of courses already set out for me to teach in the "history" category, as well as a geography course. And naturally, there were textbooks ready to go to work with. But I soon found that the different courses and their textbooks just did not quite add up to the comprehensive view that interested me the most, and what it was that I wanted to get over to my students. I wanted to build in them a broad and deep Christian worldview, based on a wide investigation of the broader world out there that awaited them. And that world, to me, was both highly international, and deeply historical across the world's many cultures. In short, I wanted to teach them how as a Christian they were to appreciate and go at the larger world, in a rather sophisticated fashion.

Thanks to my website, some of the material I wanted to teach was already available, easy to download and then print out on the school's copy machine. And I intended to build up that material in the days (and years) ahead of me.*

When I had things organized the way I wanted (actually by my second year there) I started them out with an historical survey of Western Civilization. Then I introduced them to the world's other cultures, past and present, reaching even all the way back to paleolithic and neolithic times. I also directed them in an in-depth study of America's own history. And then finally, in their senior year, I finished the series with a broad study of "social dynamics," that is, the social, economic and political dynamics in the life of any society.

And as a supplement to this "history" series, I developed a 4-year French language course of study (at least two years of foreign language study was required for graduation anyway), writing my own material for the first-year startup, and then quickly switching to some rather sophisticated French reading, including a full novel the senior year.

And I required a world map test, repeated each year (forcing them not to forget what they had learned), Western and American history ID tests (being able identify the century that a cited event took place, and, if occurring since the beginning of the 20th century, the exact decade that this occurred), and then an extensive written essay on a number of questions I required of them.

But each of these grading events was preceded by games and other exercises to get them ready. I would even review for them the essay questions, and what it was I was looking for in their responses. I tried to make things as easy as possible, because I knew that I was asking them to

---

*It is still there in abundance, with lots of accompanying pictures, on one of my websites, spiritualpilgrim.net.

demonstrate a level of knowledge that would be more likely expected in a college course. But I refused to dumb things down just because these were high schoolers (I was teaching only high school after the first two years there). I rather preferred to bring them up to the high expectations that I knew full well awaited them as they moved on in life.

And I can say, the response was amazingly positive on the part of my students, for word soon got back to TKA about how all of this advantaged them greatly when they moved on to college. For instance, one young lady was so happy to be the only one in a college course that knew where Syria was, and proved herself when the teacher challenged her to go to a world map and actually point out the country. No big deal for her.

And my students used to laugh when fellow college students complained about having to write a college essay of some five to ten pages. They had been doing that all the way through their high school days. In fact I finally had to put a page limit on their essays, when some of them presented essay papers 20 to 25 pages in length. Having to grade 50 to 80 essays each quarter, I found myself totally consumed for over a full week in just grading these essays.

My own daughters and sons were of course in those classes. And, just as much as I wanted to give them the very best education possible before they headed onward in the world of learning, so too I was just as interested in seeing their classmates highly prepared in that same way.

And we all sensed that this was what this learning process that we were engaged together on was ultimately about. These students were not just young people I was paid to teach. These were my "offspring", both biologically and by academic adoption. We were family!

The Paris (and also London) trip abroad. I soon challenged them to go abroad with me, just for a week (ultimately ten-days) over spring break, to discover the simple path that leads to the larger world. Beginning in 2005, and every-other year after that, I took them to Paris (soon adding London on the return) to show them how to get around easily in a world that was totally new to them.

We did some touring together in the mornings – not by any tour bus but rather by having to get around using the subway system – and then I turned them loose in the afternoons to explore the city on their own (actually at least in small groups, because solo-touring was a big no-no), with the instructions to meet at such-and-such metro stop if they wanted to have dinner at a restaurant we had reserved. They always showed up on time! Then they were free to explore the city on their own in the evenings (again, in small groups), with the warning that the metro system shut down at 11:00 at night. And unless they wanted a long walk back to the hotel, they had better find themselves on the metro by that time. And I had no "lights-out" night-time limit, only the warning that if they did not want to be zombies dragging around the next morning, they would want to get themselves to bed at a decent hour. And they were to remember to keep things quiet in their hotel-room gatherings, as there were others on their same floors. And they proved to be quite respectful of these "boundaries."

We had a great time, visiting the Louvre museum, shopping at book stores and resting at cafes in the Latin Quarter, exploring the Champs Elysees, etc. We would also head out to the castle at Fontainebleau (about an hour outside of Paris), similar to the Versailles Palace, though a bit smaller in size… and with usually few other visitors there. We had the beautiful place virtually to ourselves! And as it was over the Easter Season, we would find ourselves in the Notre Dame Cathedral (usually Palm Sunday) for Sunday morning worship. Actually, it used to grieve me deeply over how easy it was to find ourselves there, when it seemed that the French should have been crowding to the very limits this great place on such an important Sunday.

I soon added a few days in London to the itinerary (at first we merely changed planes there), to, again, set them loose after a morning together in this great city. By the time we got to London (by train through the "Chunnel") they considered themselves "experts" at getting around a new city. And that was ultimately what this was all about!

At first the parents were a bit nervous about how I put so much responsibility on the kids themselves in getting around in these foreign cities. But they soon came to appreciate greatly what this meant as a learning experience for their kids.   And we always had a great time!

I always had another adult helping me on the trip, at first my friend Bob (who had been part of the New Geneva team, and who had actually done some study in Paris himself during his college days), then a couple of teachers from school (for them also a new learning experience), then the head of the school himself, Dan, with Kathleen also joining the team on several of our trips. And on my last two trips, helping out as additional chaperones, were also son Paul and then daughter Elizabeth, each now in college and each having previously taken this same trip twice (as had also their older sister Rachel in the first years of this enterprise and then also as their younger brother John during the last two of our visits.)

At first we started off with about a dozen TKA students making the trip. But as time went by, the number increased to twenty or so students, including even some of our foreign students attending TKA (we were getting a lot of international students at the school by that time).

Foreign students living with us. Indeed, one of the goals of both the

Hodges family and ultimately TKA was to connect ourselves with the larger world, by bringing that world to us right there in Pennsylvania. Our first such event happened when TKA brought in for about two weeks during the spring of 2006 a group of about a dozen French students, traveling under a special exchange program. One of the girls, Justine, stayed with us, and in doing so also connected us with some of her group's other doings at the same time. It was fun.

So we signed ourselves up to do some more hosting, again, French students, coming to America through the Nacel exchange program to stay with American families for about a month during the summers. Thus it was that we had another French girl, Céline, stay with us during the summer of 2007.

Then we hosted for the 2007-2008 school year John, not a foreign student but instead the son of my Mobile friend, Bill – whose Mobile home I had made my own during my Princeton days. John and my son Paul were the same age, and spent the year hanging out together, both at school and obviously also at home. John in fact became a goalie for the recently assembled school varsity soccer team (Paul being one of its organizers). This merely brought our two families even closer together.

That summer (2008) we were joined again by another French girl, Julie (good friends ever since!). Then that fall a girl from Ukraine, Irishka (or just Ira) joined us for the 2008-2009 school year, also a dear friend ever since!

Then in the summer of 2010 another French girl, Eléanore, joined us, and likewise in 2012, a French boy, Bastien. That fall, a Norwegian boy, Håkon, joined us for the 2012-2013 school year. He was about half-way in age between Paul and John, and became close to both, though Paul was already off in college at that point. And he too joined (along with John) the TKA soccer team. He also joined us in our Paris-London trip that spring.

There would be a bit of a break in scheduling at that point, and it would not be until the 2017-2018 school year that we found ourselves serving again as international hosts, this time a Vietnamese student, Dat, a very quiet young man that seemed more like a shadow than an active participant in our family life, part of the reason being that all of our own kids had moved on from home by that point.

Foreign students at TKA. The school's director, Barbara, was very involved in the international exchange idea (personally connected in such exchange with China), especially after she stepped down from the school's leadership to focus specifically on that part of the school's academic dynamics. On they came, from Brazil, Bolivia, Korea, China, India, Armenia, Germany, Norway, Italy, Spain, Tanzania, etc. In fact the international component in the high school became quite high, making my task of bringing the larger world to the cornfields of eastern Pennsylvania all the easier!

And it certainly did not hurt our soccer teams any (we had a very active girls soccer team as well)! In fact, we did quite well, with this high international makeup of our soccer teams.

Dan takes leadership of the school. In 2005 TKA got itself a new director or "Headmaster," one that I would grow quite close to. Dan and I would often linger a bit after school to discuss matters impacting our world, that is, our larger American world. That was particularly the case when he set up a last-period contemporary affairs seminar with the seniors, located in my classroom, with me sometimes brought into the conversation, a conversation that would continue onward after school was over.

We had the same goal in mind: to prepare our students to be ready to take on that world as well-informed Christians, dedicated to the task of making the world a bit of a better place, regardless of what particular talents our students brought to such a task, or what particular place they found themselves in in the process.

... and connects us to the Heritage Foundation. Because of his own earlier affiliation with the organization, he was the one able to bring our students to the Heritage Foundation in DC each spring, and have them attend seminars set up just for them by this or that particular research expert, mornings and early afternoons (the rest of the afternoons to visit the city a bit). One year we even had an additional visit and a full day of seminars offered to us in the fall. The Heritage Foundation was very impressed with our students.

And he was one of the adults accompanying Kathleen and me (and Paul and Elizabeth) on our 2011 Paris-London trip. He was always great company!

In the fall of 2014, he moved on to a new position in Virginia, and very sadly, the dynamic I enjoyed so much went with him.

In fact, when we went on our own a year or two later to the Heritage Foundation, instead of the serious seminars with their experts, we were treated by one of their interns to some kind of brief and bland high-school-level "Welcome to the Heritage Foundation" presentation. We never went back.

MAKING PENNSYLVANIA OUR PERMANENT HOME

A deep housing makeover. In accepting the position at TKA, it quickly became apparent that we needed to look beyond the small miner's home we were renting and find some place more permanent, able to better accommodate a family of six. John and Paul were sharing a room, and Rachel and Elizabeth had a room together in what was merely the attic, having to sleep on air mattresses placed on the living-room floor in the summers when the attic became as hot as a furnace. So, with a realtor in tow, we began the search, far and wide, in the area (the fall of 2003).

Of course our finances were such – as the realtor well knew – that what she continued to show us was hardly any better than the place we were renting. It was very discouraging, as we went from one unpleasant possibility to another.

Finally I undertook to do some searching online myself, and found (January 2004) an old two-story farmhouse whose huge dairy farm had been subdivided as a large neighborhood with some quite nice new homes, probably built in the 1970s and 1980s. So the farmhouse, built in 1890, stood out quite boldly in the neighborhood.

I showed the listing to the realtor, and off we went. Thanks to a large amount of money passed on to Gina and me by our mom – because of the sale of our Collinsville home, money that we had put into savings for just such an event – we could offer a huge down-payment and take on a 15-year mortgage, with monthly payments less than what we had been paying for our rental home. So it was that we quickly closed the deal.

But the farmhouse was in bad shape. It had been cut up into some four apartments, which were in need of a deep makeover. It also had a separate 2-story garage, rented by a builder who kept a lot of his tools and material there.

When I brought my friend Bob and then Kathleen's brother John to look over our new purchase, they both agreed that I had lost my mind. But I saw not what it was, but instead what it might become. It had a beautiful bay window on the front facing the main street, a large porch facing the side street, and the apartment attached to the back part of the home being newer and needing only some paint, new floor covering, and some work in the kitchen and bathroom to get it ready to continue to serve as a rental home, helping to cover the costs of the deep upgrade that would be needed elsewhere in our new home. And as far as that was concerned, I knew I could do nearly all that work myself.

But what a surprise when we turned our attention that summer to the main house, and began our work on it. When we went to strip the walls of layers of wall-paper, we were abruptly presented with the problem that the plaster beneath quickly turned to powder when brought to the light of day. So all of that had to go, including the lathe strips beneath, so that we found ourselves back to the wall studs everywhere. We could thus stand at one end of the house and see through all the rooms to the back of the house.

But this stripping of the walls actually allowed me to rebuild entirely the electrical system and plumbing needed to bring the home up to standard. We took out the several kitchens and baths, took out a central staircase that had been put in place when the home was subdivided into three internal apartments, and relocated walls here and there, both upstairs and down. And I installed a central fireplace with glass surround that opened to both our new living room and dining room. And we built a very large and quite modern kitchen and breakfast area, as well as a number of new bathrooms.

And the whole family pitched in to do the work. Paul was a big help in installing the drywall to both our walls and high ceilings, as well as some of the electrical work. Kathleen and the girls were wood-trim strippers (we kept as much of the quite elegant antique wood-trim as possible), wall painters, etc. John, however, was only seven at the time, and mostly just observed quietly the work being done on his new home.

Finally, a year later, with Paul helping me sand and varnish the old wood floors, we were ready to move in, helped by numerous friends to fill the place with our furnishings. We had a home of our own now.

There was still work to be done. The floors of the five bedrooms on the second floor needed to be sanded and varnished (the summer of 2007). One of the rooms off the living-room had been set aside to eventually (the summer of 2008) become a huge library, to hold my extensive book collection, and a massive desk (we called it "superdesk") which I built, with two computers and numerous file drawers. And the kitchen still needed cabinet doors, which I took on as a special project (the summer of 2009), working from oak boards, cut, glued and molded into beautiful cabinet doors, a job I enjoyed greatly! And the outside of the totally white house needed final painting, and the addition of dark green shutters and doors (also the summer of 2009).

Finding a place in the area's religious community. One of the absolute rules of interim pastoring is that you do not stay at the church you have just served once a permanent pastor has been called. But we were now staying in the community itself (or at least nearby), and thus we would have to find a new church to call our own. But there were no other Presbyterian churches within reasonable reach.

As it turned out, the decision as to where we would henceforth be worshiping was not all that difficult, as I had become personally very close to Bill, the pastor who had started up nearby his own evangelical (and non-denominational) Lighthouse Church. Even my friend Bob and his wife Sue had just moved there themselves, and convinced me to lead a Wednesday night Bible study (the Gospel of John) at that church. So it was quite easy.

We simply became "members" of the Lighthouse Church.

As far as my Presbyterian involvement (I was still listed as a member of the regional presbytery) things quickly faded away. First of all, presbytery meetings were held in the afternoons, and I was teaching at TKA during that same time, thus unable to attend presbytery meetings.

I did agree to do some Sunday pastoring for a Presbyterian church about an hour away in Hazleton, for about a year, 2005-2006, but preaching there only every-other week. I was glad to help out. But I kept my participation to this every-other-week basis in order not to become their interim pastor. I was already fully involved in teaching at TKA!

But beyond that, I found that I was distancing myself not only from the doings of the presbytery, but also even of the denomination itself. I was not very happy with the "progressive" direction it was headed in, the denomination being unwilling to understand why that very direction was a big part of the reason for the loss of its former place, its traditional voice, in the life of the nation. Anyway, I knew that what I understood to be the real dynamics driving the life of our people was not something that the "peace and social justice" warriors now directing the Presbyterian denomination wanted to have to answer to. So, I simply dropped further activity with the denomination, the one that I was born in, schooled within, and served as pastor, during those many years.

My heart and soul now belonged elsewhere.

✳ ✳ ✳

RELATING TO THE LARGER WORLD

"Baby Bush." I developed the habit of referring to our newest President (2001-2009) as "Baby Bush" in contrast to his father, "Daddy Bush" (US President 1989-1993). Actually I liked Daddy Bush very much. But Baby Bush was a huge disappointment to me. What bothered me was the way he let His Secretary of Defense Rumsfeld take over the hunt for Bin Laden. That should have been the job of the CIA, who knew how to find local support in Afghanistan – and vital secret information needed to run the monster Bin Laden down. I knew how vast the Hindu Kush mountains were, and sending American soldiers into those mountains looking for Bin Laden was a total waste of time. Not only could Bin Laden easily hide in those hills, he was most likely to slip into nearby Pakistan if he stood in any obvious danger of discovery. And there was no way we were going to send troops into Pakistan after him, short of nuclear war with our suppposed ally Pakistan!

But into Afghanistan our troops went, the purpose of which I could never understand. Bush had been so critical about Clinton's "nation-building"– which had been quite cautious – and yet Bush's nation-building (making Afghanistan a "democracy") seemed to be about the only possible purpose such a massive US military invasion of Afghanistan could possibly serve. But I also knew enough about Afghanistan to know that Bush was way in over his head on this matter, as other European powers had discovered to their detriment in previous eras.

But what really bothered me about Baby Bush was his obvious desire to bring down Iraqi dictator Saddam Hussein. This made no sense at all, in even a more dangerous way. Iraq was a powder keg of sectarian explosives (Sunni Arabs hating Shi'ite Arabs, with Sunni Kurds wanting out of the whole Iraqi deal, and our allies, the Turks fuming over the way American involvement would stir up big problems within Turkeys' own Kurdish population). The only thing holding Iraq together (a post-World-War-One British creation) was Saddam Hussein himself. Taking him out would throw the whole area into turmoil, leaving opportunities for all kinds of political mischief, rather than some idyllic "democracy" as the result. Even Vice President Cheney himself had earlier confessed that we had not gone into Iraq itself after chasing Saddam out of Kuwait, because Iraq was a "quagmire", that is, a bottomless pit to sink into and lose everything. But Baby Bush was determined to be the one to bring Saddam "to justice", and (in keeping with DC political, intellectual and moral standards) now Cheney stood strongly with Bush in this plunge into the same quagmire.

I was upset, as Bush tried one excuse after another to justify his Saddam "takeout." And my students knew how upset I was. So apparently were some of the parents. So Dan came to me to tell me to ease up. He felt pretty much the same way I did over the matter. But it was upsetting these parents because I seemed so "anti-American" in not supporting our President. Anti-American? I loved my country. I just wanted my country not to do something disastrously stupid. But stupid it did. , And there was not much I really could do about it!

Obama's "change." When Baby Bush left office, with the American economy in near-melt-down status, I was hoping that the country would turn its leadership over to a proven patriot of the bravest kind, John McCain. But I also realized that the Republican Party would take a huge hit because of the economic disaster Bush left behind. And also, much was made by the Democrats of McCain's age, running for office at age 72. But they couldn't find much dirt to hit him with (besides his age) so they went after his running mate, Alaska governor, Sarah Palin, whom they accused of being no more than a beauty-queen bimbo.   And with McCain so old, the Democrats made as much as possible about how dangerously close the country was to coming under the presidency of a beauty-queen bimbo if the McCain-Palin ticket were to win the election.

However, my students and I attended a rally put on by both candidates, where from my point of view, they were both impressive in the way they addressed the major issues facing the country. And we also attended a Clinton rally, in which only Hillary's husband Bill was present. At this point Hillary had already been defeated by Obama in the race for the Democratic Party nomination, and the event was more a celebration of "Clintonness" than any presentation of the major issues of the campaign.

As far as Obama went, I could not make out much about the man, except that he rode big his "Blackness" (despite being raised by a White mother and White grandparents), and that he intended to "change" America. I was a bit nervous that Obama's goal was to bring the country back to the days of the late 1960s, when race became a very divisive issue, even violently so. But I was willing to give him the benefit of the doubt on this matter.

But little by little his program of "change" saddened me. He really wanted to bring Middle America down because of all of its failings. He rightly understood the Supreme Court (not Congress) to be the most pivotal institution in getting his changes in place. When he appointed two unmarried and childless women to the Supreme Court, I knew Middle America was in for trouble.

Then too, Obama couldn't stay out of local tragedies, first the shooting of a Black youth in Florida, which Obama went before the public announcing that if he himself had a son, he would have been like the Black youth killed in this struggle with a White (actually mixed race himself) in a neighborhood-watch event. And later, he would go full force against a White cop in Ferguson Missouri, when the cop shot a Black youth, Obama doing so, well before the facts in the matter were fully assembled. This event in turn birthed the Black Lives Matter Movement, which got full support from Obama, and his Attorney General, Eric Holder – who Obama sent to Ferguson to make sure that the final verdict on the matter went against the White cop. But the actual facts ultimately supported the cop, to the grand disappointment of Holder, who could not resist issuing deep criticism of the (White) racism that underlay the whole mess.

And so it was that America was back in the business of issuing racist accusations across American society, something that the country definitely did not need. But it seemed to serve some strong, but very narrow, political interests quite well, as racism (and for that matter nationalism, religious sectarianism, tribalism and now even sexism) always does. But serving such narrow political interests is always guaranteed to undercut the larger social order, disastrously so.

I was also saddened that Obama had America back trying to export its democratic idealism abroad, especially in the Middle East – when the "Arab Spring" of 2011 broke out, and country after country went through the disruptions of mob uprisings (the mob hysteria even spread to Greece, Italy, and ultimately even Great Britain).

Obama sent air support to the heavy European involvement in the takedown of Libyan dictator Gaddafi, which threw that country into deep civil war. This would turn around and bite us a year later when our American ambassador to a post-Gaddafi Libya and two other American officials were killed in the very region that we had been supporting, in the largely anti-Gaddafi East (Cyrenaica) versus the largely pro-Gaddafi West (Tripolitania). Ironic, not to mention tragic.

And Obama did everything he could to take down Syrian president Assad, not only helping to throw that country into ever-deeper civil war (several million people forced to flee the country) but giving Russia and Iran the excuse to come big into Syria to make themselves very useful to Assad, and find a new position of political influence right there on the shores of the Mediterranean! Wow! That was a big political loss for America.

And Obama came close to doing the same in Egypt, after the overthrow of Egyptian dictator Mubarak, with Obama's enthusiastic support of a Muslim Brotherhood leader, Morsi, when he narrowly won new Egyptian elections as the country's president, and then immediately issued an arrest warrant for his largely Secular opponent (who had to flee the country)! The election was so divisive, and Morsi so dictatorial, that this in turn threw the country into even deeper disorder, until the Egyptian military finally stepped in and restored order in the country, to the great disapproval of Obama!

But America really had little say in what was going on in Egypt at this point.

And I was unhappy with Obama's non-response to China's building a military base in the South China Sea, just offshore from the Philippines, in order to enforce its claim that this vital waterway was actually Chinese territory. No, all the rest of the world, and the many countries surrounding the South China Sea knew it to be "high seas", belonging to no one. And Obama also loudly claimed this point, but did nothing to put military muscle behind that claim. Building our own military base somewhere near the Chinese base would have been what I would have done, though no one was asking me what to do on the matter!

Overall, in the same way that Bush left America hurting deeply both economically (the meltdown) and diplomatically (Afghanistan and Iraq) I felt the same hurt for America in what Obama left behind morally and spiritually (as well as diplomatically) in departing from office after serving eight years as president. Not only had America further weakened its position internationally, the country itself was once again bitterly divided across not only racial lines but now also across unbending ideological lines as well.

Wanting to see America get back on course. What America needed badly at that point was healing, not more ideological divisiveness. That's why I so much wanted to see someone like the famous surgeon Ben Carson take the American presidency. Although he was even more "Black" by birth than Obama, in his go at life, he had become entirely Middle American in spirit, living well-above the crude racial divisions that were now tearing at the country. Having Carson as our American president would have served greatly in inspiring the country to rise once again to some kind of grander social purpose, and sense of unity.

Dr. Carson was a wonderful example to put before all Americans of traditional American "rags to riches" development through hard work (rather than just standing around complaining about how unfair life was). He was self-taught, demonstrating an ability to take on most any challenge and going at it wisely. He was an outstanding team player. And he was deeply and most authentically Christian.

America needed someone like Carson to get the nation back on track politically, socially, morally and spiritually. Otherwise the county was in danger of going further down this road not only of ideological hostility, but also that of social class, race, and even sexual and generational hostilities – the very things that self-serving politicians love to exploit for personal gain*, but also the very things that destroy social unity – and thus a society's ability to achieve and sustain greatness.

But in the 2016 Republican Presidential Debates, Carson was given little attention, because Trump kept swinging the TV cameras back to himself with his loud comments and running attacks and insults aimed at his competitors. I was deeply saddened that, in the end, this was the basis on which the Republican Party made its choice of candidates.

I must say that after this, I found myself rather removed from what was further unfolding at the political heart of my beloved America. I was

---

*Cheap-shot White racist politics employed by Southern politicians in the 1950s and 1960s served no good purpose to the poor Whites that these politicians were seeking votes from. It only gave poor Whites an excuse to accept their status, because of the supposedly impassable social barriers placed in front of them by the so-called "Black Threat." But the same holds true today when "Progressive" politicians also play the same race card – except now against Whites – in an effort to broaden their political base within the Black community. Such appeal to Black racism is guaranteed to be no more of an aid to poor-Black development than Black-baiting was to poor-White development in the previous century.

tired of listening to self-serving political "Reason" loudly proclaimed by this or that group.

My prayers for Divine rescue. My heart was breaking for the country I loved dearly. It seemed to me that, since the beginning of the 21st century, we had gone so far down the very destructive "silly road", that short of divine intervention by God himself (another Great Awakening), America would no longer be able to self-correct in its social plunge downwards.

And thus it became my daily prayer (and my beloved family's prayer) that God would intervene, and bring Middle America back on course, the one that was set out four centuries ago by the Puritans who came to America to make this new social venture one of setting up a City on a Hill, a Christ-like Light to the Nations.

And it was ultimately why I made the decision finally to take on the task of telling just that story, in my three-volume history of *America - The Covenant Nation, A Christian Perspective.*

CHAPTER NINE

OUR KIDS' PLACE
IN THE HODGES DYNAMIC!

✳ ✳ ✳

RACHEL

Our eldest, Rachel, was something of a workhorse, taking on one challenge after another. She made top grades at school, became fluent in French, took on the flute and subsequently played that instrument in the county's youth symphony. At the same time, she worked at various part-time jobs in high school, from clerking at a grocery store to food service at an elder-care home. And upon graduation from TKA, she headed off to Penn State, where she continued to do excellent work.

But her second year was very hard for her, for purely social reasons. She did not get along with her apartment mates, who constituted a pre-existing social circle, one that would give her no admission to their ranks. She lived off campus and found it difficult to get to classes on time (bus service was most unpredictable), and just in general found the new experience very depressing. When she came home at Christmas, it was clear that she simply did not want to go back. But she also did not know what she then proposed to do. She did finally decide to finish out that sophomore year at Penn State.

But the next fall she transferred to St. John's College in Annapolis, which was based entirely on a most unusual humanities program... and which put her back at the beginning of the academic process as something of a freshman, studying ancient Greek and taking on the classics (philosophy, politics, science and math) of the Greek and Roman period.

But for some reason, her Greek teacher selected her to give a hard time to, for reasons that Rachel could never understand. He criticized her for the bright red dress she was wearing the first day, and it went downhill for her from there. And then she got sick, and found herself in trouble – because the college did not have a grading policy, but had just instituted an attendance policy, and her sickness put her over the limit (she had also not gone to class a few days, not feeling able to put up with her teacher's insults). She could continue some of her other classes during the coming spring semester, but would have to start over with the Greek the next fall.

But rather than just continuing part-time, Rachel decided to come home, and start again from scratch the next year. Overall, she loved St. John's and its particular approach to learning (the classics in all fields of human learning, from ancient times down to the present) and planned simply to start over, if that was what was required of her.

In the meantime, life seemed rather depressing for Rachel. She could not figure out why now her life was having such a hard time moving forward, when it all had been so easy, or at least manageable, previously.

RIMI

I had first met this young man who came to TKA for a chapel presentation, part of a team taking a break from a YWAM (Youth with a Mission) training program in Hawaii that we brought to the school. Rimi was most unusual, though I had only small knowledge at the time of how unusual.

This would not be the only time he would come across my path. A year later, on his return from the Hawaii program, he was staying briefly at the home of our friends, Bob and Sue. At a New Year's party they hosted, I found out from Rimi that he was heading home, to Kosovo (the southernmost portion of the former Yugoslavia). I knew quite a bit about Kosovo, thanks to America's earlier involvement in the area when the United Nations called on America to intervene to end the ethnic cleansing or slaughter going on in that country.

I also came to learn that Rimi was originally of a Muslim family (actually rather tepidly Muslim) and had many family members slaughtered by Serbian "Christians", and had to go into flight to avoid all of them being murdered (also nearly happening to him at one point) – and then having to live in a refugee camp.

After things settled down in Kosovo (thanks in great part to Clinton) Rimi would then continue on in life simply as a rather cynical Secularist, but one hungering to know why life had to be the way it was. He thus became a philosophy major at Kosovo's University of Pristina. There he also took a couple of courses in American history offered by an American professor, Bill, who fascinated Rimi because Bill was so different from everyone else Rimi had ever known. Rimi came to know Bill as a man of incredible peace, and a special dedication to his teaching that reached beyond mere professorial professionalism. Finally Rimi asked him why he was so different. And he was completely shocked when Bill answered simply, "Jesus Christ." Bill (quite understandably in largely-Muslim Kosovo) had given no prior indication of any particular Christian foundations to his life. Quite naturally, the answer merely perplexed rather than satisfied Rimi. Finally Rimi got up the courage to try the question again. And the teacher, seeing Rimi's sincere interest, began (very carefully) to explain what Jesus (not "Christianity," such as the Serbs were famous for) meant to him personally.

Finally Rimi decided to test God on this matter of a Christ-based faith, and the answer God gave him was immediate and highly impacting. Rimi was coming home from class on a horribly rainy-snowy day with the wind so fierce that when he stepped off the bus it destroyed his umbrella. Rimi's challenge was: Jesus, if you are real, you can make this weather cease. And most abruptly it cleared immediately around and above him. It shocked Rimi.

From that point on, Rimi found himself on a spiritual journey, that was so different from his former life – and the lives of those around him. And that was what finally had brought him to America (thanks to the encouragement of Bill, who would continue to remain close to Rimi, even from afar), and into the Hodges world.

It was on this second visit to our area that I asked Rimi if he would return to TKA for its weekly chapel service and tell us more of his spiritual journey. He agreed. But there was a problem, in that chapel service was just after lunch, and I had no way of getting him via the half-hour trip to the school, unless someone (like Rachel who was at home at this point) could bring him there at the appointed time.

Rachel rather reluctantly agreed. She had the feeling that Rimi was more than just intellectually interested in her.* But thanks to Rachel, we indeed had him at chapel, easily delivering a most powerful message to our students.

It was on the trip back from school that Rachel mentioned to Rimi the kind of spiritual battle she seemed to find herself deeply involved in. Rimi then challenged her: do you seriously want to know about real spiritual warfare? Come to Kosovo. You'll learn a lot more about spiritual warfare in doing so.

And wouldn't you know, that very evening Rachel informed us that she thought that God himself wanted her to take up Rimi's challenge. Not

---

*Rachel did not know that when Rimi was back in Hawaii, a prophetess of sorts informed Rimi that she had a vision of him meeting and marrying a tall, dark-haired beauty from Pennsylvania. Rimi's reaction was " No! I don't want to marry a woman from Transylvania", thinking the woman was talking about someone coming from northern Romania, a gypsie most likely. He finally had to have it explained to him that it was Pennsylvania, not Transylvania, she was talking about. Rimi was thus given an American geography lesson right then and there! Needless to say, after that, the thought never left Rimi.

sure what to make of the idea, Kathleen and I agreed to go into prayer on the matter that night. And indeed, the next morning both Kathleen and I knew that this was exactly what Rachel was called to do.

Can you imagine sending your daughter off to Kosovo? But that's exactly what we did.

✳ ✳ ✳

RACHEL AND RIMI

This venture turned out to be a real life-changer for both. Rachel came to take on a peace of mind and spirit that she needed badly, a new empowerment even in the face of life's toughest challenges.

And all this also brought Rimi back into an American world he thought he had said his goodbyes to permanently. The two really connected. And thus several months into the adventure, we heard from Kosovo that the two would be returning to Pennsylvania in July, to get married. And indeed, Pastor Bill was more than glad to perform the ceremony at the Lighthouse Church.

Once married, they headed on to Hawaii, for Rimi to undertake theological studies for an MA degree at the University of the Nations, living off various grants that people had extended to them to be able to do so. After a year, they returned and took residence in the apartment at the back of our home, while Rimi took on hard work at a food-distributors warehouse to cover their living expenses. That same year their daughter Anna was born, and Rimi was able to finish his master's thesis on Christian evangelism. And as if that weren't enough for them to be carrying, Rimi also took on part-time work as a youth pastor (with Rachel a big part of the program) at the same Presbyterian church in Pottsville that I had once pastored.

But Rimi wanted to go further on his spiritual journey, and applied for and was admitted to the Gordon-Conwell Seminary in the Boston area. And thus off they went, Rimi, Rachel, and Anna – with Rachel also taking on more college courses in the area (Gordon College and elsewhere).

And wouldn't you know that after two years in seminary, Rimi would then find a job as youth pastor at a Methodist Church located just one block from our home in Pennsylvania (but they would now live in the parsonage near the church).

Over the next five-year period (2015-2020) Rachel would quickly finish online course work at Penn State for a BA degree in literature, and Rimi would not only finish his thesis work for his Gordon-Conwell MA degree, but would undertake and then complete doctoral work at the University of

Birmingham (England) in the process. And in the meantime, a son, Peter, was also born to them.

Anyway, we'll get back to their story a little further along in this narrative.

✳ ✳ ✳

PAUL

Paul came along two years after Rachel, and just as Rachel was the very picture of a young lady, Paul also became that of a young gentleman. He took an early interest in sports, especially soccer, something that remained a passion for him through his TKA and Temple University years. In fact, not only did he and a fellow student put together TKA's new soccer team, he later even helped start up a local soccer team in Bethlehem, Pennsylvania (at the same time he was undertaking his new business venture there as well).

Things seemed also to come easy to Paul, although I knew that there was a lot of work that he put into his many ventures. Like Rachel, he became quite adept at French, spending the summer before his senior year at TKA in Paris with the family of the young lady, Julie, whom we ourselves had hosted the year previously.

Heading on to college, he had been offered a soccer scholarship, but knew that he would have then been expected to be a PE major. Instead, he continued his interest in international affairs, majoring in political science and minoring in history.

He also got to witness the rougher part of life living in Philadelphia, where crime was not exactly an uncommon occurrence. Once he got called to the window of his apartment when he heard arguing going on outside on the street, in time to witness one young man shooting and killing another before running off. Another time he was driving to school, stopped at a light, just as a man came running out of a Chinese restaurant, shooting at a bunch of kids who had just run out of the restaurant ahead of him. One of the boys went down in the firing, before Paul scooted off to get out of the shooting gallery! He subsequently moved on to campus, hoping to find this to be a safer environment. But when he was away in Europe, a group of masked young men broke into a neighboring campus apartment at gunpoint, to take whatever they could from the guys gathered there. These were close friends of Paul's, and most likely Paul would have been among that group if he had been back in the States.

None of this of course made the papers, as such events happened regularly on a daily basis in Philadelphia (the "city of brotherly love")!

Paul spent part of his junior year in Europe, at first studying German at the Goethe Institute in Freiburg, then moving on to Florence to study Italian. It was in Florence that he truly settled into the surrounding life, becoming quite close to a number of British students also studying there, including Princess Diana's niece, Kitty, who became a close friend of Paul's and who helped host his 21st birthday party while he was there in Florence.

Also while he was there he put together a research paper, one he had convinced a Temple University professor to allow him to do for college credit, focused on the action of the European Union in the overthrow the previous summer of Libya's dictator Muammar Gaddafi. Paul too like to study actual political dynamics, just like his father! And he got to see a lot of that up close!

Then in May, his younger sister, Elizabeth, joined him for a month in Florence, before the two headed off together to spend the rest of the summer touring much of Western Europe. This was easy for them, as both had also been to Europe twice previously with our TKA visits, and of course by this time Paul was fully familiar with life in Europe.

Upon graduation, Paul and a TKA friend of his, Mikey, decided to join together in an enterprise designed to bring solar power to schools in Third World countries. Paul, in order to give their Solar for Academics enterprise some support, took a position on the board of directors of an organization that sponsored just such Third World enterprises. But even then, Paul and Mikey knew that they would still need to find their own funding to put the enterprise into actual operation. And thus it was that they decided to build and sell (quite pricey) solar lights as a means of financing this larger operation.

But actually, the solar light business (Soltech Solutions) became itself the major focus for them. Things started off very slowly. They decided to set up their operations in nearby Bethlehem, where, to pay the bills, Paul was able to get a job as a waiter at the Hotel Bethlehem (he had previously worked summers as a host at the Nassau Inn's restaurant in Princeton). Eventually they were able to move their operations to a building dedicated to supporting startup businesses. Here they received a lot of wise counsel and personal encouragement in their undertaking.

Gradually their business began to grow. They then took on a third partner, Chris, a young man that Paul had worked with at the Hotel Bethlehem. And thus Mikey served as the company's solar engineer who designed, improved and diversified their products, Clark was in charge of their on-line presence, and Paul was the overall director of the enterprise, growing the company through his widening world of business contacts and operations

They quite early took on students from nearby Lehigh University as business interns, showing these students the actual challenges of a business startup.

Then their product got noticed by the media, and became featured on various shows. Their business now took off, greatly! At this point they had to take on a much larger staff (at the present around 15 employees) to meet a growing demand (for instance, Google bought a large number of their lights for their new offices in New York City).

And thus it was that Paul's world became that of business, even though his heart still wants to go into the world of helping struggling nations get on their feet economically. And thus he and Mikey (Mikey is very familiar with the world of China) are presently looking into ways to expand their operations abroad, in order to bring into being their dream of being of great assistance to the larger world.

✳ ✳ ✳

ELIZABETH

Elizabeth came along not quite two years after Paul. And although she did not suffer greatly because her older sister and brother were relatively notable personalities ahead of her in her world, she would have to work a bit harder to bring notice her way. She was, like her brother and sister, quite good academically. She was musical like her brothers and sisters, like them taking up piano at an early age, and then eventually becoming a violinist on the Schuylkill Youth Symphony, as her sister had been a flutist for the same organization and Paul a cellist there – as well as a drummer and guitarist for small groups. She too played soccer at TKA, like her brother before her, though not quite as passionately as Paul. She too learned French and went abroad twice with the TKA groups, like her brother and sister.

But most importantly, she was quite artistic, way ahead of her brother and sister in that category!

She got a huge scholarship allowing her to take up study (computer science mostly) at Lafayette College in Easton (eastern Pennsylvania), though tuition still tended to be quite pricey. And thus it was there that she spent her first two years in college, finally able to do her own thing, out from under the shadow of her sister and brother!

But when the third year rolled around, the college hiked its tuition considerably (it had fancy street surfacing to improve!) and I blew up. This was pure nonsense (or just plain academic greed). Thus I pulled her out of Lafayette College. What then? It was already a couple of weeks into the fall term, and too late to get her entered elsewhere. So, she found herself back at a job at the dealership of our friend Bob's, cleaning the floors in the extensive service shop (actually, she had started that work that same summer as a way of earning a bit of spending money). Most oddly, she loved the work, or was it just that she loved the enormous appreciation she received from the male workers for the way no one had ever cleaned the floor before!

Needless to say, that was not quite the world we had designed for her. And thus somewhat reluctantly, she headed off early the next year to take up in Florence where she had left off earlier. And thankfully, she came to once again love academic life, especially when it involved a side course in art and sculpture that she took up while studying Italian.

Actually, she came to love Florence deeply – where she was extremely fortunate (her encounter with *Fortuna*!) to find an apartment for herself right in the very center of town! But not only did she come to love Florence, Florence came to love her – not only by the circle of friends she acquired in the venture but also in the form of the many shop owners in the area that she came to know quite well, and love! That was Elizabeth being Elizabeth!

So she finally forgave her dad (me) for having yanked her around so much in her effort to move ahead in life!

When she returned to the States, she signed up to attend Indiana University (of Pennsylvania), way over on the other side of the state (probably also another aspect of her hunger for self-sufficiency), to continue her computer studies. And she would finish out there two years later.

During her last semester, as graduation approached, she signed up for some job interviews. Her first interview was with the PNC bank, headquartered in Pittsburgh, an interview which she undertook as something of a "practice session" in the art of interviewing. She had never interviewed before, and knew that she needed to develop some interviewing skills.

But actually, her interviewer loved his interview with her, and recommended her forward to some follow-up interviewing, which ended up with the same impression of Elizabeth. Thus her "practice session" landed her a job in Pittsburgh (also on the opposite side of the state from us), to where she would be moving immediately after graduation, to undertake work as a mainframe computer engineer.

She fell in love with Pittsburgh, loved the computer team she worked with, and at this point made Pittsburgh a true home. It was distant, but Kathleen and I made the trips west to visit as often as possible (about a 4 to 5-hour trip depending on the traffic and the route we chose) to see how Elizabeth was doing in her new world.

But more recently her world of art also found its way forward, when she started doing some art work for friends, then had some of her work displayed at a local pub, subsequently noticed by the director of an art studio in the neighborhood. He invited her to join a small group of fellow artists who gathered at his studio and had their work displayed there. And so this new world opened up for Elizabeth, becoming increasingly important to her, not only as a personal interest but also as a supplement to her income, for her work found sales quite easily.

And Elizabeth proved to be quite the adventurer as well. At one point she took some vacation time to fly to Iceland, rent a car, and do a full tour around the island, many days without seeing much by way of human life, sleeping in the car at one point. But that's the way she liked things. Then we were shocked to learn one day that she had gone up in a plane, just to take a parachute jump from the plane (accompanied by an instructor, of course). She also liked to jump in the car and head out from Pittsburgh, heading west or south, into neighboring states or beyond, just for an extended weekend!

Then more recently she decided to take some vacation time to drive all the way to the American West, swinging south to New Mexico and Arizona before then heading north to join Paul (who flew, not drove, there!) in Wyoming and Montana. Then on the way back she decided to swing by Kansas City, running into President Eisenhower's grandson at a tiny bar in the city, and his good friend, Ryan. And it was Ryan that would invite her to stay on for a bit, so he could show her more of his city.

And thus a relationship was born, which now has them headed in the direction of marriage, and ultimately making Pittsburgh their home together. So, Ryan will be bringing to the Hodges family more knowledge and experience in the business world (linking him closely to both Paul and John), plus a personal interest in social-political matters that fits right in with where the rest of the family finds itself.

JOHN

As the "baby of the family" John had the usual dynamics to deal with, although he handled these quite nicely.

Where he ran into trouble was at TKA, where for reasons we never were able to understand, the primary school teachers came to some kind of mutual agreement to make life as hard as possible for John.* Part of the problem was that John is very intelligent, making schoolwork a largely

---

*One of them, his 5th grade teacher, came up to me on the last day of school (she was also finishing up at TKA), and totally surprised me by telling me tearfully that God had told her to apologize to John for the way she had treated him. That meant a lot to John!

boring experience for him. This got him in constant trouble with his teachers (just as was the case for me in the third and fourth grades!), who would punish him for his inattention by making him do remedial schoolwork during recess, rather than play with the other kids, about the worst thing you could think of doing to John. And our protests got things nowhere. Even Barbara, the school director, appealed to the teachers to let up. But that was just not going to happen. So John had to learn early-on just to take punishment quietly as part of his world. It left a rather deep impression on him.

Once John reached high school, he found the pace to be more to his liking.

As far as French was concerned, I started up a new French series only every other year (teaching a full load of French, history and social studies forced me to be selective in how I structured the development of each of these fields), and I had only French 2 (and French 4) scheduled for the coming year. So rather than wait until the following year to start up the French series with French 1(which would have allowed him only three years of French study) he undertook to study French on his own during the summer before his freshman year, and thus was able to jump into French 2 that fall.

And that would be typical of how John would go at things. John would come to understand that his best teacher was himself! And that would extend through his college years.

Like Elizabeth, John did all the standard Hodges stuff – soccer, music (trumpet and piano), travel abroad with TKA, and a deep interest in everything from history to computers. But, like Elizabeth, computers would become his primary focus, though interestingly, the social-political aspect of the world of computerized communications.

Once again, in his senior year (2015-2016), he ran into trouble with a teacher – who was in charge of guiding and grading the writing of the student senior thesis and its public defense (public as far as the school itself went). He picked the subject of internet security, and all the problems that came with the growing world of internet communications. He even created a virus and showed how easily these kinds of things can get into the program. But his teacher accused John of stirring up hysteria, of "McCarthyism", and threatened to flunk him. Of course she knew not the first thing about the subject itself.

She was not very supportive of him at his oral defense, more grudging than happy at giving him a "pass", so he could then graduate. But John took matters like the moral soldier that he had over the years learned to become, never arguing back, but just pushing forward.

Indeed at the graduation ceremony, when the 20-or-so graduates were asked to summarize thoughts they had about their TKA experience – and all the fellow students gushed on about how wonderful it had all been – when it came to John, he offered only a single word on the matter: "perseverance." All his classmates laughed. They knew exactly what he meant.

That fall John too went west like Elizabeth, all the way to Indiana University (of Pennsylvania) – but only for a semester. He quickly transferred to Penn State – but the Lehigh Campus in Allentown, taking up residence in neighboring Bethlehem, not far from Paul's apartment, John sharing an apartment with a number of Lehigh University students, older than him, but becoming good friends. He became especially close to an upperclassman named "Miles!"

John's field was a blend of computer science and communications, John creating some kind of major of his own design. But again, it was not easy for John, because he seemed already to know about as much (if not more) concerning his subject as did his teachers, John being so completely self-taught, constantly taking on more and more knowledge as some kind of personal challenge.

We were never certain exactly where John stood on the academic road toward graduation, as he took on all kinds of courses that interested him – but avoided what he considered "idiot" courses, courses in particular areas that nonetheless he was going to have to take to graduate.

Anyway, in the fall of 2018, during what might have been considered his "junior year," he headed off to Shanghai to study Chinese, living with a Chinese family – under a special arrangement involving inexpensive housing in exchange for his offering of English lessons to the Chinese family's daughter. That worked out very nicely. And he picked up a lot of international (mostly European) friends at the school in the process, and came to really appreciate his young Chinese instructors.

And his 21st birthday just happened to come around while he was there. And to celebrate it with him, Elizabeth and Paul (and a friend Ben) joined him for that celebration in Hong Kong, Paul and Elizabeth having also combined that visit with a trip to India (and Elizabeth with a visit to Thailand just before that as well) before arriving in Hong Kong.

✳ ✳ ✳

PHUONG, AND JOHN

Phuong was a Vietnamese young lady who came to TKA her sophomore year, and graduated with John's class her senior year as its valedictorian. It was during that senior year that John and Phuong grew close, not really evident in any particular way however prior to the senior prom at which they went together as a couple.

Then John went off to college in Pennsylvania, and Phuong started up a 6-year doctoral program in pharmacy at the University of Rhode Island.

But the two remained close, and during the summer of 2017, John joined Phuong for an extensive visit to Vietnam, not only to her home in Hanoi but also widely across the entire country, visiting not only ancient archeological sites but also more recent battle areas in the South of the country. They especially came to love Danang, located about midway along Vietnam's long north-south coast.

Upon their return it became obvious where their relationship was headed, even though both of them were quite young. And thus two years later (2019), at the end of May, they got married here in Pennsylvania, officiated by the pastor of the Methodist Church that Rimi now served as associate pastor. And it was a huge affair, with fellow TKA students attending in large numbers, coming even from China to do so. And his friend Miles came down from Rhode Island, to serve as the DJ at a wonderful reception held on a local restaurant's huge patio.

Then John and Phuong headed off to Rhode Island to start their new home together.

John would, meanwhile, continue his Penn State studies online, and is presently completing his last required course for graduation. Ugh!

But he also became increasingly busy consulting with a new startup business in the area of computer research and marketing, an activity which at present occupies him full time (and more!).

Just recently, Phuong started the internship part of her program, which has them in Providence for the remainder of the year, with the likelihood that they then will be moving to Pennsylvania (the Allentown-Bethlehem area) for her to finish up the coming year (2022).

CHAPTER TEN

LIFE GOES ON

✳ ✳ ✳

MY HUGE AMERICAN HISTORY PROJECT

The decision to "retire." When the spring of 2019 came around, and a TKA teacher's contract for the 2019-2020 school year sat unsigned on my desk – something most exceptional for me, as I usually signed it as soon as I got it – I sensed that something was up. I had a feeling that God was possibly drawing me in a new direction, though I hardly knew what that could be. But I was used to God having me go at things this way. I just needed to stay alert for some kind of door God might be opening, and approach the matter prayerfully. And pray I did, joined by Kathleen in the process.

And bit by bit the message became ever clearer. I was to devote myself fulltime to putting together for publication the considerable research and writing I had built up over the years, most of it online on my Spiritual Pilgrim website. But I was to focus specifically on the American history portion of that mass of information.

Thus when TKA commencement came around in early June, I knew I would be saying goodbye to everyone, not just the graduates but the teachers as well. I was "retiring" as a classroom teacher.

The three-volume history. As I looked over all the material, I came to understand that I was to take all this on as an American story or narrative, focusing especially on how the nation had come to develop under the challenge of working closely with God, on sort of a covenant basis – like Israel of old. And this narrative indicated quite clearly how that American covenant had its ups and downs, also like Israel of old. And America's own ups and downs depended heavily on the status of that covenant. That was also most clear.

And being a political scientist rather than an historian, I found myself focusing particularly on the lessons we might therefore learn from that long narrative, lessons needed badly today, as we seem to be off on one of our "wandering" periods again, wandering from this precious covenant

243

with God.

Anyway, that summer (2019) I began the process of assembling, expanding and editing that huge American narrative, discovering that the depth that I wanted to take the narrative proved to be enormously extensive. Thus I decided to break it up into three volumes. The first volume, *Securing America's Covenant with God*, went into great detail on the birth and early development of the nation, all the way through the Civil War – which more or less settled the issue of what exactly the American nation was supposed to look like or be. The second volume, *America's Rise to Greatness under God's Covenant*, focused on how America joined the world of competing nations, from the rising Age of Imperialism in the late 1800s all the way up to America's place of leadership with the development of the Cold War following World War Two. The third volume, *The Dismissing of America's Covenant with God*, then took up in the 1960s, principally with America's Washington government trying to take command of the nation, pushing God out of the picture, and also instituting something of what I termed "democracy from above" – obviously a contradiction in itself! And with this volume I brought things up to date (at least as far as mid-2020 would take me), and then concluded, with my "lessons learned" laid out more specifically.

Publication. Rather than going from publisher to publisher with my proposal, I decided from the very first that I would undertake "self-publishing" in order to get this project up and moving quickly. But of course, there are many ways, many companies, to go with this idea. And after much searching, and with some advice from my daughter Rachel, I decided to go with Westbow Press, actually a subsidiary of the well-known Zondervan Press. Thus as it turned out, I would be working with a publishing company that sort of stood halfway between self-publication and professional publication.

That meant also that I would have to follow editorial lines they, as a Christian publishing company, set out. No words such as "bloody" (too British?), "hell" (such as Sherman's comment on the nature of war, or Bryan's closing argument in the 1925 Scopes Monkey trial), and just in general a certain "tone" required of the whole effort – something that I found not too hard to adjust to.

But this process took quite a bit of time, especially as I myself did all the editing (a slow and painful process), and then put it all together (including extensive bibliography and index) in both Microsoft Word and Adobe InDesign, the latter easily ready-to-print. Well almost. We did go a bit back and forth on this matter of final copy, especially the second volume (which came out about the time that the Coronavirus hit hard) which I had to get the editor-in-chief to intervene in the process to get it finally moving forward.

But anyway the volumes finally made their public appearance, the first one in February (2020), the second and third ones in April.

Marketing. Westbow made sure that these volumes made their appearance not only on their own booklist, but also on Amazon, Barnes and Noble, Christian Books, Cokesbury, etc.

But of course, bringing these three volumes to public notice would be my responsibility. And this was an area in which I had absolutely no experience. I did create a very nice and quite extensive website, thecovenantnation.com. But even here, I would need to find a way to bring the website itself to public notice. I joined LinkedIn and created a special Facebook page devoted to the series. That helped a little. Sales started to move slowly on Amazon.com.

✳ ✳ ✳

THE NEW AWAKENING CHURCH

Rachel and Rimi move on. But at the same time, I found myself deeply involved in a grand development in the lives of my daughter Rachel, her husband Rimi, and their kids, Anna and Peter.

It was becoming increasingly clear with time that Rimi had completed his useful service at the nearby Methodist Church (which Kathleen and I were now also attending). It was time for Rimi to move on to a new calling.

It was all a bit awkward, as Rimi was way overqualified in the position he held at the church, which itself was becoming less and less significant, as certain individuals wanted for themselves the position as head of the church's youth program, and Rimi also found himself called on less and less to preach.

It probably was Rachel that felt the hurt most deeply. Or maybe it was just that Rimi seemed to handle such political maneuvering amazingly quietly, something like the way John took on adversity.

But Rimi had seen much in his life that was cruel, and which he learned to overcome with a spirit that stood way apart from the manner that most people reacted to such things. He wasn't passive. Just not reactive. He just kept going, quietly taking on whatever steps seemed to be required of him next. And, I knew that this had a lot to do with the way he personally had come to take on Jesus Christ in his own life.

For instance, he and Rachel and the kids were back and forth from Pennsylvania to England, for Rimi to take on doctoral studies at the

University of Birmingham. And he carefully researched and wrote (with Rachel doing the extensive editing to make it English-perfect!) on America's Second Great Awakening (early 1800s), describing in detail the many key circuit riders and revivalists who brought Christ to the American frontier, and the many signs and wonders that accompanied their ministries. His doctoral supervisor loved the final product. But under the English system, his supervisor could not be part of the board that finally reviewed and decided Rimi's dissertation as qualifying him for the PhD degree.

And there's where another attack on Rimi came to take place. One of the professors, drawn from another British university, who himself had been a student of Rimi's supervisor, took great exception to the way Rimi combined his study of the frontier preaching with his close attention to the signs and miracles that came with that preaching. This man was actually furious that Rimi would even attempt what he saw as an absurd misrepresentation of the facts of the event (the signs and miracles Rimi described in detail), not that he really knew all that much about America's Second Great Awakening – and what it meant to the American nation. Thus he vetoed Rimi's entrance into the doctoral ranks. That should have killed Rimi's effort to get the doctorate.

Actually, not only was Rimi shocked (speechless, actually, for there was nothing he could say to satisfy this professor) but so was also his supervisor. But his supervisor then did something that he said he had never done before, which was to simply take the professor's criticisms (eventually expressed in six pages of comments), have Rimi go back to his dissertation to do some updating in answer to the man, and then present a rewrite of his dissertation to a new panel that would go over the revised project. And this Rimi did. And with the objecting professor not part of the new panel, Rimi's doctoral effort went ahead beautifully.

But more than that, this adversity actually strengthened his work, by requiring Rimi to answer the questions that skeptics might have had about his findings. And thus revised, a publishing house decided to take on the publication of his work, just now hitting the bookshelves.* And the book has been endorsed by a large number of highly reputable Christian authors, including Mark Noll, the master of American Christian history.

Looking for another Methodist church. Meanwhile, the Methodist bishop of the region was most anxious not to lose Rimi, once it became known that he was looking to move on. Oddly enough, the Methodist Church higher-ups had told Rimi that they could not ordain him because he did his seminary education at Gordon-Conwell (one of the highest ranked

---

The Supernatural and the Circuit Riders: The Rise of Early American Methodism. Eugene, OR: Pickwick Publications, 2021.

seminaries in the country), because the Methodist denomination no longer accepted Gordon-Conwell certification.* They thus had told Rimi that he would have to get a degree from a Methodist-approved seminary. Just how many MA and PhD degrees did Rimi need, and how many books on the birth and growth of Methodism did Rimi need to write in order to satisfy the Methodists that he was a competent candidate for ordination in their denomination?

But somehow the bishop moved ahead as if this would be no problem and set up interviews in an area ranging from central Pennsylvania south to Delaware. But the pickings were very marginal (churches in deep trouble, sort of like the Garfield church). So nothing really developed.

The Lighthouse Church. Then in the fall of 2019 Rimi got a call from (supposedly retired) pastor Bill to see if he would be interested in pastoring the Lighthouse Church. Well that was a no-brainer. Rachel and Rimi had a long history with the church. Thus the answer was an enthusiastic "yes."

Consequently Rimi was interviewed by a committee (the church's newly constituted "bylaws committee") headed up by pastor Bill's brother-in-law, Jim. And so it was that Rimi negotiated salary and job details with the committee, and was thus hired as their new pastor.

Of course Rimi would need some time to make the transition from church to church.

Most importantly, they would need to find a new home (they were living in the Methodist church's parsonage and would thus have to move on). But most amazingly (really?) they found a fantastic home not far from the Lighthouse Church, at clearly a bargain price – the very day it came on the market. And it was fully furnished (not that they needed all the furniture) and included an old Buick, with very low mileage, owned by the elderly lady living there (who had just died, thus the house sale). Now they would have two cars, which they would need badly. So the matter of a new life was taken care of most beautifully. Clearly, this was another one of God's "signs and wonders!"

But there was a huge problem with the church deal. The opening had suddenly occurred at the Lighthouse Church because the previous pastor, who had been there only two years, suddenly quit, largely due to the maneuvering of Bill's brother-in-law, Jim, a maneuvering designed to put the running of the church more tightly into the hands of this by-laws committee that Jim headed up. Things had finally exploded over this matter of exactly who it was that was supposed to be leading the church. And not only had the new pastor just quit, half of the congregation also left

---

*Gordon Conwell had not moved to the Left socio-politically the way the Methodist denomination had done so over recent years.

in disgust. Unfortunately, Rimi knew very little of the deeper elements of this dynamic at the time.

He did know however that a similar split had happened several years earlier, helping Kathleen and me make the decision to move on to the Methodist church where, anyway, Rimi had begun to serve. This had all come about because pastor Bill announced his "retirement" – but stayed on to "help" the young assistant (who had been with him for nearly 20 years) run the church.

As a former interim pastor, I well understood that this in itself was a situation designed for disaster. And indeed, it was not long before the younger pastor and a good portion of the congregation – including most of the members of the very active men's organization – left the church, to start up a new congregation nearby. And it had taken over a year for the Lighthouse Church to pull itself together to make the call to bring on a new pastor (the one who had himself just quit) to take over the church. But again, the question remained unresolved as to who really was in charge – which no longer seemed to be Jesus Christ himself!

And now it was Rimi's turn to step into this dynamic.

For a while things seemed to be working fairly well, and Jim and his committee seemed to be supportive of Rimi in making the transition. After all, Rimi was a newbie – or so they chose to believe – and needed their supervisory assistance.

Actually, as an experienced associate pastor, Rimi needed no such help. So the horrible political dynamic that seemed to continuously haunt the Lighthouse Church began to make itself felt again. And within the matter of only a half a year, things began to get quite ugly. In fact, it got to the point where Jim and his group were clearly moving to either put Rimi under their total mastery, or force him out. Rimi was simply undertaking too much of the developmental dynamic (the church was actually growing again), and there was no way Jim and his group were going to let Rimi get ahead of them in the running of the church.

Sadly, Rimi got no help from pastor Bill, or his wife, Sandy – the latter who at one point even told Rimi that he preached the worst sermons she had ever heard, which not surprisingly was exactly the style that was bringing in new blood to the church.

Then there was the problem of the young musical director that was brought in to help Rimi (actually a young man raised in that church). At first he was cooperative with Rimi in working with the music that Rimi wanted presented, in order to lead into the day's message. But it soon appeared that he had ambitions of his own to direct worship, running music and praying at such length that it forced Rimi to shorten up his sermons in order to stay within a certain online limit.

But then things turned even worse when the young man also took over the sound and online presentation of Sunday worship. While he was very artistic, he was not technologically very adept, and technical problems began to multiply.

By this time, summer (2020) was coming on, and John and Phuong were back living with us, at least for that summer. And Rimi asked John if he would take over the running of the sound booth. The problem child was not happy about that, and fought back, developing a natural alliance with Jim and his committee.

Worse, he decided abruptly to take a "vacation", and did everything he knew to do to shut down the sound and lighting system, as well as block access to the internet, before he left. But John figured out rather quickly how to get around these blockages. And by that Sunday John had things back in working order.

When the young man returned, full war was on, conducted not only by him but also by Jim and his committee.

A new church board was put in place (largely designed by Jim's committee) that July, and moved immediately to put Rimi in his "proper" place." Rimi was repeatedly brought before the new board to give account for his ways. Actually Rimi was working very hard at the church, counselling and visiting extensively, and the efforts of the new board (of some of the board anyway, because not all of them were part of Jim's anti-Rimi group) to find fault with Rimi's ministry reached the point of being totally ludicrous in character. Rimi found it hard to offer this group any answers that would satisfy them. But did they really want such satisfaction in the first place?

Things finally reached such a state that the new board decided (with some very strong opposition on the part of a couple of the members) that Rimi was not to preach the coming Sunday. In fact, church service would not be held at all.

That was ironic because Rimi had an excellent candidate to head up their new music ministry coming that Sunday to lead musical worship (the problem child had recently walked off the job, hoping to make worship seem pathetic without him leading it).

But there was no way that Rimi was simply going to call off worship. And thus he held worship. The next day he was told he was fired.

Actually, he found out that the ruling majority on the board had actually made the decision to fire him a few days earlier, even before he went ahead and held worship.

The New Awakening Church. But immediately a number of people from the church pleaded with Rimi not to give up his ministry, but to find a place elsewhere to preach, because they loved his preaching and did not want to lose him.

The decision thus was made to hold a small service the following Sunday at their new home, outside on their large lawn (almost 2 acres in size). And to Rimi and Rachel's shock, about 25 people had somehow got the word and showed up to support him.

Rimi's preaching thus would go on!

Rimi would never have started up a church on his own. Simply trying to find a handful of people to get a new church started was itself a very difficult matter. And how would Rachel and Rimi have supported themselves in such slender startup days, for they were deeply invested in their new home? Where would they have found the people, and the funds needed to keep going?

But as things worked out, he didn't have to do any of that. He was able to start up his own ministry with a couple of dozen people in person (and soon more) – and numerous people online – excited to get that ministry up and running. And they were most generous in their financial support.

Thus once again, what was meant to destroy Rimi (basic evil), God turned into a miraculous good. It's as if everything had been set up to go that way. And all Rimi and Rachel needed to do was simply go through the doors as God himself opened them.

From August into September Rimi held worship outside on the lawn. But cooler weather was coming on, and Rachel and Rimi made the decision to bring worship inside. They had a point in their house where Rimi could preach and be seen and heard in the large family room, the huge kitchen and breakfast area, and the glassed-in back porch, all at the same time. More than 30 people could be accommodated this way.

Also, as things quickly settled into something of a routine, Rimi and Rachel knew that it was time to give their ministry a name. It was going to need one anyway in order to secure its place not only online but also to find itself in accordance with state law. And being as Rimi was very interested in the realm of America's great awakenings, the decision to name this ministry The New Awakening Church (and Ministry) came easily.

But it soon became clear that the house was not going to be able to accommodate the growth that was happening with the ministry. So Rachel and Rimi began to make calls to various local organizations and civic institutions concerning the availability of a place for them to meet with their growing congregation. And somehow a huge racquetball and recreation center nearby came to their notice. And in contacting the director, René, their request was met with enthusiasm, because she herself had just come to the thought that one of the huge rooms at the center (with padded and carpeted flooring) would be a perfect place for a Christian congregation to meet on a Sunday morning.

What a coincidence (really?)! And so it was that in early November, the New Awakening Church found itself gathering in its new home at the racquetball and recreation center.

It was a perfect place. People came early to visit and stayed late for the same purpose. And the kids (soon to number 15 to 20 in number) could run around wildly before and after service and not get hurt when they tumbled (they held Sunday School in another room at the center), loving every minute of it!

And the growth continued, and is continuing even with this writing.

Rachel moves ahead: Oxford. Meanwhile, Rachel decided to resume her educational journey, not only in helping Rimi's research by bringing her own editorial skills to excellent use in the process, but deciding at the same time to apply for a master's program at Oxford University.

Are you kidding? She was already homeschooling Anna and Peter, serving as something of a business manager at their new church, and head of the church's Sunday School program, as well as editing Rimi's work.

But she was accepted, and started classes there, solely online (thanks to the Coronavirus). And she came to love every minute of it, and doing so well that the department director asked her if she would be interested in taking up PhD studies at Oxford. They would love to have her.

She's thinking about it!

$$* \quad * \quad *$$

KATHLEEN

Not a whole lot has been said about Kathleen in these pages. That is because Kathleen is not the grand adventurer like the rest of the Hodges family. Where Kathleen plays so importantly in the whole picture is the way she has loved to serve as an enabler to the rest of the adventurers in the Hodges family.

Kathleen has been the supermom and superwife who has made sure that the family remains well-founded and strong in its larger pursuits. The home front is a place of incredible peace and easy joy, because of all the work she puts into making it the home we have all learned to know as the most awesome of base camps for all our doings. She delights in setting up the table with the most exquisite dishes and beautifully prepared table settings. She loves to find small gifts to delight us, especially the grandchildren, who love her dearly. And she keeps the home and gardens beautiful with all the flowers, ferns and bushes she carefully nourishes. Thus the home is not only a beautiful place spiritually, it is a beautiful place physically, thanks to her close attention to that very beauty.

And she is quiet and wise counsel, especially when one or another of the Hodges activities seems to be headed down the road of confusion. The kids check in with her constantly on this matter and that. And she loves to message them with daily devotionals that she attends to regularly. She prays for them constantly. And they know who to come to when they feel they need special prayers.

And she is still gorgeous! I don't understand how the process of aging has not diminished her beauty one bit!

God is so good in the way he has put this wonderful family together!

✳ ✳ ✳

REACHING BEYOND

I have absolutely no experience in marketing anything, especially in the realm of ideas. Reaching beyond the world immediately in front of me (a classroom or church sanctuary) is very new to me. But as my children point out to me, in today's world of the internet, on your computer screen the world is also immediately in front of you. You just have to look at that world a bit differently now. So I'm working on that!

A new single-volume American history. I was also told that reducing the amount of material I want to bring to that world would make it more attractive to those who would have an interest in the matter of America and its historical destiny. Thus I have been working on a single-volume presentation of the American narrative, entitled America's Story - a Spiritual Journey. The message is the same as the three-volume series. It's just that there's less historical detail, yet the same amount of spiritual analysis. The work is almost finished. So I am looking to see how I can reach the public this time. Self-publishing seems to be the best option. We'll see.

Social Truth through historical narrative. I remain deeply concerned that I am leaving for my children a very messy nation to have to deal with, a nation trying to move forward without the slightest idea of what actually works, and what likewise is always destined to fail in the world of social-political choices. I am deeply aware that the truly wise ones that have graced human life – from those ancient souls who assembled the Jewish Testament (Christianity's Old Testament) and the many philosophers of the Greco-Roman world (especially Aristotle, Cicero and Marcus Aurelius) down to modern times (Winthrop, Franklin, Lincoln, Truman and others) – have always understood the importance of living boldly, but at the same time always according to social rules built into nature – especially human nature itself.

And it is exactly those same rules – which are as "spiritual" as they are "material" – that I am trying to put forward in my writings, through the process of story-telling – the most ancient and most reliable form of presenting the Great Truths – or rules of life.

Living by the "Rules of Life." My own kids have caught on to these rules, and how to make them work for themselves. And they have done quite well, despite all the human confusion circling around them. They are not ones to be swayed from their paths by clever reasoning, reasoning that our modern American culture has been dumping on our dear society, especially its youth. They know very well the enormous – and highly critical – difference between authentic Truth, and mere well-reasoned ideological opinion.

They know that reason can be very inventive. It usually is. In any case, it is always clever. But they have come to understand (sometimes the hard way) that human social-reasoning is seldom anything more than crude self-promotion, self-interest, driven by personal motivation willing to use the world of "others" to get what it wants.

No, they are deeply understanding of the truths that make for real social success – that is, success not only for themselves but also for those around them – the kind of success that endures not only over the years but also over the generations. They know that real success in life will never be found outside of the social truths that have led their people over many generations, rules and social patterns that have proven themselves in the tough laboratory of time and circumstance.

So, please, America. Take a cue from the Hodges family. Look upward. Look beyond the immediate. The Hodges family wants you to succeed.

Lightning Source UK Ltd.
Milton Keynes UK
UKHW012018170821
388973UK00001B/36